BASIC ARABIC: A GRAMMAR AND WORKBOOK

Basic Arabic: A Grammar and Workbook comprises an accessible reference grammar with related exercises in a single volume.

This book presents 51 units, covering the key grammar points which students would expect to encounter in their first year of learning Arabic. Examples and exercises are provided throughout, allowing students to reinforce and consolidate their learning.

Key features include:

- clear, accessible format
- many useful language examples
- jargon-free explanations of grammar
- abundant exercises with full answer key
- subject index.

Clearly presented and user-friendly, *Basic Arabic* is an ideal grammar reference and practice resource for both beginners and students with some knowledge of the language. It is suitable for both class use and independent study.

Waheed Samy, PhD, was a professor of Arabic language for over 30 years, teaching Arabic at the American University in Cairo (AUC) and the Center for Arabic Study Abroad (CASA), Egypt, and the University of Michigan, USA. Dr. Samy was Director of AUC's Summer Intensive Arabic Language Program for 10 years. He was also Founder and Director of AUC's Arabic Computer-Aided Language Learning Lab.

Leila Samy, MPH, currently directs a Government program to help rural communities across the US leverage health information technology to improve health care quality and fuel economic development. As an expert in Arabic language, Ms Samy has provided technical services to a range of institutions, including the University of Michigan and the World Health Organization.

Other titles available in the Grammar Workbooks series are:

Basic Cantonese
Intermediate Cantonese

Basic Chinese
Intermediate Chinese

Basic German
Intermediate German

Basic Irish
Intermediate Irish

Basic Italian

Basic Japanese
Intermediate Japanese

Basic Korean
Intermediate Korean

Basic Persian

Basic Polish
Intermediate Polish

Basic Russian
Intermediate Russian

Basic Spanish
Intermediate Spanish

Basic Welsh
Intermediate Welsh

Basic Yiddish

BASIC ARABIC: A GRAMMAR AND WORKBOOK

Waheed Samy and Leila Samy

Routledge
Taylor & Francis Group
NEW YORK AND LONDON

First published 2014
by Routledge
2 Park Square, Milton Park, Abingdon, Oxon OX14 4RN

Simultaneously published in the USA and Canada
by Routledge
711 Third Avenue, New York, NY 10017

Routledge is an imprint of the Taylor & Francis Group, an informa business

British Library Cataloguing-in-Publication Data
A catalogue record for this book is available from the British Library

Library of Congress Cataloging-in-Publication Data
A catalog record for this book has been requested

ISBN: 978-0-415-58772-3 (hbk)
ISBN: 978-0-415-58773-0 (pbk)
ISBN: 978-1-315-84890-7 (ebk)

Typeset in Times New Roman
by Apex CoVantage, LLC

CONTENTS

Contents v
List of tables ix

1 **Word boundaries in written Arabic** 1

2 **Meaning and grammatical categories encapsulated in a word** 4

3 **Arabic grammar paradigm قواعد اللغة العربية نحو وصرف** 6

4 **The Arabic language writing system** 7

5 **Function of diacritics التشكيل وعلامات الإعراب** 20

6 **Agreement تطابق** 27

7 **Pronouns الضمائر** 29

8 **Demonstratives أسماء الإشارة** 37

9 **Case marking: noun words الإعراب** 39

10 **Noun type words: syntactic function, case name, and case marking** 40

11 **Syntactic functions and their case markers الحالة الإعرابية و علامات الإعراب** 60

12 **Noun types** 61

13 **The "human" vs "non-human" classification of nouns** 67

14	The human category nouns	71
15	The non-human category nouns	82
16	Noun attributes: number, gender, case, definiteness	89
17	Numbers and counting الأعداد و المعدود	107
18	The sentence الجُملَة – the basics	109
19	The noun–adjective phrases	120
20	Adjectives: agreement with nouns	122
21	The ’idafa phrase الإضافة	141
22	The ’idafa-adjective phrase	155
23	The definite article ال	157
24	Prepositions	158
25	Adverbials	167
26	To have عِندَ، لِ، مَع، في	178
27	Questions	185
28	Negation	190
29	About the Arabic verb الفِعل	191
30	Conjugating the perfect تصريف الماضي	195
31	Conjugating the imperfect تصريف المُضارع	199
32	Subject and mood markers of the imperfect verb	203
33	Verb patterns أوزان الفعل	207
34	The perfect, Form I فَعَل	214
35	The perfect, Form II فَعَّل	218

36 The perfect, Form III فاعَل 220

37 The perfect, Form IV أَفعَل 223

38 The perfect, Form V تَفَعّل 227

39 The perfect, Form VI تَفاعَل 229

40 The perfect, Form VII اِنفَعَل 231

41 The perfect, Form VIII اِفتَعَل 233

42 The perfect, Form IX اِفعَلّ 237

43 The perfect, Form X اِستَفعَل 238

44 Noun–verb paradigm chart 240

45 Time 243

46 Verb–subject agreement 245

47 Constituents of verb-type words 246

48 Verb types (sound, hamzated, doubled, weak radicalled) 247

49 Adverbs marked by the accusative case 250

50 The passive voice 251

51 Inflecting the verb for the passive voice 254

Workbook and answers 259

Unit 4: The Arabic language writing system 259

Unit 5: Function of diacritics التشكيل و علامات الإعراب 265

Unit 6: Agreement تطابق 269

Unit 7: Pronouns الضمائر 270

Unit 8: Demonstratives - أسماء الإشارة 274

Unit 10: Noun type words: syntactic function, case name, and case marking 274

Unit 12: Noun types 283

Unit 13: The "human" vs "non-human" classification of nouns 285
Unit 14: The human category nouns 287
Unit 15: The non-human category nouns 295
Unit 16: Noun attributes: number, gender, case, definiteness 299
Unit 18: The sentence الجُملَة – the basics 304
Unit 20: Adjectives: agreement with nouns 313
Unit 21: The 'idafa phrase الإضافة 313
Unit 22: The 'idafa-adjective phrase 320
Unit 26: To have عِندَ، لِ، مَع، في 321
Unit 27: Questions 325
Unit 30: Conjugating the perfect verb 327
Unit 31: Conjugating the imperfect 328
Unit 33: Verb patterns أوزان الفعل 331
Unit 34: The perfect, Form I فَعل 334
Unit 35: The perfect, Form II فَعّل 335
Unit 36: The perfect, Form III فاعَل 337
Unit 37: The perfect, Form IV أَفعَل 339
Unit 38: The perfect, Form V تَفَعّلَ 342
Unit 39: The perfect, Form VI تَفاعَلَ 342
Unit 40: The perfect, Form VII اِنفَعَلَ 343
Unit 41: The perfect, Form VIII اِفتَعَلَ 345
Unit 42: The perfect, Form IX اِفعَلّ 347
Unit 43: The perfect, Form X اِستَفعَلَ 347
Unit 44: Noun–verb paradigm chart 349
Unit 48: Verb types (sound, hamzated, doubled, weak radicalled) 351
Unit 50: The passive voice 352
Unit 51: Inflecting the verb for the passive voice 353

Index 355

LIST OF TABLES

(Key tables are featured in **bold**)

Phonological characteristics and transcription of letters **8–9**
Letter shapes and context **10–11**
Phonological characteristics and transcription of diacritics **19**
Free-standing and suffixed pronouns **34–35**
Dual pronouns 34
Singular pronouns 34
Plural pronouns 35
Demonstratives **37**
Subject marker suffixes of the perfect verb in the singular **195**
Subject marker suffixes of the perfect verb in the dual **196**
Subject marker suffixes of the perfect verb in the plural **196–197**
Perfect verbs, summary 197
Subject markers of the imperfect verb in the singular **199**
Subject markers of the imperfect verb in the dual **200–201**
Subject markers of the imperfect verb in the plural **201**
Subject and mood markers of the imperfect verb **203–206**
Mood marking **205–206**
Verbs, derivational system of 207–208
Verb forms **208–209**
Form IX, colours 209
Perfect verb forms, summary **210**
Imperfect **212**
Noun-verb paradigm chart **240**
Typical arrangement of constituents of verb-type words **246**
Voice, perfect tense verb 254–255
Vowel transformations to inflect active for passive **254**
Active and passive forms of the perfect tense **255**
Vowel transformations to inflect active imperfect for passive **256**
voice, imperfect tense verb 256
Active and passive forms of the imperfect tense **257**
Imperfect Form I-X stems (Forms I-X without subject marker) **333**

UNIT 1
Word boundaries in written Arabic

Number of words in a message

The same message typically requires fewer words in Arabic than English.

If someone said to you, "I am very happy because she gave me her telephone number", as a speaker of English you would understand the message.

If someone were to say to you in Modern Standard Arabic,

أنا سعيدٌ جداً لأنّها أعطتني رقم تليفونها

as a speaker of Arabic you would understand the same message.

The written representation of the spoken message consists of words delineated by whitespace. Contrast the difference between English and Arabic:

I am very happy because she gave me her telephone number.	11 words
أنا سعيدٌ جداً لأنّها أعطتني رقم تليفونها	7 words

Instead of "she gave me the number" consider the following example with a preposition (حَرف جَرّ):

She gave the number to me	6 words
أعطت الرقم لي	3 words

The following is an account for the difference in the number of words that are expressed by the message above: in "I am very happy," Arabic requires no copula (I am, you are, he is). So you have:

I am very happy	أنا سعيد جداً
you are very happy	أنت سعيد جداً
he is very happy	هو سعيد جداً

The word "because" takes a pronoun suffix, not an independent pronoun.

Examples:

because she	لأنّها
because we	لأنَّنا
because he	لأنَّه
because they	لأنّهم

Arabic verbs always have an integral subject marker (see About the Arabic verb). Consequently, only one Arabic word is required to express each of the following English phrases that require two-word combinations:

2 words	1 word (verb and subject marker)
I "gave"	أعطَيتُ
you "gave" (m.)	أعطَيتَ
you "gave" (f.)	أعطَيتِ
he "gave"	أعطى
she "gave"	أعطَت
we "gave"	أعطَينا
you "gave" (d., m. and f.)	أعطيتُما
you "gave" (pl. m.)	أعطَيتُم
you "gave" (pl. f.)	أعطَيتُنَّ
they "gave"	أعطَوا، أعطَينَ
it "gave"	أعطى، أعطَت

A direct object pronoun must be a suffix (see Pronouns):

she gave me	3 words
أعطتني	1 word

Possessives – her telephone – are done with a pronoun suffix (see The 'idafa phrase). Consequently, the two-word expression, "her telephone", is تليفونها.

The definite article ال is not an independent word; it is always a prefix:

the	number
	الرقم

Pronominal suffixation contributes to the difference in the number of words that are needed to express the same message in Arabic and English. A pronoun that is the object of a preposition must be a suffix (see Pronouns):

to me → لي

The above examples illustrate that written English and Arabic pack the same information differently. Whereas English seems to use whitespace to encapsulate syntactic units, whitespace often encapsulates Arabic compound units, such as verb + subject + object.

The following summarizes the cases enumerated above where written Arabic may employ fewer words than English:

- Arabic has no copula.
- The definite article is a prefix, not an independent word.
- Arabic verbs have integral subject markers.
- Pronouns (as objects of verbs and prepositions, and in possessive expressions) are not independent.

Word count: computational linguistics

Word count may be used to measure relative complexity, value (e.g. price of a translation) or readability of written products. Particularly in academia, word count may be applied as a standard measurement when designing curricula and authoring language textbooks, for example. The boundaries of words in both Arabic and English are similarly marked by whitespace. However, Arabic words and English words tend to hold and package information differently. For example, the boundaries of individual words in English tend to encapsulate individual syntactic units (e.g. either an object or a verb or a subject). The boundary of a single word in Arabic may encapsulate compound units (e.g. a verb and a subject and an object). Computer programs that generate lists or counts of words may not offer seamless, interchangeable support for Arabic and English. For example, computer programs seeking to generate a count of "words" as delineated by whitespace will actually generate a count of compounds when analysing Arabic text.[1]

Note

1. Waheed Samy, PhD. "Computer Word Frequency Counting in Arabic." Chapter 15, page 259, *Understanding Arabic: Essays in Contemporary Arabic Linguistics in Honor of El-Said Badawi.*

UNIT 2

Meaning and grammatical categories encapsulated in a word

In addition to their core (root) meaning, Arabic words are marked for the following grammatical categories:

1 Syntactic function (case or mood) (الحالة الإعرابية)
   a) For nouns (including adjectives):
      The nominative case (حالة المَرفوع)
      The accusative case (حالة المنصوب)
      The genitive case (حالة المَجرور)
   b) For imperfect verbs
      Indicative mood (حالة المرفوع)
      Subjunctive mood (حالة المَنصوب)
      Jussive mood (حالة المَجزوم)
2 Gender (الجِنس)
   Masculine (مذكّر)
   Feminine (موئنّث)
3 Definiteness (التَعريف والتنكير)
   Definite (مَعرِفة)
   Indefinite (نَكِرة)
4 Humanness
   Human (عاقِل)
   Non-human (غير العاقِل)
5 Tense
   Perfect tense (الماضي)
   Imperfect tense (المُضارِع)
   Imperative tense (الأمر)
6 Person
   First person (المُتكلِّم)
   Second person (المُخاطَب)
   Third person (الغائب)

7 Voice: active/passive
8 Number (عَدد)
   Singular (مُفرَد)
   Dual (مُثَنّى)
   Plural (جَمع)
9 Pattern/form (وزن)

That is, implicit within a word (verb, noun or pronoun), aside from its core (root) meaning, are the following characteristics:

> Verbs: tense, person, voice, mood, gender and number.
> Pronouns: person, gender, number and case.
> Nouns and adjectives: gender, number, case, definiteness.

UNIT 3

Arabic grammar paradigm

قواعد اللغة العربية نحو وصرف

The meaning and morphology (structure) of words stem from:

Roots
Patterns, including:

Foms (I–X) (الأوزان) (See Verb patterns; Noun–verb paradigm chart)
Conjugation (التصريف)
Syntax (النحو)

How words are formed:

Arabic words are derived by root radicals and pattern systems. A root assigns the core meaning to the word and may be bound to patterns of letters and diacritics to generate words with different meanings and functions within a sentence.

Roots contain the core meaning and are the primary entries in the Arabic dictionary. Patterns carry information and specific features (e.g. gender, a type of place, a type of profession, someone carrying out an action, a tool). The pattern may be combined with the inherent meaning in a root to generate nouns and verbs.

Examples:

Deriving a noun: The root كتب (pertaining to write/wrote) is combined with the pattern for the doer of a verb, فاعل to generate the noun كاتب (writer).

Deriving a verb: The root فهم (pertaining to understand/understood) is combined with the pattern for the action of doing something together تَفاعَل to generate the verb يَتَفاهَم (to understand each other or to work toward an understanding together).

How words interact with syntax:

Case or mood markings (علامات الإعراب) affix to a word and assign to the word its functions in a sentence or context (الحالة الإعرابية).

UNIT 4
The Arabic language writing system

Arabic writing: order and style

Order

Written Arabic goes from right to left. To illustrate, see the letters below:

os ekil ,tfel ot thgir morf seog gnitirw cibarA

Starting from right to left, they read:

Arabic writing goes from right to left, like so.

Style

Arabic writing is cursive and letters join to form words. Within a word, symbols may be added above or below (and slightly after) the letters (see Diacritics).

Example: يُقَسِّم

Constituents of the writing system

The Arabic writing system includes an alphabet and diacritics (i.e. small symbols above or below individual characters/letters).

Alphabet

Arabic uses an alphabet comprising 28 characters. Two of these 28 are semi-vowels, one is a long vowel, and the remaining 25 are consonants. In the first row in the table below is the همزة, which is not always included in Arabic alphabet charts. Thus the table shows 29 characters.

Diacritics

Diacritics are small symbols appearing above or below a letter. More specifically, a diacritic is written above or below a letter, and slightly after (i.e. to the left).

Unfortunately diacritics are – by convention – considered optional, which is a problem because diacritics supplement letters by providing a more accurate indication about how a word is pronounced.

Letters

The shape of an Arabic letter depends on its context. Unlike English, the Arabic letters have no upper case and lower case, such as A a, G g, and R r. However, some letters have different shapes depending on whether they standalone or are joined to other letters within a word. Letters can take an initial position (preceded by whitespace and followed by a letter), a medial position (with letters on either side), or a final position (preceded by a letter and followed by whitespace).

For example, consider the letter ي. Here are the shapes of the letter based on different contexts:

- يـ At the beginning of a word and when it is preceded by a type of letter that does not link directly to following letters.
- ـيـ In the middle of a word and directly linked to letters on both sides.
- ـي At the end of a word and directly connected to the preceding letter.

Phonological characteristics and transcription of Letters

Phonological characteristics	*Transcription*	*Letter*	*Name*
consonant, glottal stop, no equivalent English letter, but it is the unwritten sound at the beginning of English words beginning with a vowel, such as: and, egg, in, old, and under	'	ء	هَمزة
long front vowel, as in: mad; or long back vowel, as in: mar	ā	ا ى	ألف (ألف مقصورة)
consonant, voiced bilabial stop, as in: bring	b	ب	باء
consonant, voiceless alveolar stop, as in: true	t	ت	تاء
consonant, voiceless interdental fricative, as in: three	th	ث	ثاء
consonant, has regional varieties: voiced velar stop, as in: girl; or voiced post alveolar fricative, as in: *jolie* (French); or voiced post alveolar affricate, as in: joy	g, j, or dj	ج	جيم
consonant, voiceless pharyngeal fricative, no equivalent English sound	ḥ	ح	حاء

consonant, voiceless velar fricative, no equivalent English sound	kh	خ	خاء
consonant, voiced alveolar stop, as in: drink	d	د	دال
consonant, voiced interdental fricative, as in: this	dh	ذ	ذال
consonant, alveolar trill, as in: ring	r	ر	راء
consonant, voiced alveolar stop, as in: zoo	z	ز	زاي
consonant, voiceless alveolar fricative, as in: stand	s	س	سين
consonant, voiceless post alveolar fricative, as in: shout	sh	ش	شين
consonant, velarized/emphatized voiceless alveolar fricative, perhaps equivalent to salt	ṣ	ص	صاد
consonant, velarized/emphatized voiced alveolar stop, perhaps equivalent to dull	ḍ	ض	ضاد
consonant, velarized/emphatized voiceless alveolar stop, perhaps equivalent to tall	ṭ	ط	طاء
consonant, velarized/emphatized voiced interdental fricative, perhaps equivalent to thus	ẓ	ظ	ظاء
consonant, voiced pharyngeal fricative, no equivalent English sound	c	ع	عَين
consonant, voiced velar fricative, similar to rouge (French)	gh	غ	غَين
consonant, voiceless labiodental fricative, as in: front	f	ف	فاء
consonant, voiceless, uvular stop, no equivalent English sound	q	ق	قاف
consonant, voiceless velar stop (kind)	k	ك	كاف
consonant, voiced or voiceless alveolar lateral approximant, as in: let	l	ل	لام
consonant, voiced nasal bilabial (man)	m	م	ميم
consonant, voiced nasal alveolar (net)	n	ن	نون
consonant, voiced or voiceless glottal fricative, as in: hotel	h	ه	هاء
semivowel, voiced labiovelar approximant, as in win; or long back vowel, as in fool	w or ū	و	واو
semivowel, voiced labiopalatal approximant, as in yell; or long close front vowel, as in feel	y, or ī	ي	ياء

Letter shapes and context

As mentioned above, the shape of an Arabic letter depends on its context, i.e. its position in a word and the shapes of letters, if any, that precede or follow it. Any letter can be in the word-initial position, except for the hamza (see Hamza below). Any letter can be in the word-final position.

The letters ا، د، ذ، ر، ز، و can only be joined on one side; they can only join to a preceding letter and never to following letters. A small horizontal dash-like line, ـ, is used to join a letter that can be joined to a preceding or following one. The tables below compare the shape of letters when:

standing alone (preceded and followed by whitespace)
in a word and in the following positions
  word-initial (preceded by whitespace)
  in the middle of a word (with letters on either side), and
  word-final (followed by whitespace).

This first table shows the shapes of letters that can link directly to preceding and following letters. Each of these letters has four shapes.

Shape of letter			
In a word (based on position within the word)			*Alone*
word-final; or followed by a letter that does not link directly	*middle of a word; preceded and followed by letters that also link directly*	*word-initial; or preceded by a letter that does not link directly*	
ـب ...	... ـبـ ...	... بـ	ب
ـت ...	... ـتـ ...	... تـ	ت
ـث ...	... ـثـ ...	... ثـ	ث
ـج ...	... ـجـ ...	... جـ	ج
ـح ...	... ـحـ ...	... حـ	ح
ـخ ...	... ـخـ ...	... خـ	خ
ـس ...	... ـسـ ...	... سـ	س
ـش ...	... ـشـ ...	... شـ	ش
ـص ...	... ـصـ ...	... صـ	ص
ـض ...	... ـضـ ...	... ضـ	ض
ـط ...	... ـطـ ...	... طـ	ط
ـظ ...	... ـظـ ...	... ظـ	ظ
ـع ...	... ـعـ ...	... عـ	ع
ـغ ...	... ـغـ ...	... غـ	غ
ـف ...	... ـفـ ...	... فـ	ف
ـق ...	... ـقـ ...	... قـ	ق

Final	Middle	Initial	Alone
...ك	...كـ...	كـ...	ك
...ل	...لـ...	لـ...	ل
...م	...مـ...	مـ...	م
...ن	...نـ...	نـ...	ن
...ه	...هـ...	هـ...	ه
...ي	...يـ...	يـ...	ي

This second table illustrates the shape of the hamza with and without a seat. When it occurs without a seat, the hamza takes only one shape and never links directly to any letter. The hamzas ا or و seats only link directly to preceding and never to following letters. The ى seat links directly to both preceding and following letters.

Shape of letter			
In a word (based on position within the word)			*Alone*
Final	*Middle*	*Initial*	
ء	ء	NA	ء (with no seat)
...أ		أ	ء (with a seat)
...إ		إ	
ؤ		NA	ء (with a seat)
...ؤ			
...ئ	...ئـ ...ئـ...	NA	ء (with a seat)

This third table shows the shapes of six letters that never link directly to letters that follow.

Shape of letter		
In a word (based on position within the word)		*Alone*
word-final; or middle of a word and preceded by a letter that does link directly	*word-initial; or preceded by a letter that does not link directly*	
...ـا	ا	ا
...ـد	د	د
...ـذ	ذ	ذ
...ـر	ر	ر
...ـز	ز	ز
...ـو	و	و

Exercises: letter shapes and context

Exercise 1

Join the sets of letters to form words. Write the words in the space provided.

a) فَ + و + ا + ك + ه

____

b) كِ + ت + ا + بِ + ك

____

c) رُ + ف + و + ف

____

d) يَ + ك + ثُ + ب

____

e) نُ + ق + و + د

____

f) كِ + ت + ا + ب + ي

____

g) يَ + ن + ا + م

____

h) ل + ي + ب + ي + ا

____

Exercise 2

Match each of the two groups of letters to one of the statements below. Draw a line under (a) or (b) to indicate your answer.

1 Letter(s) that cannot be joined by a following letter (i.e. the next letter to the left)
   a) ا، د، ذ، ر، ز، و
   b) ي

2 Letter(s) that cannot be in a word initial position
   a) ا، د، ذ، ر، ز، و
   b) ء

Exercise 3

Write examples of words with each of the following letters in the beginning, middle and end of the word. Write your words in the blank spaces in the table below.

Letter	End of a word	Middle of a word	Beginning of a word
ك كـ			
ق قـ			
ل لـ			
م مـ			
س سـ			
ش شـ			
ص صـ			

Hamza

Hamza and hamza seat

When the hamza is not standing alone, it has a so-called "seat"; that is, the hamza combines with one of the following three letters: ألِف , واو , ياء.

Alone	ء
Above ي	ئـ، ـئـ، ئ
Above و	ـؤ، ؤ
Above or below ا	أ، إ

Hamza sound with different seats and alone

The table below illustrates how the seat of the hamza is pronounced when it takes the ي seat, the و seat, the ا seat, or when it stands alone.

ئ ـئـ ئـ إ	أُ ـؤ ؤ	أَ	ء
'i or i'	'u or u'	'a	'

Note that when it takes the ا seat, it can be pronounced in three different ways.

Hamza shapes and context

Hamza shape with different seats and alone

The table below illustrates the hamza in four contexts: unjoined and standing alone, as well as directly linked to preceding letters, letters on both sides and letters that follow.

directly linked to following	*directly linked to letters on both sides (middle of a word)*	*directly linked to preceding letter*	*unjoined*
ئـ...	...ـئـ...	ـأ، ـأ؛ ـؤ، ـئ	ء، أ، أُ، إ

Exercise: hamza shape with different seats and alone

Exercise 4

Join the following letters to form words. Write the correct answer in the blank spaces below.

Read from right to left.

1 رِ + ئَ + ةٌ   ri'atun

____

2 ب + ي + ئِ + يٌّ   bii'iyyun

____

Exercise: hamza shape with different seats and alone

3 ق + ا + رِ + ئ + و + ن — qaari'uuna

4 بِ + ئ + س — bi'sun

5 رُ + ؤَ + س + ا + ء — ru'asaa'un

6 رُ + ئِ + يَ — ru'iya

7 رُ + ؤْ + ي + ةٌ — ru'yatun

8 رُ + ؤ + و + س — ru'uusun

9 لُ + ؤ + م — lu'mun

10 رَ + أ + سَ — ra'asa

11 تَ + ق + رَ + ئ + ي + نَ — taqra'iina

12 تَ + ق + رَ + ؤ + و + نَ — taqra'uuna

13 رَ + أ + يٌ — ra'yun

Hamza shape based on position in a word

The hamza can be written with and without a seat. However, there are some rules.

At the beginning of a word, the hamza can only have an ا as a seat; all other seats are never word initial. In the middle and at the end of a word, the hamza can have any seat.

1 on no seat and unjoined when it occurs

between two long vowels
at the end of a word
if preceded by a long vowel
if preceded by a sukūn

2 on the ا seat when it occurs

at the beginning of a word
in the middle of a word
at the end of a word

3 on the و seat when it occurs

in the middle of a word
at the end of a word

4 on the ي seat when it occurs

in the middle of a word
at the end of a word

Exercise: hamza shape based on position in a word

Exercise 5

Below are examples of words that contain a hamza. Match each word to the corresponding statement describing the context of the hamza and write the word in the space provided.

1 باءات	4 سوء	7 أسرة	10 مئة
2 لاءات	5 قَميء	8 سأل	11 شيء
3 شاء	6 درْء	9 قرأ	

a) on no seat and unjoined between two long vowels:

____

b) on no seat and unjoined at the end of a word and preceded by a long vowel:

____

c) on no seat and unjoined at the end of a word and preceded by a sukūn:

____

d) on the ا seat at the beginning of a word:

____

e) on the ا seat in the middle of a word:

____

f) on the ا seat at the end of a word:

____

g) in the middle of a word:

____

Exercise: hamza shape based on position in a word

Hamza shape based on surrounding diacritics

1 At the beginning of a word, the hamza can only have the ا as a seat.

The hamza appears above the ا when it takes either a فَتحة or ضَمَّة.

Examples: أُسرة، أَحمر

The hamza appears below the ا when the hamza takes a كَسرة.

Examples: إِذا، إِسعاف

2 In the middle of a word, the hamza can take any seat or stand alone.

When the hamza is preceded by ا or و, it stands alone.

Examples: تساءَل، وتفاءَل، ولن يسوءَه وإن وضوءَه

When the hamza is preceded by a كَسرة or ي, it appears above the ي seat.

Examples: مشيئة، وبريئة، وإن مجيئك

When the hamza takes a كَسرة, it appears above the ي.

Examples: رُئِي، يُئِس، رَئيس

When the hamza takes a ضَمَّة, it appears above the و seat,

except when it is preceded by either a ي or كَسرة.

Examples: قرؤُوا، وشؤُون، ويستهزِئُون، وبريئُون

When the hamza takes a فَتحة, its seat corresponds to the preceding diacritic.

If preceded by a كَسرة, it takes ي as a seat.
If preceded by a ضَمَّة, it takes و as a seat.
If preceded by a فَتحة, it takes ا as a seat.

Examples: بُؤَساء، رَأس، رِئَة

If it is preceded by a سُكون, it takes ا as a seat.

Examples: يسْأل، يَيْأس

When the hamza takes a سُكون, it takes a seat that corresponds to the preceding diacritic.

Examples: فَأْس، بِئْر، سُؤْل

3 At the end of a word, the hamza can have any seat.

The hamza takes the seat that corresponds to the preceding diacritic.

Examples: يجرُؤُ ويبدَأُ ويستهزِئُ

When the hamza is preceded by a سُكون, it takes the ي seat.

Examples: بطْئاً، وشيْئاً جزْءٌ

Exercise: hamza shape based on surrounding diacritics

Exercise 6

أ or ؤ or ئ? Which will be the seat of the hamza in the following contexts? To the right and to the left of the blank spaces below are vowels before or after the hamza. Fill in the blanks below with the correct hamza seat. The first answer is provided as an example.

Read from right to left			transcribed word
1 … + a +	________	+ i + …	ri'atun
	… + a + ئ + i + …		
2 … + i +	________	+ i + …	bii'iyyun
3 + u +	________	+ i +	qaari'uuna
4 … + ° +	________	+ i + …	bi'sun
5 … + a +	________	+ u + …	ru'asaa'un
6 … + i +	________	+ u + …	ru'iya
7 … i + ° +	________	+ u + …	ru'yatun
8 + u +	________	+ u +	ru'uusun
9 … + ° +	________	+ u + …	lu'mun
10 … + a +	________	+ a + …	ra'asa

11 … + i +	________________	+ a + …	taqra’iina
12 … + u +	________________	+ a + …	taqra’uuna
13 … + ْ +	________________	+ a + …	ra’yun

Variations in hamza shapes

The hamza appears above or below the ا when embedded with prepositions in words like: فإن، بأن، لأنَّ، لإنْ

Diacritics التشكيل

Diacritics are symbols that are not part of the alphabet. They can be considered optional. Indeed by convention diacritics are most often not used in print or in handwriting. However, sometimes they are included to clarify the meaning of the word or its role within a phrase.

Phonological characteristics and transcription of diacritics

Phonological characteristics	*transcription*	*diacritic*	*name*
short vowel /a/, as in: pleas<u>a</u>nt or short vowel /ɑ/, as in: ab<u>u</u>ndant	a	َ	فتحة
short vowel /a/ or /ɑ/, as above, but followed by /n/	an	ً	تنوين فَتح
short vowel /u/, as in: f<u>oo</u>t, c<u>oo</u>k, f<u>u</u>ll, p<u>u</u>ll	u	ُ	ضمّة
short vowel /u/, as above, but followed by /n/	un	ٌ	تنوين ضَمّ
short vowel /i/, as in: f<u>i</u>t	i	ِ	كسرة
short vowel /i/, as above, but followed by /n/	in	ٍ	تنوين كَسر
denotes an absence of a vowel sound	none	ْ	سكون
doubles the time interval of a consonant, as in English when the last sound in a word is the same as the following one: ni<u>c</u>e <u>s</u>andwich, coo<u>l</u> <u>l</u>ady, boo<u>k</u> <u>c</u>ase	none	ّ	شدة

The three تنوين diacritic types above – rows 2, 4, and 6 – only appear at the end of a noun, and indicate that it is indefinite (see Definiteness – Indefiniteness).

UNIT 5

Function of diacritics
التشكيل وعلامات الإعراب

Diacritics have three functions:

Diacritics integral to a word: add meaning
Diacritics mark case (indicate syntax for nouns, علامات الإعراب)
Diacritics mark mood (indicate syntax for verbs, علامات الإعراب)

Diacritics as an integral part of a word

Diacritics are typically short vowels interleaved between consonants in any word. Diacritics can also be used to indicate the lack of a vowel after a consonant or to indicate that a consonant is doubled. They are always present when a word is spoken. Although in the written form such internal diacritics are frequently not written, they are understood to be there. The two sentences in the chart below provide an illustration. The first sentence shows no internal diacritics, and is the common print form. The second is the same sentence showing internal diacritics:

Comment	*Transcription*	*Sentence*
The written sentence has no diacritics, but cannot be spoken without them.	shrb mhmd alqhwa	شرب محمد القهوة
The spoken sentence includes diacritics.	shariba muham-mad alqahwa	شَرِبَ مُحَمَّد القَهوَة

The first sentence is missing internal diacritics. Native speakers reading the first sentence will understand what it means – Mohamed drank the coffee – but they will have to provide the missing vowels before they are able to *say* it. Being an imperfect symbolic system of representing the spoken word, a writing system is only an approximation. With the absence of diacritics, saying an unfamiliar *written* word is a problem because one does not know what vowels to say. For example, the word شرب, as in the above example, can theoretically have any one of three vowels – a, u, or i – between the first letter ش, and the second one ر.

Similarly, any one of the same three vowels can be inserted between the second letter ر, and the last one ب. The total number of possibilities is nine:

شَرَب، شَرُب، شَرِب،
شُرَب، شُرُب، شُرِب،
شِرَب، شِرُب، شِرِب،

The following headline from a prominent newspaper is missing internal diacritics:

٤٢ قتيلا ٣٥٠ مصابا ضحايا الأمطار[1]

A person who is not familiar with the word قتيلا would not know the diacritic immediately following the first consonant of this word; is it قَتيلا, قُتيلا, or قِتيلا? The words مصابا, and ضحايا, would provide the same problem.

Exercises: diacritics as an integral part of a word

Exercise 1

What are the differences between the two words below?

يَدْرُس
يُدَرِّس

____

____

____

____

____

____

Diacritics marking case of nouns علامات إعراب الأسماء

Case-marking diacritics provide an indication – i.e. an overt mark – to the syntactic function of nouns (see Case marking: noun words, and case names). They are located at the end of a noun, as shown in the examples that follow.

A noun has three cases (see Case names). These cases are:

المرفوع (nominative case)
المنصوب (accusative case)
المجرور (genitive case)

By convention:

المرفوع case is marked by ضمّة or تنوين ضَم,
المنصوب case is marked by a فتحة or تنوين فَتح, and
المجرور case is marked by كَسرة or تنوين كَسر (see Diacritics).

Diacritics marking case for definite and indefinite nouns

For the مرفوع case, a ضمّة indicates a noun is definite, تنوين ضَم indicates a noun is indefinite (see Noun: definiteness/indefiniteness).

Similarly, for the منصوب and the مجرور cases, a فتحة indicates a noun is definite, تنوين فَتح indicates a noun is indefinite; and a كَسرة indicates a noun is definite, تنوين كَسر indicates a noun is indefinite.

Examples:

Diacritic case marking with definite feminine and masculine nouns.

Definite			
Case	مَجرور	مَنصوب	مَرفوع
Feminine	السيارةِ	السيارةَ	السيارةُ
Masculine	الشارعِ	الشارعَ	الشارعُ

Diacritic case marking with indefinite feminine and masculine nouns.

Indefinite			
Case	مَجرور	مَنصوب	مَرفوع
Feminine	سيارةٍ	سيارةً	سيارةٌ
Masculine	شارعٍ	شارعاً	شارعٌ

Diacritic case marking for the first term of the 'idafa phrase: سيارة أميرة

In the first table, the second term in the 'idafa is a proper noun.

Case	*'idafa phrase*
مَرفوع	سيارةُ أميرة
مَنصوب	سيارةَ أميرة
مَجرور	سيارةِ أميرة

In the second table, the second term in the 'idafa is a pronoun suffix.

Case	*'idafa phrase*
مَرفوع	سيارتُها
مَنصوب	سيارتَها
مَجرور	سيارتِها

Exercises: diacritics marking case of nouns (الأسماء علامات إعراب)

Exercise 2

In the blank spaces below, add the diacritic case marking for the first terms of the 'idafa phrase: شارع محمد. First, fill the blank spaces below with the 'idafa phrase شارع محمد so the second term in the 'idafa is the standalone proper noun محمد. Then add the diacritic case marking to the first term of the 'idafa phrase. As a reminder, please place the diacritic immediately before the possessives (i.e. the proper, standalone noun).

مَرفوع ______ ______
مَنصوب ______ ______
مَجرور ______ ______

Exercise 3

In the blank spaces below, add the diacritic case marking for the first terms of the 'idafa phrase: شارع محمد. In this exercise, the second term in the 'idafa is a pronoun suffix ـه. So, first, fill the blank spaces below with the 'idafa phrase شارعه. Then add the diacritic case marking to the first term of the 'idafa phrase. As a reminder, please place the diacritic immediately before the possessive (i.e. pronoun suffix).

مَرفوع ______ ______
مَنصوب ______ ______
مَجرور ______ ______

Diacritics marking mood of verbs علامات إعراب الأفعال

Mood-marking diacritics provide an indication (i.e. an overt mark) to the mood of imperfect verbs (see Mood markings of imperfect verbs).

By convention, an imperfect verb has three moods:

1 المرفوع (the indicative),
2 الـمَنصوب (the subjunctive), and
3 الـمَجزوم (the jussive)

For imperfect form verbs with one subject marker, mood-marking diacritics are located immediately following the last radical. (See Conjugating the imperfect تصريف المُضارع, and Subject markers of the imperfect verb).

By convention, imperfect verbs with only one subject marker are marked by a:

1 ضمّة to show that they are in الـمرفوع mood
2 فتحة to show that they are in الـمنصوب mood
3 سُكون to show that they are in المجزوم mood

Examples:

Diacritic mood marker of imperfect verbs with one subject-marker

المرفوع	المنصوب	المَجزوم	
أفعلُ	أفعلَ	أفعلْ	أنا
تـفعلُ	تـفعلَ	تـفعلْ	أنتَ
يـفعلُ	يـفعلَ	يـفعلْ	هو
تـفعلُ	تـفعلَ	تـفعلْ	هي
نـفعلُ	نـفعلَ	نـفعل	نحن

Exercises: diacritics marking mood of verbs علامات إعراب الأفعال

Exercise 4

Add the mood marker of the imperfect verbs below. Reminder: please make sure the mood marker is in the appropriate locations.

المرفوع	المنصوب	المَجزوم	
يقوم	لن يقوم	لم يقم	هو
أقول	لن أقول	لم أقل	أنا
تكتب	لن تكتب	لم تكتب	أنتَ
ندعو	لن ندعو	لم ندعو	نحن
تتكلّم	لن تتكلّم	لم تتكلّم	هي

Exercise 5

Study the following sentences. The underlined words are imperfect verbs in المرفوع mood. Add the mood marker for the underlined verbs. Reminder: please make sure the mood marker is in the appropriate location.

A تزيدها تحتاج

فإنَّ كُلَّ أُمَّةٍ تحتاج إلى لُغَةٍ مُوَحَّدَةٍ

تزيدها تَجاوُباً وتَماسُكاً، فتكون مُوَحِّدة

Every nation needs a unified language (one language) that would make it more (mutually) responsive and more joined/connected/fused/fastened together, and thus be a unifying language.

B تختلف تختلف

تختلف اختلافاً بَيِّنا

حتّى إنّها تختلف بَعضَ الاختلافِ من حارةٍ إلى حارة.

They differ considerably;
they are even somewhat different from one alley to another.

Exercise 6

Study the following sentences. The underlined words are imperfect verbs in المنصوب mood. Add the mood marker for the underlined verbs. Reminder: please make sure the mood marker is in the appropriate location.

A تبسّط

من اللازِم أنْ تبسّط لُغَتَك عندما تتكلّمُ مع الأطفال

You must simplify your language when speaking with children.

B أغيّر

أحبّ أن أخرج معكم ولكنّي أريد أنْ أغيّر ملابِسي أوّلاً

I would like to go out with you, but I would like to change my clothes first.

C تدخل

إذا تأخَّـرْتَ أكثر من خمس دقائق

فلا تستطيع أن تَدخل إلى الصف

If you are more than 5 minutes late, you will not be able to enter the class.

D تتحقّق

أتَمَنّى أنْ تتحقّق كلُّ أحلامي

I hope (I wish) that all my dreams will come true.

E تستمع

أظُنُّ أنَّها لم تُرِيدْ أنْ تستمع إلى رأيي في الموضوع

I think that she does not want to listen to my opinion on the subject.

Exercise 7

Study the following sentences. The underlined words are imperfect verbs in المَجزوم mood. Add the mood marker for the underlined verbs. Reminder: please make sure the mood marker is in the appropriate locations.

A يعرّب

لم يعرّب تَدريسُ الطِّب في مُعظَم الجامعات العربية حتّى الآن

The teaching of medicine was not done in Arabic ("Arabized") in most Arab universities until now.

B تعتاد

انتَ لا تُحبّ القهوة لأنّك لم تعتاد عليها

You do not like coffee because you are not used to it.

C يتغيّر

مَطَر مَطَر مَطَر ! إذا لم يتغيّر الطقسُ قريباً
فلا أعرف ماذا سأفعل

Rain, rain, rain! If the weather does not change soon, I do not know what I will do.

D يحضر

أنا غاضِبةٌ مِنهُ لأنَّهُ لم يحضر لِزيارتي مُنذُ وقتٍ طويل

I am angry with him because he has not come to visit me in a long time.

E تريد

أظُنُّ أنَّها لم تريد أنْ تَستَمِعَ إلى رأيي في الموضوع

I think that she does not want to listen to my opinion on the subject.

Note

1. Al-Ahram (الأهرام), url: http://www.ahram.org.eg/420/2011/01/22/38/index.aspx, accessed 22 January 2011.

UNIT 6
Agreement تطابق

In Arabic, as in other languages, agreement is important. Words within a clause or sentence take on features that conform to each other.

For example:

Verbs and their subjects agree. This is true whether the subject is implied (i.e. affixed as a subject marker within the same word), a pronoun, or a standalone noun.

Nouns and their adjectives or pronouns agree.

Grammatical categories contibuting to agreement

The following are the grammatical categories that contribute to agreement:

Syntactic function (case or mood) (الحالة الإعرابية)
Gender (الجِنس)
Definiteness (التَعريف والتنكير)
Humanness (عاقِل و غير العاقِل)
Tense
Person
Voice
Number (عَدد)

Exercises: agreement تطابق

Exercise 1

Read the following passage carefully, then rewrite it in Arabic substituting محمّد for ياسمين. Rewrite the new passage in the blank spaces below. Make all the necessary changes to ensure agreement.

ياسمين تسكن في مدينة نيويورك، وهي طالبة تدرس الأدب الإنجليزي في جامعة نيويورك. والدها مصري، وهو يعمل في الأمم المتحدة، ووالدتها فلسطينية وهي سكرتيرة في نفس الجامعة. محمود وعادل وفاطمة أقارب ياسمين، وهم يسكنون في مدينة القاهرة

____

____

____

____

____

____

Exercise 2

Use the vocabulary in the glossary of adjectives below to fill in the blanks in the sentences. Make all the necessary changes to ensure agreement.

Glossary:

كبير	big	واسع	wide, broad
مصريّ	Egyptian	جَديد	new

a) I am a new student ______________ أنا طالِبة

b) New York is a big city ______________ نيويورك مدينة

c) I live in a new house ______________ أسكن في بيت

d) My dad is Egyptian ______________ والدي

e) This is a wide road ______________ هذا شارع

UNIT 7
Pronouns الضمائر

Pronominal suffixation

In English, pronouns are free-standing words; they are never suffixed to other words.

Possessive pronouns: my, your, his, her, our, and their
Object pronouns: me, you, him, her, us, you, and them

In Arabic, pronouns can be suffixed to other words. Possessive pronoun suffixes attached to nouns are the same as object pronoun suffixes attached to prepositions.

Possessive pronoun suffixes attached to nouns and object pronoun suffixes attached to prepositions:

ـي، ـكَ، ـكِ، ـهُ، ـها، ـكُما،
ـهُما، ـنا، ـكُم، ـكُنَّ، ـهُم، ـهُنَّ

Below, the pronoun suffixes are matched with their English pronoun equivalents to illustrate how number (i.e. singular, dual, plural), gender (i.e. masculine, feminine) and person (i.e. first, second, third) are reflected in Arabic suffixes.

ـي	(my/me)
ـكَ	(your/you, s., m.)
ـكِ	(your/you, s., f.)
ـهُ	(his/him)
ـها	(hers/her)
ـكُما	(your/you, d., m. and f.)
ـهُما	(their/them, d., m. and f.)
ـنا	(our/us, d. and pl.)

ـكُم	(your/yours, pl., m.)
ـكُنَّ	(your/yours, pl., f.)
ـهُم	(their, them, pl., m.)
ـهُن	(their, them, pl., f.)

Again, the possessive pronoun suffixes attached to nouns are the same as the object pronoun suffixes attached to prepositions. These suffixes (listed above) are also used for object pronoun suffixes attached to verbs, with one exception: the suffix for the first person object pronoun is ـني ("me") when affixed to verbs and ـي ("my") when affixed to prepositions.

Object pronouns: me, you, him, her, us, them
Pronouns suffixed to verbs:

نـي، كَ، كِ، هُ، ها، كُما، هُما، نا، كُم، كُنَّ، هُم، هُنَّ

Below, the noun suffixes are matched with their English pronoun equivalents to illustrate how number (i.e. singular, dual, plural), gender (i.e. masculine, feminine) and person (i.e. first, second, third) are reflected in Arabic suffixes.

نـي	(me)
كَ	(you, s., m.)
كِ	(you, s., f.)
هُ	(him)
ها	(her)
كُما	(you, d., m. or f.)
هُما	(them, d., m. or f.)
نا	(us, d. or pl.)
كُم	(you, pl., m.)
كُنَّ	(you, pl., f.)
هُم	(them, pl., m.)
هُنَّ	(them, pl., f.)

Possessive pronouns ضمائر الملكيّة

Possessive pronouns in Arabic are suffixed to nouns, adding a measure of specificity to the nouns. The nouns are therefore definite nouns that do not accept the تنوين diacritics.

Example:

Your (s., m.) book is on the chair	كتابُكَ على الكرسي
Your (p., f.) book is on the chair	كتابُكُنَّ على الكرسي

Exercise: possessive pronouns ضمائر الملكيّة

Exercise 1

Fill in the blanks below with the Arabic noun and possessive pronoun suffixes that correspond to the underlined English words. The first answer is offered as an example.

Glossary

Word	Meaning	Gender
كِتاب	a book	m.
بَيت	a house	m.
سَيّارة	a car	f.
شقّة	an apartment	f.

a) Whose book is this? — This is his book

هذا ________

هذا كِتابه

b) Whose car is this? — This is her car

هذه ________

c) Whose house is this? — This is my house

هذا ________

d) Whose apartment is this? — This is their (pl., f.) apartment

هذه ________

Object pronouns

Object pronouns are suffixed to verbs and some prepositions.

Examples:

Object pronoun suffixed to verb:

He helped you (s., m). — ساعدكَ

Object pronoun suffixed to preposition:

She went to the station with me.	ذهبَت معي إلى المحطّة
He greeted (said hello to) her at the airport	سَلَّم عليها في المطار

Exercise: object pronouns

Exercise 2

Fill in the blanks below with the Arabic words and object pronoun suffixes that correspond to the underlined English words.

Glossary

He loves	يُحِب
We heard	سَمِعنا
with	مع

a) He loves the girl — هو يُحب البنت

He loves her — هو ________

هو يُحِبها

b) We heard Samia — نحن سَمِعنا سامية

We heard her — نحن ________

c) The girl is playing with her friend — البنت تلعب مع صديقتها

The girl is playing with her — البنت تلعب ________

d) The boy is playing with the neighbours — الوَلد يلعب مع الجران

The boy is playing with them — الوَلد يلعب ________

Free-standing pronouns الضمائر المُنفَصِلة

Below, the free-standing Arabic personal pronouns are matched with their English pronoun equivalents. Note the differences in pronouns based on number (i.e. singular, dual, plural), gender (i.e. masculine, feminine) and person (i.e. first, second, third).

أنا	I
أنتَ	you (s., m.)
أنتِ	you (s., f.)

هُو	he
هِى	she
أنتُما	you (d., m. or f.)
هُما	they (d., m. or f.)
نَحنُ	we (d. or pl.)
أنتُم	you (pl., m.)
أنتُنَّ	you (pl., f.)
هُم	they (m.)
هُنَّ	they (f.)

Exercise: Free-standing pronouns الضمائر المُنفَصِلة

Exercise 3

Study the underlined subject pronouns in the statements. For each underlined subject pronoun, choose the correct person, gender and number.

	Person, gender, number	Statement
a)	____________	هَل أنتَ جَوعان؟
b)	____________	نَعَم، أنا جَوعان
c)	____________	مِن أينَ أنتُم يا شَباب؟
d)	____________	نَحنُ مِن مِصر
e)	____________	هَل أنتِ مِصريّة يا عائشَة؟
f)	____________	لا. أنا سودانِيّة
g)	____________	مَن نادية؟ هِيَ خالَة عائشَة
h)	____________	أينَ يَعمَل والِد مَها؟ هو يَعمَل في الأُمَم المُتَّحِدة
i)	____________	أدرُس في جامِعة ميدلبِري، وهي جامِعة صَغيرة في وِلايَة فيرمونت
j)	____________	أسكُن في مِنطقة المَزَّة، وهي مِنطقة قريبة مِن جامِعة

Free-standing and suffixed pronouns
الضمائر المُنفَصِلة والمُتَّصِلة

The following three tables show the independent personal pronouns in the single, dual, and plural, and the corresponding pronoun suffixes. Specifically, the tables show the possessive pronoun suffixes that attach to nouns, and the object pronoun suffixes that attach to prepositions and verbs. The tables also show the subject markers for the perfect and imperfect verbs for reference.

					Singular
Possessive pronoun: noun suffixes	*Object pronoun: preposition suffixes*	*Object pronoun: verb suffixes*	*Subject markers: imperfect verbs*	*Subject markers: perfect verbs*	*Independent pronoun*
... ي	... ي	... ـني	أ...	... ـتُ	أنا
... ـكَ	... ـكَ	... ـكَ	تـ...	... ـتَ	أنتَ
... ـكِ	... ـكِ	... ـكِ	تـ... ـي	... ـتِ	أنتِ
... ـهُ	... ـهُ	... ـهُ	يـ...	... َ	هُو
... ـها	... ـها	... ـها	تـ...	... ـتْ	هِي

					Dual
Possessive pronoun: noun suffixes	*Object pronoun: preposition suffixes*	*Object pronoun: verb suffixes*	*Subject markers: imperfect verbs*	*Subject markers: perfect verbs*	*Independent pronoun*
... ـكُما	... ـكُما	... ـكُما	تـ... ا	... ـتُما	أنتُما
... ـكُما	... ـكُما	... ـكُما	تـ... ا	... ـتُما	أنتُما
... ـهُما	... ـهُما	... ـهُما	يـ... ا	... ـا	هُما
... ـهُما	... ـهُما	... ـهُما	تـ... ا	... ـتا	هُما

Plural					
Possessive pronoun: noun suffixes	*Object pronoun: preposition suffixes*	*Object pronoun: verb suffixes*	*Subject markers: imperfect verbs*	*Subject markers: perfect verbs*	*Independent pronoun*
...ـنا	...ـنا	...ـنا	نـ...	...ـنا	نَحنُ
...ـكُم	...ـكُم	...ـكُم	تـ ... و	...ـتُم	أنتُم
...ـكُنَّ	...ـكُنَّ	...ـكُنَّ	تـ ... نَ	...ـتُنَّ	أنتُنَّ
...ـهُم	...ـهُم	...ـهُم	يـ ... و	...ـوا	هُم
...ـهُنَّ	...ـهُنَّ	...ـهُنَّ	يـ ... ن	...ـنَ	هُنَّ

Exercises: Free-standing and suffixed pronouns
الضمائر المُنفَصِلة والمُتَّصِلة

Exercise 4

Fill in the blanks with the correct forms of the pronouns or noun and pronoun suffix combinations. The first answer is given as an example.

Glossary

صورة	picture
سوريا	Syria
والدة	mother

a) Your (s., m.) picture is pretty

جميلة ________

صورَتُكَ جميلة

b) My mother is Syrian

سوريّة ________

c) I live in Beirut and it (s., f.) is a large city in the Middle East.

أسكن في مدينة بيروت و ______ مدينة كبيرة
في الشرق الأوسط

d) Are you (s., f.) a translator? Yes, I specialize in Arabic.

هل ________ مترجمة؟

نعم. ______ متخصِّصة في العربيّة

Exercise 5

Change the statements below from the first person to the third person feminine. Make all other necessary changes. The first answer is provided as an example.

a) I am hungry (m.) — أنا جعان

She is hungry — هي جَوعانة

b) I am from Egypt — أنا مِن مِصر

She is from Egypt — ________ مِن مِصر

I am Dalia's aunt — أنا خالَة داليا

She is Dalia's aunt — ________ داليا

I work at the United Nations — أنا أعْمَل في الأُمَم المُتَّحِدة

She works at the United Nations — ________ في الأُمَم المُتَّحِدة

UNIT 8
Demonstratives أسماء الإشارة

The attributes of each noun determine which demonstrative must be used to refer to that noun. The table below identifies the demonstratives that correspond to nouns based on the number, gender and case of the nouns as well as whether they are human or non-human.

	Non-human ("irrational")	*Human*
Singular		
Masculine	هذا	هذا
Feminine	هذه	هذه

Dual	*Non-human ("irrational")*		*Human*	
	مرفوع	منصوب مجرور	مرفوع	منصوب مجرور
Masculine	هذان	هذين	هذان	هذين
Feminine	هاتان	هاتين	هاتان	هاتين

Plural	*Non-human ("irrational")*	*Human*
Masculine	NA	هؤلاء
Feminine	هذه	هؤلاء

Exercise: demonstratives – أسماء الإشارة

Exercise 1

Fill in the blanks below with the appropriate pronoun and demonstrative. The first couple of answers are completed for reference.

Glossary

فنجان	tea cup (s., m.)
شَجَرة	tree (s., f.)
مُمَثِّل	actor (s., m.)

a) This is a man. This is the man.

______ رَجُل. ______ الرَجُل

هذا رَجُل. هذا هو الرَجُل

b) This is a tea cup. This is the tea cup.

______ فنجان ______ الفنجان

c) This is a tree. This is the tree.

______ شَجَرة ______ الشَجَرة

d) These are actresses (dual). These are the actresses (dual).

______ مُمَثلتان ______ المُمَثلتان

UNIT 9

Case marking: noun words الإعراب

In Arabic, as in other languages, the grammatical environment affects the form a noun takes. In other words, concepts can be expressed in different word forms. For example, in English, there exists "I" vs "me", "he" vs "him", "she" vs "her", "we" vs "us", "they" vs "them" and "who" vs "whom". Although "I" and "me" refer to the same person, and "she" and "her" also refer to the same person, the different forms are not interchangeable; it would be grammatically incorrect to say:

*Me spoke to she

or

*Her gave it to I

The corrected versions are:

I spoke to her

and

She gave it to me

UNIT 10

Noun type words: syntactic function, case name, and case marking

Syntactic function, case name, and case marking are three interrelated topics that taken together determine how a noun "should" be (I vs me, we vs us, . . .).

Syntactic function

A noun-type word can have different syntactic functions. For the purpose of illustration, it is useful to examine three such functions: subject of a verb, object of a verb, and object of a preposition. Later, some other functions will be presented. See Syntactic functions and their case markers.

1) Subject of a verb (فاعِل)
   In an instance where someone or something performs an action, that someone or something is called "subject", and the action is called "verb".

   Example of a فاعل:

   The <u>monkey</u> ate the banana in an instant أكل <u>القرد</u> الموزة في لحظة
2) Object of a verb (مفعول به)
   In an instance where an action affects someone or something, that someone or something is called "object", and the action is called "verb".

   Example of a مفعول به:

   The monkey ate the <u>banana</u> in an instant أكل القرد <u>الموزة</u> في لحظة
3) Object of a preposition (اسم مجرور:)
   A noun that immediately follows a preposition (see Prepositions) is called the object of a preposition.

   Example of an اسم مجرور:

   The monkey ate the banana in <u>an instant</u>. أكل القرد الموزة في <u>لحظة</u>

For a more complete list of different syntactic functions see Syntactic functions and their case markers.

Exercise: syntactic function of nouns

Exercise 1

Identify the syntactic function of the underlined words as subject of a verb (فاعِل), object of a verb (مفعول به), or object of a preposition (اسم مجرور). For each underlined word, select the appropriate syntactic function from the three options provided.

A Mohamed travelled to Yemen in the winter of 2009.

سافر محمد إلى اليَمن في شتاء ٢٠٠٩.

i) محمد
   a) subject of verb (فاعِل),
   b) object of verb (مفعول به),
   c) object of preposition (اسم مجرور)

ii) اليَمن
   a) subject of verb (فاعِل),
   b) object of verb (مفعول به),
   c) object of preposition (اسم مجرور)

iii) شتاء
   a) subject of verb (فاعِل),
   b) object of verb (مفعول به),
   c) object of preposition (اسم مجرور)

B The wife listens to the radio while she has breakfast in the morning.

تستمع الزوجة إلى الإذاعة وهي تفطر في الصباح.

i) الزوجة
   a) subject of verb (فاعِل),
   b) object of verb (مفعول به),
   c) object of preposition (اسم مجرور)

ii) الإذاعة
   a) subject of verb (فاعِل)
   b) object of verb (مفعول به)
   c) object of preposition (اسم مجرور)

iii) الصباح
   a) subject of verb (فاعِل)
   b) object of verb (مفعول به)
   c) object of preposition (اسم مجرور)

C When I visit the family during the weekends, we eat dinner and watch TV together.

عندما أزور العائلة في نهاية الأسبوع نأكل العشاء ونُشاهد التلفزيون معا.

i) العائلة
   a) subject of verb (فاعِل)
   b) object of verb (مفعول به)
   c) object of preposition (اسم مجرور)

ii) نهاية
   a) subject of verb (فاعِل)
   b) object of verb (مفعول به)
   c) object of preposition (اسم مجرور)

iii) العشاء
   a) subject of verb (فاعِل)
   b) object of verb (مفعول به)
   c) object of preposition (اسم مجرور)

iv) التلفزيون
   a) subject of verb (فاعِل)
   b) object of verb (مفعول به)
   c) object of preposition (اسم مجرور)

D She saw the accident on TV then read an article about it.

شاهدَت الحادثة في التلفزيون ثُمّ قرأت مقالة عنها.

i) الحادثة
   a) subject of verb (فاعِل),
   b) object of verb (مفعول به),
   c) object of preposition (اسم مجرور)

ii) التلفزيون
   a) subject of verb (فاعِل),
   b) object of verb (مفعول به),
   c) object of preposition (اسم مجرور)

iii) مقالة
   a) subject of verb (فاعِل),
   b) object of verb (مفعول به),
   c) object of preposition (اسم مجرور)

E The two friends met in the evening and had dinner, then went into the "Shuruuq" bookstore where Mustafa bought a magazine and Mahmoud bought a book.

تقابل الصديقان في المساء وأكلا العشاء
وبعد ذلك دخلا مكتبة «الشروق» حيث اشترى
مصطفى مجلة واشترى محمود كتابا.

i) الصديقان
   a) subject of verb (فاعِل),
   b) object of verb (مفعول به),
   c) object of preposition (اسم مجرور)

ii) المساء
   a) subject of verb (فاعِل),
   b) object of verb (مفعول به),
   c) object of preposition (اسم مجرور)

iii) العشاء
   a) subject of verb (فاعِل),
   b) object of verb (مفعول به),
   c) object of preposition (اسم مجرور)

iv) مكتبة
   a) subject of verb (فاعِل),
   b) object of verb (مفعول به),
   c) object of preposition (اسم مجرور)

v) مصطفى
   a) subject of verb (فاعِل),
   b) object of verb (مفعول به),
   c) object of preposition (اسم مجرور)

vi) مجلة
   a) subject of verb (فاعِل),
   b) object of verb (مفعول به),
   c) object of preposition (اسم مجرور)

vii) محمود
a) subject of verb (فاعِل),
b) object of verb (مفعول به),
c) object of preposition (اسم مجرور)

viii) كتابا
a) subject of verb (فاعِل),
b) object of verb (مفعول به),
c) object of preposition (اسم مجرور)

Case name

There are three cases for Arabic nouns. Here are their Arabic names, followed by English equivalents:

1 حالة المَرفوع the nominative case
2 حالة المنصوب the accusative case
3 حالة المَجرور the genitive case

By convention, a noun functioning as:

1 a subject of a verb (فاعِل) is in the nominative case (المرفوع),
2 the object of a verb (مفعول به) is in the accusative case (المنصوب), and
3 the object of a preposition (اِسم مجرور) is in the genitive case (المجرور).

Examples:

1 Noun in the nominative case (المرفوع)
(because its syntactic function is subject of a verb – فاعل):

أكل القرد الموزة في لحظة The monkey ate the banana in an instant.

2 Noun in the accusative case (المنصوب)
(because its syntactic function is object of a verb – المفعول به):

أكل القرد الموزة في لحظة The monkey ate the banana in an instant.

3 Noun in the genitive case (المجرور)
(its syntactic function is object of a preposition – مجرور بحرف جر):

أكل القرد الموزة في لحظة The monkey ate the banana in an instant.

Exercise: case name

Exercise 2

Identify the case name of the underlined words as مرفوع (nominative), منصوب (accusative), or مجرور (genitive). For each underlined word, select the appropriate case name from the three options provided.

A Mohamed travelled to Yemen in the winter of 2009.

سافر محمد إلى اليَمن في شتاء ٢٠٠٩.

i) محمد
   a) مرفوع (nominative)
   b) منصوب (accusative)
   c) مجرور (genitive)

ii) اليَمن
   a) مرفوع (nominative)
   b) منصوب (accusative)
   c) مجرور (genitive)

iii) شتاء
   a) مرفوع (nominative)
   b) منصوب (accusative)
   c) مجرور (genitive)

B The wife listens to the radio while she has breakfast in the morning.

تستمع الزوجة إلى الإذاعة وهي تفطر في الصباح.

i) الزوجة
   a) مرفوع (nominative)
   b) منصوب (accusative)
   c) مجرور (genitive)

ii) الإذاعة
   a) مرفوع (nominative)
   b) منصوب (accusative)
   c) مجرور (genitive)

iii) الصباح
   a) مرفوع (nominative)
   b) منصوب (accusative)
   c) مجرور (genitive).

C When I visit the family during the weekends we eat dinner and watch TV together.

عندما أزور العائلة في نهاية الأسبوع نأكل العشاء ونُشاهد التلفزيون معا.

i) العائلة
   a) مرفوع (nominative)
   b) منصوب (accusative)
   c) مجرور (genitive)

ii) نهاية
   a) مرفوع (nominative)
   b) منصوب (accusative)
   c) مجرور (genitive)

iii) العشاء
   a) مرفوع (nominative)
   b) منصوب (accusative)
   c) مجرور (genitive)

iv) التلفزيون
   a) مرفوع (nominative)
   b) منصوب (accusative)
   c) مجرور (genitive)

D She saw the accident on TV then read an article about it

شاهدَت الحادثة في التلفزيون ثُمّ قرأَت مقالة عنها.

i) الحادثة
   a) مرفوع (nominative)
   b) منصوب (accusative)
   c) مجرور (genitive)

ii) التلفزيون
   a) مرفوع (nominative)
   b) منصوب (accusative)
   c) مجرور (genitive)

iii) مقالة
   a) مرفوع (nominative)
   b) منصوب (accusative)
   c) مجرور (genitive)

E The two friends met in the evening and had dinner, then went into the "Shuruuq" bookstore where Mustafa bought a magazine and Mahmoud bought a book.

تقابل الصديقان في المساء وأكلا العشاء وبعد ذلك دخلا مكتبة "الشروق" حيث اشترى مصطفى مجلة واشترى محمود كتابا.

i) الصديقان
   a) مرفوع (nominative)
   b) منصوب (accusative)
   c) مجرور (genitive)

ii) المساء
   a) مرفوع (nominative)
   b) منصوب (accusative)
   c) مجرور (genitive)

iii) العشاء
   a) مرفوع (nominative)
   b) منصوب (accusative)
   c) مجرور (genitive)

iv) مكتبة
   a) مرفوع (nominative)
   b) منصوب (accusative)
   c) مجرور (genitive)

v) مصطفى
   a) مرفوع (nominative)
   b) منصوب (accusative)
   c) مجرور (genitive)

vi) مجلة
   a) مرفوع (nominative)
   b) منصوب (accusative)
   c) مجرور (genitive)

vii) محمود
  a) مرفوع (nominative)
  b) منصوب (accusative)
  c) مجرور (genitive)

viii) كتابا
  a) مرفوع (nominative)
  b) منصوب (accusative)
  c) مجرور (genitive)

Case marking

Only words are given case marks, not phrases or sentences.

Case marking means providing a "clue" indicating the case or function of a noun. When the English first person singular pronoun functions as a subject, it becomes "I", otherwise it is "me". The marking thus involves a pretty obvious "clue" – a complete change of the word from "I" to "me". In other instances English case marking is by only changing a letter:

<u>They</u> went to John → John went to <u>them</u> (y → m)
She's the one <u>who</u> saw me → She's the one <u>whom</u> I saw (o → m)

There are two ways to mark the case of Arabic nouns:

1 Diacritics
2 Letters

Exercises: case marking

Exercise 3

Are case marks applied to any of the words or phrases below? Give the answer نعم (yes) or لا (no) in the blank spaces below.

	نعم	لا
a) singular, feminine noun	______	______
b) singular, masculine noun	______	______
c) dual, feminine noun	______	______
d) sound, plural masculine	______	______
e) verbal phrase	______	______
f) nominal phrase	______	______

Case marking by diacritics

Case-marking diacritics – if present – (see Case-marking diacritics in the Arabic language writing system) are as follows.

Nominative case (المرفوع) is generally marked by the following diacritics:

1 ضَمّة /u/ for a definite noun

2 تنوين ضَم /un/ for an indefinite noun

Examples:

Number	*Definiteness*	*Masculine*	*Feminine*	*Meaning*
Single	Definite	المهندسُ	المهندسةُ	The engineer
Single	Indefinite	مهندسٌ	مهندسةٌ	An engineer
Plural	Definite		السَيّاراتُ	The cars
Plural	Indefinite		سَيّاراتٌ	Cars

Accusative case, المنصوب, is generally marked by the following diacritics:

1 فتحة /a/, for a definite noun (exceptions include plural feminine nouns)

2 تنوين فتح /an/ for an indefinite feminine noun (exceptions include plural feminine nouns)

3 the letter ا and تنوين فتح /an/ for an indefinite masculine noun

Examples:

Number	*Definiteness*	*Masculine*	*Feminine*	*Meaning*
Single	Definite	المهندسَ	المهندسةَ	The engineer
Single	Indefinite	مهندساً	مهندسةً	An engineer

Genitive case (المجرور) is generally marked by the following diacritics:

1 كسرة /i/ for a definite noun

2 تنوين كسر /in/ for an indefinite noun

Examples:

Number	*Definiteness*	*Masculine*	*Feminine*	*Meaning*
Single	Definite	المهندسِ	المهندسةِ	The engineer
Single	Indefinite	مهندسٍ	مهندسةٍ	An engineer
Plural	Definite		المهندساتِ	The engineers
Plural	Indefinite		مهندساتٍ	Engineers

Exercise: case marking by diacritics

Exercise 4

Study the sentence below. Add the appropriate case marker to the underlined words. If necessary, refer to sections on agreement, case marking, and syntactic functions of nouns and their case markers.

استجابت الحكومة الأمريكية لدعوات الاتصال المباشر بسوريا وإيران، وقبلت، للمرة الأولى، الجلوس على طاولة واحدة مع مسئولين من البلدين في شهر مارس الماضي، وفي إطار مؤتمر بغداد الذي شارك فيه وفود أمريكية وعربية بهدف إيجاد حل لوقف دوامة العنف في العراق.

Exercise 5

Study the phrases below. Identify the syntactic function of the underlined words as subject of a verb (فاعِل), object of a verb (مفعول به), object of a preposition (اسم مجرور). For each underlined word, select the appropriate name of the case-marking diacritic (ضَمّة, فَتحة, كسرة).

a) ذهبت المهندسة للمرة الثانية
b) استجابت الحكومة لدعوات الاتصال المباشر في ظل الضغوط
c) استجابت الحكومة الإطالية
d) قبلت (هى) الجلوس

For each of the four underlined words, fill in the blanks below with 1) the appropriate syntactic function and 2) the name of the case-marking diacritic. If necessary, refer to sections on case marking and syntactic functions of nouns and their case markers.

	Syntactic function	Case-marking diacritic
a) المرّة	____________	____________
b) ظل	____________	____________
c) الحكومة	____________	____________
d) الجلوس	____________	____________

Case marking by letters

Whereas diacritics are often by convention left out of written Arabic, case-marking letters cannot be left out of written words because letters are never left out of written Arabic.

Letters are used for case-marking nouns in the dual (see Dual) and nouns in the sound masculine plural (see Sound plurals).

Nominative case (المرفوع) is marked by the letters:

ا /aa/, for dual nouns

و /uu/, for sound masculine plural nouns

Examples:

Number	*Definiteness*	*Masculine*	*Feminine*	*Meaning*
Dual	Definite	المهندسانِ	المهندستانِ	The two engineers
Dual	Indefinite	مهندسانِ	مهندستانِ	Two engineers
Plural	Definite	المهندسونَ	NA	The engineers
Plural	Indefinite	مهندسونَ	NA	Engineers

Accusative case (المنصوب) is generally marked by:

the letter ا /an/ + diacritic تنوين فتح for a single indefinite masculine noun
the letter ي /y/ for dual and sound masculine plural nouns

Examples:

Number	*Definiteness*	*Masculine*	*Feminine*	*Meaning*
Single	Indefinite	مهندساً	NA	An engineer
Dual	Definite	المهندسَيْنِ	المهندستَيْنِ	The two engineers
Dual	Indefinite	مهندسَيْنِ	مهندستَيْنِ	Two engineers
Plural	Definite	المهندسينَ	NA	The engineers
Plural	Indefinite	مهندسينَ	NA	Engineers

Genitive case (المجرور) is marked by the:

letter ي /y/ for dual and sound masculine plural nouns

Examples:

Number	*Definiteness*	*Masculine*	*Feminine*	*Meaning*
Dual	Definite	المهندسَيْنِ	المهندستَيْنِ	The two engineers
Dual	Indefinite	مهندسَيْنِ	مهندستَيْنِ	Two engineers
Plural	Definite	المهندسينَ		The engineers
Plural	Indefinite	مهندسينَ		Engineers

Letters marking case of dual nouns

With dual nouns there is no distinction between the منصوب (accusative) and the مجرور (genitive) markers. Thus, case cannot be determined on the basis of the marking; rather case is determined on the basis of the syntactic function of the noun.

With dual nouns, case-marking letters – always present – are the following:
The nominative case (المرفوع) is marked by the:

letter ا /aa/,

Examples:

Definiteness	*Masculine*	*Feminine*	*Meaning*
Definite	المهندسانِ	المهندستانِ	The two engineers
Indefinite	مهندسانِ	مهندستانِ	Two engineers

Accusative and **genitive** cases (المنصوب و المجرور) are marked by the:

letter ي /y/

Examples:

Definiteness	*Masculine*	*Feminine*	*Meaning*
Definite	المهندسَيْنِ	المهندستَيْنِ	The two engineers
Indefinite	مهندسَيْنِ	مهندستَيْنِ	Two engineers

Letters marking case of sound masculine plural nouns

With sound masculine plural nouns there is no distinction between the منصوب (accusative) and the مجرور (genitive) markers. Thus, case can't be determined on the basis of the marking; rather case is determined on the basis of the syntactic function of the noun.

With sound masculine plural nouns, case-marking letters – always present – are the following:

Nominative case (المرفوع) is marked by:

the letter و /uu/

Examples:

Definiteness	*Masculine*	*Meaning*
Definite	المهندسونَ	The engineers
Indefinite	مهندسونَ	Engineers

Accusative and **genitive** (المنصوب و المجرور) cases are marked by:

the letter ي /ii/

In the plural, there is no distinction in case marking between **accusative** and **genitive** (المنصوب و المجرور).

Examples:

Definiteness	*Masculine*	*Meaning*
Definite	المهندسينَ	The engineers
Indefinite	مهندسينَ	Engineers

Exercises: case marking by letters

Exercise 6

Rewrite the sentences below by transforming the underlined singular nouns into their dual form. Place the correct answer in the blank spaces below. Remember to make all necessary changes and add the letters marking the case of dual nouns.

a) وَجَدتُ عائلةً في هذه البناية

____

b) الكتابُ على الكرسي

____

c) الأستاذةُ في الكُلّيّة

____

d) البنت كَسّرة قَلَمٍ

____

e) كتبت الرسالة إلى الرجُلِ

____

Exercise 7

Rewrite the sentences below by transforming the underlined singular nouns into their plural, masculine form. Place the correct answer in the blank spaces below. Remember to make all necessary changes and add the letters marking the case of plural nouns.

a) وَجَدتُ الرجلَ الطَيِّبَ في هذا الشارع

____

b) يصومُ المسلمُ شهرَ رمضان

____

c) المواطنُ معتادُ على دفع الضرائب

____

Variations in case marking

The majority of circumstances requiring case marking by diacritics for nouns are outlined above. The following, however, are some variations that are marked slightly differently:

i) Sound plural feminine nouns, ending with the suffix ات
ii) Diptotes (الممنوع من الصرف)
iii) Nouns with the following letters in final position:

(ألف) ا
(ألِف مَقصورة) ى
(ياء) ي

Case marking: Feminine sound plural nouns ending in ات

For the feminine sound plural, there is no distinction in case marking between المنصوب and المجرور.

Examples:

Case	*Definiteness*	*Feminine*	*Meaning*
المرفوع	Definite	السَيّاراتُ	the cars
المرفوع	Indefinite	سَيّاراتٌ	cars
المنصوب/المجرور	Definite	السَيّاراتِ	the cars
المنصوب/المجرور	Indefinite	سَيّاراتٍ	cars

Case marking of diptotes الممنوع من الصرف

Diptotes are a class of nouns which do not display تنوين when they are indefinite. In addition, when they are indefinite, there is no distinction in case marking between المنصوب and المجرور.

Examples:

Case	*Number*	*Definiteness*	*Feminine*	*Meaning*
المرفوع	Plural	Definite	الشَوارِعُ	the streets
المرفوع	Plural	Indefinite	شَوارِعُ	streets
المنصوب/المجرور	Plural	Definite	الشَوارِعَ	the streets
المنصوب/المجرور	Plural	Indefinite	شَوارِعَ	streets

Case marking of nouns ending with ألِف – ا

Nouns ending in ألِف can't have case markers.

Examples:

مرفوع	منصوب	مَجرور	*Meaning*
عَصا	عَصا	عَصا	a stick
العَصا	العَصا	العَصا	the stick

Case marking of nouns ending with ألِف مَقصورة – ى

There can be no case markers for nouns ending in ألِف مقصورة.

Examples:

مرفوع	منصوب	مَجرور	*Meaning*
مَقهى	مَقهى	مَقهى	a coffee shop
المَقهى	المَقهى	المَقهى	the coffee shop

Case marking of nouns ending with ياء – ي

For nouns ending in ياء, only the منصوب (accusative) can be assigned a case marker indicating the actual case. The other two cases can't have a marker indicating their actual cases; the indefinite مرفوع and مجرور both have the same marker (ٍ), while neither the definite مرفوع nor مجرور can have any marker.

Examples:

مرفوع	منصوب	مَجرور	*Meaning*
مُحامٍ	مُحامِياً	مُحامٍ	a lawyer
المُحامي	المُحاميَ	المُحامي	a lawyer

Exercise: variations in case marking

Exercise 8

Study the eight sentences below. The underlined words are diptotes (ممنوع من الصرف). First add the appropriate case marker to the underlined words. Then write the case name for each of these eight words in the blank spaces below. The first answer is offered as an example.

a) case name: منصوب

مع أنّي لا أكتُب رسائل عادةً،
فإنّي أحياناً أكتُبُ إلى صديقة طفولتي.

b) case name: ______________

لماذا لا تُوجَدُ كَنائس كثيرةٌ في الأحياء الحديثة بالمُدُن الغربية؟

c) case name: ______________

عملي يَضطَّرُني أن أُقيمَ في البحرين عدّةَ أسابيع من كلّ سنة.

d) case name: ______________

مَرَرْتُ بِتَجارِب صَعبةٍ كثيرةٍ في حياتي جعلتني أكتَشِف نَفسي.

e) case name: ______________

الناس الذين تعرّفتُ عليهم في العالم العربي كانوا لُطَفاء جِدّاً معي.

f) case name: ______________

خَرَّجَت الجامعة الأمريكية في بيروت وُزَراء ورُؤَساء عرباً كثيرين.

g) case name: ______________

عِندما زُرنا الشامَ رأَيْنا عِدَّةَ مَساجِد قَديمةً في منطقة" باب توما.

h) case name: ______________

ناقَشَت المُتَحَدِّثَةُ باسم الحُكومة عِدّةَ مَشاريع جديدة تَنوي الحُكومةُ القيامَ بها.

An overview of case markings

Examples:

		المرفوع	
Definiteness	*Masculine*	*Feminine*	*Meaning*
Definite	المهندسُ	المهندسةُ	The engineer
Indefinite	مهندسٌ	مهندسةٌ	An engineer
Definite	المهندسانِ	المهندستانِ	The two engineers

Indefinite	مهندسانِ	مهندستانِ	Two engineers
Definite	المهندسونَ	المهندساتُ	The engineers
Indefinite	مهندسونَ	مهندساتٌ	Engineers

المنصوب

Definiteness	*Masculine*	*Feminine*	*Meaning*
Definite	المهندسَ	المهندسةَ	The engineer
Indefinite	مهندساً	مهندسةً	An engineer
Definite	المهندسَيْنِ	المهندستَيْنِ	The two engineers
Indefinite	مهندسَيْنِ	مهندستَيْنِ	Two engineers
Definite	المهندسينَ	المهندساتِ	The engineers
Indefinite	مهندسينَ	مهندساتٍ	Engineers

المجرور

Definiteness	*Masculine*	*Feminine*	*Meaning*
Definite	المهندسِ	المهندسةِ	The engineer
Indefinite	مهندسٍ	مهندسةٍ	An engineer
Definite	المهندسَيْنِ	المهندستَيْنِ	The two engineers
Indefinite	مهندسَيْنِ	مهندستَيْنِ	Two engineers
Definite	المهندسينَ	المهندساتِ	The engineers
Indefinite	مهندسينَ	مهندساتٍ	Engineers

Exercise: an overview of case marking

Exercise 9

Complete the three tables below by making all necessary changes to the noun مُمَثِّلٌ (an actor).

A Fill in the blanks in this table with the noun in the singular. Please make all necessary changes to reflect all combinations of the following attributes: definite, indefinite, masculine, feminine, nominative case, accusative case, genitive case.

The singular (المُفرَد)				
Definite (مَعرِفَة)		Indefinite (نَكِرَة)		Case
Feminine (مُؤَنَّث)	Masculine (مُذَكَّر)	Feminine (مُؤَنَّث)	Masculine (مُذَكَّر)	
______	______	______	مُمَثِّلٌ	المرفوع
______	______	______	______	المنصوب
______	______	______	______	المجرور

B Fill in the blanks in this table with the noun in the dual. Please make all necessary changes to reflect all combinations of the following attributes: definite, indefinite, masculine, feminine, nominative case, accusative case, genitive case.

The dual (المُثَنَّى)				
Definite (مَعرِفَة)		Indefinite (نَكِرَة)		Case
Feminine (مُؤَنَّث)	Masculine (مُذَكَّر)	Feminine (مُؤَنَّث)	Masculine (مُذَكَّر)	
______	______	______	______	المرفوع
______	______	______	______	المنصوب
______	______	______	______	المجرور

C Fill in the blanks in this table with the noun in the plural. Please make all necessary changes to reflect all combinations of the following attributes: definite, indefinite, masculine, feminine, nominative case, accusative case, genitive case.

The plural (الجَمع)				
Definite (مَعرِفَة)		Indefinite (نَكِرَة)		Case
Feminine (مُؤَنَّث)	Masculine (مُذَكَّر)	Feminine (مُؤَنَّث)	Masculine (مُذَكَّر)	
______	______	______	______	المرفوع
______	______		______	المنصوب
______	______	______	______	المجرور

UNIT 11

Syntactic functions and their case markers الحالة الإعرابية و علامات الإعراب

The function of a word determines its case (see Syntactic function). The following are some main functions of words and their equivalent case names:

A The following functions of words are marked مرفوع (nominative):

الفاعِل (subject of a verb)
الـمُبتدأ (subject of a جملة اسمية)
الـخَبر (predicate of a جملة اسمية)

B The following functions of words are marked منصوب accusative:

الـمَفعول به (direct object of a verb)
الظَرف (adverb)

C The following functions of words are marked مجرور (genitive):

الـمَجرور بحرف جر (the object of a preposition)
الـمُضاف إليه (the second term of an 'idafa)

UNIT 12
Noun types

A phrasal predicate is a nominal phrase with one of the following headwords:

1 Proper noun

Examples:

سَميرةُ، مُحَمّدٌ، مُصطَفى، ليلى، سَميحةُ، ...

2 Common noun

Examples:

بابٌ، شَجَرَةٌ، مَدرَسةٌ، رَجُلٌ، اِمرأةٌ، ...

3 Adjectival noun

Examples:

مُديرةٌ، مُديرٌ، طَويلٌ، طَويلةٌ،
مُعَقَّدٌ، مُعَقَّدةٌ، جَميلٌ، جَميلةٌ، ...

4 Temporal or locative adverbial noun

Examples:

بَعدَ، قَبلَ، فَوقَ، تَحتَ، أمامَ، وَراءَ، ...

5 Gerund

Examples:

دَمارٌ، نَشازٌ، جَمالٌ، اِستِقلالٌ،
اِستِقبالٌ، تَقبيلٌ، ...

Adjectival nouns

An adjectival noun has a masculine form as well as a feminine one.

Examples of adjectival nouns in the singular:

كَبير/كبيرة
صَغير/صَغيرة
طالب/طالِبة
مُدير/مُديرة
جَميل/جَميلة
قَبيح/قَبيحة

The examples of adjectives above illustrate that an adjective has a masculine form and an equivalent feminine one. In other words, adjectives exist in masculine-feminine pairs.

The relative adjective النِّسبة

The relative adjective is formed by suffixing a يّ to the masculine noun.

Example:

Egypt	Egyptian (s., m.)
مِصر	مِصري

There are three exceptions:

If a noun ends in ة or ا or يا.

To form the adjective: First, drop the last letter ة or ا or يا, then add the ي.

Examples:

1 If the word ends in ا, such as أمريكا

America	American (s., m.)
أمريكا	أمريكيّ

2 If the word ends in يا, such as سوريا

Syria	Syrian (s., m.)
سوريا	سوريّ

3 If the word ends in ة, such as جامِعة

University	Academic (s., m.)
جامعة	جامعيّ

To form a feminine adjective, add ة after the adjectival suffix يّ.

Example:

Egypt	Egyptian (s., m.)	Egyptian (s., f.)
مِصر	مِصريّ	مِصريّة

Exercise: the relative adjective النِّسبة

Exercise 1

Fill in the blanks with the appropriate relative adjectives. First, for each statement, identify the suitable word from the glossary below. Then make all the necessary changes to each selected word from the glossary below to convert it to an adjective that agrees with the noun that it qualifies. That is, the relative adjective must agree with the noun that it qualifies in terms of number, gender, and definiteness.

Glossary

Saudi Arabia	السعودية
Italy	إيطاليا
Spain	إسبانيا
France	فرنسا
Turkey	تركيا
Egypt	مِصر

Arab	عرب (s., m.)
coffee	قهوة (s., f.)
bank	البنك (s., m.)
literature	الأَدَب (s., m.)

a) a Saudi man ________ رجل

b) the Turkish coffee (s., f.) ________ القهوة

c) the Arab bank (s., m.) ________ البنك

d) Italian girl ________ بنت

e) The book, *Alf Leila Wa Leila*, is one of the great works in the history of Arab Literature (s., m.).

كتاب "ألف ليلة وليلة" من الأعمال
العظيمة في تاريخ الأدب ________

f) I {study/am studying} Spanish literature (s., m.)

أدرُس الأَدَب ________

g) She's an Egyptian from the city of Tanta

هي ________ من مدينة طنطا

h) the Egyptian student (s., m.) ________ الطالب

Substantive nouns

Examples of masculine substantive nouns:

كِتاب	a book
شارع	a street
فِنجان	a cup
بَيت	a house

Examples of feminine substantive nouns:

سيارة	a car
طاولة	a table
شجرة	a tree
شقّة	an apartment

The masculine and feminine examples of substantive nouns above illustrate that a substantive is either masculine or feminine. There aren't masculine-feminine pairs of the same substantive.

Gerunds المصدر

Gerunds and verb

A مَصدَر can is derived from a verb. For example, the مَصدَر from the verb يُسافِر, he travels, is السَّفَر. (See Word–noun paradigm.) Depending on how it is used, it can have either the meaning "travelling", or the meaning of the English infinitive "to travel".

Gerunds and gender

A gerund is either masculine or feminine. There are no masculine-feminine pairs of the same gerund.

Examples of masculine gerunds:

شَرح	(an) explanation
وُجود	(an) existence
قُبول	(an) acceptance
مَشي	walking (e.g. Walking is beneficial.)

Examples of feminine gerunds:

قِراءة	reading
كِتابة	writing
غَباوة	stupidity
حَلاوة	sweetness

Exercises: gerunds

Exercise 2

Rewrite the following sentence by substituting the word مَشي (walking) with the prompts provided. Make all other necessary changes.

He likes walking because it strengthens the mind.

a) walking هو يحب المشى لِأنه يُقَوّى العَقل

b) reading ____________________

c) writing ____________________

Exercise 3

Study the sentences below. Underline the مصدر in each sentence.

a) أكل الفطار مُفيد

b) الطفل لا يحب الاسْتِحمام

c) البنت تستمتع بقراءة الكتب

d) التاجر يُحِّب الإقامة في المدن الكبيرة

e) ازداد عددُ المُحجّبات في هذه المنطقة

f) الأُستاذ لا يحبُّ التَدريس في الصباح

g) عقيل كان يحب شُربَ القهوة

h) الشُعور بالوحدة صعب على الجميع

i) داليا تُحِب السَّفَر

UNIT 13

The "human" vs "non-human" classification of nouns

Arabic nouns fall into two broad categories (kingdoms in other systems). The first category, العاقِل, meaning "rational", is only in reference to humans. The other category, غير العاقِل, meaning "not rational", includes everything else (i.e. animal, vegetable, and mineral).

Gender and non-human nouns

Arabic has *no neutral* category, i.e. it; there are only masculine and feminine. In the singular, the word "it" is either masculine (هو) or feminine (هي). So, a non-human noun is either:

masculine	or	feminine
هو – مُذَكَّر	or	هي – مُؤَنَّث.

Examples:

This is the chair (m.)	هذا هو الكُرسي
This is the apartment (f.)	هذه هي الشَقّة

Non-human referents are often made explicit. Thus, Arabic equivalents of English expressions such as "It is hot", "It is night", or "It is difficult" tend not to use proform equivalents of "it", such as هو and هي. Instead a commonly understood or commonly interpreted referent of "it" is used.

Examples:

الجَوّ حار	It (i.e. the weather) is hot
الوقتُ ليل	It (i.e. the time) is night
المُشكلة صعبة	It (i.e. the problem) is difficult

Exercise: gender and non-human nouns

Exercise 1

Fill in the blanks. Below is a glossary of terms for reference.

Glossary

سَيّارة	car
إسعاف	ambulance
سريع	fast

1 The car (f.) is fast — السَيّارة ________
2 It (the car, f.) is fast — ________ سَريعة
3 The ambulance (m.) is fast — الإسعاف ________
4 It (the ambulance, m.) is fast — ________ سريع

Gender and human nouns

A human noun can have a masculine and a feminine form. To make a masculine noun feminine, add a تاء مَربوطة.

Example:

Professor

أُستاذ	Masculine
أُستاذة	Feminine

Exercise: gender and human nouns

Exercise 2

Rewrite the following by turning the masculine human nouns into feminine. Please make all necessary changes to ensure agreement. Write the answers in the blank spaces below.

a) He is a professor — هو أُستاذ
She is a professor — ________

b) He is a student — هو طالب
She is a student — ________

c) He is American هو أمريكي
She is American ______________

Number in human and non-human nouns and their adjectives

Concerning the number in nouns, Arabic distinguishes between human and non-human nouns.

Non-human plural nouns are treated like singular feminine nouns in a sentence. Therefore, the adjectives for non-human plural nouns will always be singular and feminine.

Examples:

non-human noun and adjective	meaning
سيارات أمريكيّة	American (s., f.) cars (pl., f.)
سيارة أمريكيّة	American (s., f.) car (s., f.)
شوارِع واسِعة	wide (s., f.) streets (pl.)
شارِع واسِع	wide (s., m.) street (s., m.)

Only human adjectives can be plural and feminine or masculine.

Examples:

human noun and adjective	meaning
طالِب أمريكيّ	American student (s., m.)
طالِبة أمريكيّة	American student (s., f.)
طُلاّب أمريكيّون	American (pl., m.) students (pl., m.)
طالِبات أمريكيّات	American (pl., f.) students (pl., f.)

Exercise: number in human and non-human nouns and their adjectives

Exercise 3

Fill in the blank spaces below with the appropriate adjective. Use the glossary below to identify the relevant adjective. Then make all the necessary adjustments to the number and gender of the adjective to ensure agreement with the noun.

Glossary

لُغات	languages (pl.)
أوروبيّ	European (s., m.)
مُتَرجِمون	translators (pl., m.)
عَرَب	Arab (pl.)
موظّفات	employees (pl., f.)
جديد	new (s., m.)
أشياءَ	things
يابانيّ	Japanese (s., m.)
لُبنانيّ	Lebanese (s., m.)

a) Italian, Spanish, and French are European languages.

الإيطالية والإسبانية والفرنسية لُغات ________

b) Lebanese friends

أصحاب ________

c) Arab translators at the UN

مُتَرجِمون ______ في الأُمَم المُتَّحِدة

d) Miss Muna, Miss Wafa' and Mrs Mary are new employees.

الآنِسة مُنى والآنِسة وفاء والسيدة ماري موظّفات ________

e) Today, the history professor taught us new things about ancient Central Asian history.

اليومَ أستاذُ التاريخِ علَّمنا أشياءَ ________

عن تاريخِ آسيا الوُسْطَى القديم.

f) Honda, Isuzu and Toyota are Japanese cars.

هوندا وإيسوزو وتويوتا سَيّارات ________

UNIT 14

The human category nouns

I. Singular human

Reference to singular masculine human nouns

Masculine singular human nouns are referred to by the pronoun هو, or by the demonstrative هذا.

Examples:

هذا الرَجُل	This man
هذا رَجُل	This is a man
هذا هو الرَجُل	This is the man

Exercise: reference to singular masculine human nouns

Exercise 1

Study the sentences below and the pronouns and/or demonstratives in each sentence. Draw a line under each pronoun and/or demonstrative referencing a singular masculine human noun. In the blank spaces below, write the specific pronoun and/or demonstrative. Where, for example, the pronoun is affixed to part of another word, only write the independent pronoun. If there are no references to singular, masculine human nouns, write "none" in the blank spaces.

Glossary

كثيرُ الحركة	restless
بعيدةُ النظر	far-sighted
خفيفةُ الدمِ	cute/funny
وسريعةُ البديهة	quick-witted

الطويلُ القامةِ	tall
الجميلُ الوجه	handsome
قليلُ الكلام	silent, not wordy
جميلةُ المَناظِرِ	pretty, scenic
طَيّبة القلب	kind-hearted, generous
الواسعةِ الانتشار	in broad circulation
ثقيلُ الدّمِ	unpleasant
أصفرُ الوَجه	pale-faced or jaundiced

a) ______________________

لا يستطيع أخي أن يجلس في مكان واحد مدة طويلة، فهو كثيرُ الحركة

b) ______________________

والدتي إنسانة بعيدةُ النظر تُفَكّر دائماً في المُستقبل

c) ______________________

تعجبني شخصيتها لأنّها خفيفةُ الدمِ وسريعةُ البديهة

d) ______________________

مَن هذا الشابّ الطويلُ القامةِ الجميلُ الوجه؟

e) ______________________

من الصعب أن يتعرّف عليه الناس لأنّه خجولٌ وقليلُ الكلام

f) ______________________

هذه منطقة جميلةُ المَناظِرِ ولذلك يَقصِدُها ناسٌ كثيرونَ كلّ عام

g) ______________________

جريدة الـ "واشنطون بوست" والـ "نيويورك تايمز" من الجرائد الواسعةِ الانتشار

h) ______________________

يبدو أنّك تعبان جداً وأصفَرُ الوَجه، هل أنتَ مَريض؟

i) ______________________

هي طَيّبة القلب، تحبّ كلّ الناس وتحاول أن تساعدهم

j) ______________________

هو شخص ثقيلُ الدّمِ، لا أستطيع الجُلوس معه أكثر من دقيقتين

Reference to singular feminine human nouns

Feminine singular human nouns are referred to by the pronoun هي, or by the demonstrative هذه.

Examples:

هذه المَرأة	This woman
(هذه اِمرأة) هذه مَرأة	This is a woman
هذه هي المَرأة	This is the woman

Exercise: reference to singular feminine human nouns

Exercise 2

Study the sentences below and the pronouns and/or demonstratives in each sentence. Draw a line under each pronoun and/or demonstrative referencing a singular feminine human noun. In the blank spaces below, write the specific pronoun and/or demonstrative. Where, for example, the pronoun is affixed to part of another word, only write the independent pronoun. If there are no references to singular feminine human nouns, write "none" in the blank spaces.

Glossary

كثيرُ الحركة	restless
بعيدةُ النظر	far-sighted
خفيفةُ الدمِ	cute/funny
وسريعةُ البديهة	quick-witted
الطويلُ القامةِ	tall
الجميلُ الوجه	handsome
قليلُ الكلام	silent, not wordy
جميلةُ المَناظِرِ	pretty, scenic
طَيِّبة القلب	kind-hearted, generous
الواسعةِ الانتشار	in broad circulation
ثقيلُ الدّمِ	unpleasant
أصفرُ الوَجه	pale-faced or jaundiced

a) ______________________________

لا يستطيع أخي أن يجلس في مكان واحد مدة طويلة، فهو كثيرُ الحركة

b) ______________________________

والدتي إنسانة بعيدةُ النظر تُفَكّر دائماً في المُستقبل

c) ______________________________

تعجبني شخصيتها لأنّها خفيفةُ الدمِ وسريعةُ البديهة

d) ____________________

مَن هذا الشابّ الطويلُ القامةِ الجميلُ الوجه؟

e) ____________________

من الصعب أن يتعرّف عليه الناس لأنّه خجولٌ وقليلُ الكلام

f) ____________________

هذه منطقة جميلةُ المَناظِرِ ولذلك يَقصِدُها ناسٌ كثيرونَ كلّ عام

g) ____________________

جريدة الـ ''واشنطون بوست'' والـ ''نيويورك تايمز'' من الجرائد الواسعةِ الانتشار

h) ____________________

يبدو أنّك تعبان جداً وأصفَرُ الوَجه، هل أنتَ مَريض؟

i) ____________________

هي طَيّبة القلب، تحبّ كلّ الناس وتحاول أن تساعدهم

j) ____________________

هو شخص ثقيلُ الدّمِ، لا أستطيع الجُلوس معه أكثر من دقيقتين

Summary: reference to singular human nouns

Predictably, in the singular, gender determines which pronouns and demonstratives are used to reference a noun:

Masculine:

Pronoun: هو
Demonstrative: هذا

Feminine:

Pronoun: هي
Demonstrative: هذه

Exercises: summary – reference to singular human nouns

Exercise 3

Rewrite the sentences below and change pronouns and demonstratives that are singular masculine human to singular feminine human. Please make all necessary changes to ensure agreement. Write the answers in the blank spaces below.

a) ____________________

لا يستطيع أخي أن يجلس في مكان واحد مدة طويلة،
فهو كثيرُ الحركة

b) ____

مَن هذا الشابّ الطويلُ القامةِ الجميلُ الوجه؟

c) ____

من الصعب أن يتعرّف عليه الناس لأنّه خجولٌ وقليلُ الكلام

d) ____

هو شخص ثقيلُ الدّم،
لا أستطيع الجُلوس معه أكثر من دقيقتي

Exercise 4

Rewrite the sentences below and change pronouns and demonstratives that are singular feminine human to singular masculine human. Please make all necessary changes to ensure agreement. Write the answers in the blank spaces below.

Glossary

area/place منطقة (s., f.) area/place مكان (s., m.)

a) ____

تعجبني شخصيتها لأنّها خفيفةُ الدمِ وسريعةُ البديهة

b) ____

هذه منطقة جميلةُ المَناظِرِ ولذلك يَقصِدُها ناسٌ كثيرونَ كلّ عام

c) ____

هي طَيّبة القلب، تحبّ كلّ الناس وتحاول أن تساعدهم

II. Dual human

Reference to masculine dual human nouns

Masculine dual human nouns can be referred to by the pronoun هُما, or by the demonstrative هذانِ if the noun is in the nominative case, or the demonstrative هذين if the noun is either in the accusative or genitive case.

Examples:

هذانِ الرَجُلان These two men
هذانِ رَجُلان These are two men
هذانِ هُما الرَجُلان These are the two men

Exercise: reference to masculine dual human nouns

Exercise 5

Study the sentences below and the pronouns and/or demonstratives in each sentence. Draw a line under each pronoun and/or demonstrative referencing a masculine dual human noun. In the blank spaces below, write the specific pronoun and/or demonstrative. If there are no references to masculine dual human nouns, write "none" in the blank spaces.

a) ____

هذان هما المهندسان

b) ____

هذان المهندسان أسسا شركة في العام الماضي

c) ____

هاتان هما المُمَرضتان

d) ____

هاتان المُمَرضتان أسستا عيادة مجانية في العام الماضي

Reference to feminine dual human nouns

Feminine dual human nouns are referred to by the pronoun هُما, or by the demonstrative هاتان if the noun is in the nominative case, or the demonstrative هاتين if the noun is in either the accusative or genitive case.

Examples:

هاتانِ المَرأتانِ	These two women
هاتانِ مَرأتانِ	These are two women
هاتانِ هُما المَرأتانِ	These are the two women

Exercise: reference to feminine dual human nouns

Exercise 6

Study the sentences below and the pronouns and/or demonstratives in each sentence. Draw a line under each pronoun and/or demonstrative referencing a feminine dual human noun. In the blank spaces below, write the specific pronoun and/or demonstrative. If there are no references to feminine dual human nouns, write "none" in the blank spaces.

a) ____

هذان هما المهندسان

b) ____

هذان المهندسان أسسا شركة في العام الماضي

c) ____

هاتان هما المُمَرضتان

d) ____

هاتان المُمَرضتان أسستا عيادة مجانية في العام الماضي

Summary: reference to dual human nouns

With demonstratives, reference to the dual masculine requires a masculine demonstrative, while reference to the dual feminine requires a feminine one:

Masculine: هذانِ، هذاين
Feminine: هاتان، هاتين

However, reference to the masculine dual and the feminine dual is by the same pronoun:

Masculine: هُما
Feminine: هُما

Exercises: summary reference to dual human nouns

Exercise 7

Rewrite the sentences below and change the pronouns and demonstratives that are dual masculine human to dual feminine human. Please make all necessary changes to ensure agreement. Write the answers in the blank spaces below.

These are the (two m.) children

هذان هما الطفلان

These are the (two f.) children

____

These (two m.) engineers founded a company last year

هذان المهندسان أسسا شركة في العام الماضي

These (two f.) engineers founded a company last year

____

Exercise 8

Rewrite the sentences below and change the pronouns and demonstratives that are dual feminine human to dual masculine human. Please make all necessary changes to ensure agreement. Write the answers in the blank spaces below.

These (two f.) nurses founded a free clinic last year

هاتان المُمَرضتان أسستا عيادة مجانية في العام الماضي

These (two m.) nurses founded a free clinic last year

____

These are nurses (d., f.)

هاتان هما مُمَرضتان

These are nurses (d., m.)

____

III. Plural human

Reference to masculine plural human nouns

Plural masculine human nouns are referred to by the pronoun هُم, or by the demonstrative هؤلاء.

Examples:

هؤلاء الرِجال	These men
هؤلاء رِجال	These are men
هؤلاء هُم الرِجال	These are the men

Exercise: reference to masculine plural human nouns

Exercise 9

Study the sentences below and the pronouns and/or demonstratives in each sentence. Draw a line under each pronoun and/or demonstrative referencing a masculine plural human noun. In the blank spaces, write the specific pronoun and/or demonstrative. If there are no references to masculine dual human nouns, write "none" in the blank spaces.

a) ____

هؤلاء هم العلماء

b) ____

هؤلاء علماء

c) ____

هؤلاء هن المحترفات

d) ____

هؤلاء هم المحترفون

e) ____

هؤلاء هم التلاميذ

f) ____

هؤلاء تلاميذ

g) ____

هؤلاء هن مُترجمات

h) ____

هؤلاء المترجمات

Reference to feminine plural human nouns

Plural feminine human nouns are referred to by the pronoun هُنَّ, or by the demonstrative هؤلاء.

Examples:

هؤلاء النساء	These women
هؤلاء نِساء	These are women
هؤلاء هُنَّ النساء	These are the women

Exercise: reference to feminine plural human nouns

Exercise 10

Study the sentences below and the pronouns and/or demonstratives in each sentence. Draw a line under each pronoun and/or demonstrative referencing a feminine plural human noun. In the blank spaces below, write the specific pronoun and/or demonstrative. If there are no references to feminine plural human nouns, write "none" in the blank spaces.

a) ______________________________

هؤلاء هم العلماء

b) ______________________________

هؤلاء علماء

c) ______________________________

هؤلاء هن المحترفات

d) ______________________________

هؤلاء هم المحترفون

e) ______________________________

هؤلاء هم التلاميذ

f) ______________________________

هؤلاء تلاميذ

g) ______________________________

هؤلاء هن مُترجمات

h) ______________________________

هؤلاء المترجمات

Summary: reference to plural human nouns

Reference to the masculine feminine plural is by the same demonstrative:

Masculine: هؤلاءِ
Feminine: هؤلاءِ

However, reference to the masculine requires a masculine pronoun, but reference to the feminine requires a feminine one:

Masculine: هُم
Feminine: هُنَّ

Exercise: summary – reference to plural human nouns

Exercise 11

Rewrite the sentences below and change the pronouns and demonstratives that are plural feminine human to plural masculine human. Please make all necessary changes to ensure agreement. Write the answers in the blank spaces.

a) These (pl. f.) are the skilled (individuals)

هؤلاء هن المحترفات

These (pl. m.) are the skilled (individuals)

____

b) These are translators (pl. f.)

هؤلاء هن مُترجمات

These are translators (pl. m.)

____

Exercise: summary – reference to plural human nouns

Overall

Singular

Reference to the masculine and feminine using pronouns and demonstratives is on the basis of gender:

Masculine: هو and هذا
Feminine: هي and هذه

Dual

Reference to the masculine and feminine is on the basis of gender only with the demonstratives:

Masculine: هذانِ، هذين
Feminine: هاتان، هاتين

However, reference to the masculine and feminine is by the same pronoun:

Masculine: هُما
Feminine: هُما

Plural

Reference to the masculine and the feminine is on the basis of gender only with the pronouns:

Masculine: هُم
Feminine: هُنَّ

However, reference to the masculine and feminine is by the same demonstrative:

Masculine: هؤلاءِ
Feminine: هؤلاءِ

UNIT 15

The non-human category nouns

I. Singular non-human

Reference to singular masculine non-human nouns

Masculine singular non-human nouns are referred to by the pronoun هو, or by the demonstrative هذا.

Examples:

هذا الكُرسي	This chair
هذا كُرسي	This is a chair
هذا هو الكُرسي	This is the chair
هذا الشارِع	This street
هذا شارِع	This is a street
هذا هو الشارع	This is the street
هذا الفِنجان	This cup
هذا فِنجان	This is a cup
هذا هو الفِنجان	This is the cup
هذا البيت	This house
هذا بيت	This is a house
هذا هو البيت	This is the house

Exercise: singular masculine non-human nouns

Exercise 1

Fill in the blanks below with the appropriate noun and pronoun and/or demonstrative. The first example is completed for reference. For help, refer to the following glossary of objects found in a typical classroom:

Glossary

كُرسي	(s., m.) chair
باب	(s., m.) door
شُبّاك	(s., m.) window
كِتاب	(s., m.) book
قَلَم	(s., m.) pen

What is this?	ما هذا؟
This is a chair.	هذا ________
This is the chair	________ الكُرسي
What is this?	________ ؟
This is a door.	________ باب
This is the door.	هذا هو ________
What is this?	ما هذا؟
This is a window.	________
This is the window.	________ الشُبّاك
What is this?	________ ؟
This is a book.	هذا كِتاب
This is the book.	________
What is this?	ما هذا؟
This is a pen.	________
This is the pen.	هذا هو القَلَم

Reference to singular feminine non-human nouns

Feminine singular non-human nouns are referred to by the pronoun هي, or by the demonstrative هذه.

Examples:

هذه السيّارة	This car
هذه سيّارة	This is a car

هذه هي السيّارة	This is the car
هذه الشَجَرة	This tree
هذه شَجَرة	This is a tree
هذه هي شَجَرة	This is the tree
هذه الطاوِلة	This table
هذه طاوِلة	This is a table
هذه هي الطاوِلة	This is the table
هذه الشَقّة	This apartment
هذه شَقّة	This is an apartment
هذه هي الشَقّة	This is the apartment

Exercise: singular feminine non-human nouns

Exercise 2

Fill in the blanks below with the appropriate noun and pronoun and/or demonstrative. For help, refer to the following glossary of objects found in a typical classroom:

Glossary

طاوِلة	(s., f.) table
كَرّاسة	(s., f.) notebook

What is this?	ما هذِه؟
This is a table.	هذِه __________
This is the table.	__________ الطاوِلة
What is this?	__________ __________؟
This is a notebook.	هذِه __________
This is the notebook.	__________ الكَرّاسة

Summary:

Predictably, in the singular, gender determines which pronouns and demonstratives are used to reference a noun:

Masculine:
Pronoun: هو
Demonstrative: هذا

Feminine:
Pronoun: هي
Demonstrative: هذه

II. Dual non-human

Reference to dual masculine non-human nouns

Masculine, non-human dual nouns can be referred to by the pronoun هُما. These nouns can also be referred to by the demonstrative هذان if they are in the nominative case, or the demonstrative هذين if they are in either the accusative or the genitive case.

Examples:

هذانِ الشارِعانِ	These two streets
هذانِ شارِعانِ	These are two streets
هذانِ هُما الشارِعانِ	These are the two streets

Exercise: dual masculine non-human nouns

Exercise 3

Translate the English phrases below into Arabic with a noun and pronoun and/or demonstrative. Use a pronoun or demonstrative corresponding to non-human dual masculine nouns. Refer to the glossary below for the noun and make the necessary changes to ensure agreement.

Glossary

كِتاب	book (s., m.)
باب	door (s., m.)
شُبّاك	window (s., m.)
كتاب	book (s., m.)
قَلَم	pen (s., m.)

i. These are two books

____

ii. These are the two doors

____

iii. These are the two windows

____

iv. These two houses

____

v. These are the two pens

____

Reference to feminine dual non-human nouns

الشَقّتانِ Feminine dual nouns are referred to by the pronoun هُما, or by the demonstrative هاتانِ if the noun is in the nominative case, or the demonstrative هاتين if the noun is in either the accusative or genitive case.

Examples:

هاتانِ الشَقّتانِ	These two apartments
هاتانِ شَقّتانِ	These are two apartments
هاتانِ هُما الشَقّتانِ	These are the two apartments

Exercise: dual, feminine non-human nouns

Exercise 4

Transform the English phrases below into Arabic with a noun and pronoun and/or demonstrative. Use a pronoun or demonstrative corresponding to non-human dual feminine nouns. Refer to the glossary below for the noun and make the necessary changes to ensure agreement.

Glossary

سيّارة	car (s., f.)
شَجَرة	tree (s., f.)
طاوِلة	table (s., f.)
شَقّة	apartment (s., f.)

i) These two cars

____

ii) These are the two cars

____

iii) These are the two trees

____

iv) These two tables

____

Summary:

With demonstratives, reference to the dual masculine requires a masculine demonstrative, while reference to the dual feminine requires a feminine one:

Masculine: هذانِ، هذين
Feminine: هاتان، هاتين

However, reference to the masculine dual and the feminine dual is by the same pronoun:

Masculine: هُما
Feminine: هُما

III. Plural non-human

Reference to all non-human plural nouns

Plural non-human nouns form a special category. They are all exclusively referred to by the pronoun هي, or by the demonstrative هذه.

Examples:

هذه الشوارِع	These streets
هذه شوارع	These are streets
هذه هي الشوارع	These are the streets

Exercise: reference to all non-human plural nouns

Exercise 5

Translate the English phrases below into Arabic with a noun and pronoun and/or demonstrative. Use a pronoun or demonstrative corresponding to non-human plural nouns. Refer to the glossary below for the noun and make the necessary changes to ensure agreement.

Glossary

كَرّاسة	notebook
شَقّة	apartment

i) These notebooks

____

ii) These apartments

____

iii) These are the apartments

____

iv) These are apartments

____

Overall

Singular

Reference to the masculine and feminine using pronouns and demonstratives is on the basis of gender:

Masculine: هو and هذا
Feminine: هي and هذه

Dual

Reference to the masculine and feminine is on the basis of gender only with the demonstratives:

Masculine: هذانِ، هذين
Feminine: هاتان، هاتين

However, reference to the masculine and feminine is by same pronoun:

Masculine: هُما
Feminine: هُما

Plural

Reference to the masculine and the feminine is by the same pronoun:

Masculine: هي
Feminine: هي

Similarly, reference to the masculine and feminine is by the same demonstrative:

Masculine: هذه
Feminine: هذه

UNIT 16

Noun attributes: number, gender, case, definiteness

The morphological nature of the structure of Arabic words is such that, apart from its core meaning (which is determined by its roots), a noun has four attributes: number, gender, case, and definiteness.

Number (عَدد)

Singular (مُفرَد)

Dual (مُثَنّى)

Plural (جَمع)

Gender is either masculine or feminine. There is no neutral category.

Case is nominative, accusative, or genitive.

Definiteness is definite or indefinite.

Decoding attributes of an unfamiliar noun

We can discern the attributes of a noun based on its form. That is, we can read a word we have never seen before and determine the number, gender, case, and definiteness of the noun based on the form of the word.

For example, study the following two nouns in their singular feminine, indefinite forms:

سيّارة	car
مُمَثِّلة	actress (female actor)
يابانية	Japanese woman/girl

Now, study the nouns in their plural feminine, indefinite forms:

سيّارات	cars
مُمَثِّلات	actresses (female actors)
يابانيّات	Japanese women/girls

A pattern is seen in the examples above. The singular feminine indefinite nouns end in the letter ة and the plural feminine indefinite nouns end in the letters ات.

singular feminine, indefinite	plural feminine, indefinite
سيّارة	سيّارات
مُمَثِّلة	مُمَثِّلات
يابانية	يابانيّات

Exercise: decoding attributes of an unfamiliar noun

Exercise 1

Study the feminine, indefinite nouns below and determine whether they are singular or plural by underlining the correct choice.

Noun	Answer choices
مُتَرجِمة	(plural feminine, indefinite) or (singular feminine, indefinite)
مهندسة	(plural feminine, indefinite) or (singular feminine, indefinite)
سَيِّدة	(plural feminine, indefinite) or (singular feminine, indefinite)
جامعة	(plural feminine, indefinite) or (singular feminine, indefinite)
مُتَرجِمات	(plural feminine, indefinite) or (singular feminine, indefinite)
مهندسات	(plural feminine, indefinite) or (singular feminine, indefinite)
سَيِّدات	(plural feminine, indefinite) or (singular feminine, indefinite)
جامعات	(plural feminine, indefinite) or (singular feminine, indefinite)

Typical arrangement of noun constituents (number, gender, case, and definiteness)

In this section, we will examine the typical anatomy of a noun with respect to its attributes (i.e. number, gender, case, and definiteness).

The morphological nature of the structure of Arabic nouns is such that the attributes are intertwined in a single word. Therefore, we cannot easily examine them in isolation. The typical anatomy of a noun can be represented morphologically by columns showing a noun and the relative position of each of its attributes.

The tables below illustrate the typical arrangement of the constituents of a noun.

Singular: typical arrangement of noun constituents (number, gender, case, and definiteness)

ممثلٌ

definiteness	*noun*	*gender*	*case*	*definiteness*	*number*
	mumaththil		u	n	

الممثلُ

definiteness	*noun*	*gender*	*case*	*definiteness*	*number*
al	mumaththil		u		

ممثلةٌ

definiteness	*noun*	*gender*	*case*	*definiteness*	*number*
	mumaththil	at	u	n	

المُمَثِّلةُ

definiteness	*noun*	*gender*	*case*	*definiteness*	*number*
al	mumaththil	at	u		

Dual: typical arrangement of noun constituents (number, gender, case, and definiteness)

ممثلانِ

definiteness	*noun*	*gender*	*case*	*number*
	mumaththil		aa	ni

الممثلان

definiteness	*noun*	*gender*	*case*	*number*
al	mumaththil		aa	ni

ممثلتان

definiteness	*noun*	*gender*	*case*	*number*
	mumaththil	at	aa	ni

الممثلتان

definiteness	*noun*	*gender*	*case*	*number*
al	mumaththil	at	aa	ni

Plural: typical arrangement of noun constituents (number, gender, case, and definiteness)

ممثلون

definiteness	*noun*	*gender*	*case*	*number*
	mumaththil		uu	na

الممثلون

definiteness	*noun*	*gender*	*case*	*number*
al	mumaththil		uu	na

ممثلاتٌ

definiteness	*noun*	*gender*	*case*	*definiteness*
	mumaththil	aat	u	n

المُمَثِّلاتُ

definiteness	*noun*	*gender*	*case*	*definiteness*
al	mumaththil	aat	u	

The following sections contain details illustrating number, gender, case, and definiteness in nouns.

Number العَدد

As noted above, Arabic nouns are either singular, dual, or plural.

Morphology

Plurals are more than two. Plurals are formed by suffixation (sound plural) or inter-digitation (broken plural).

For masculine plural nouns, add a suffix to the noun stem.
For feminine plural nouns, add a suffix after removing the (at) suffix.

The dual is a separate morphological entity. For the dual, the suffix is added to the noun stem. In the case of the feminine, the (at) suffix is not removed.

Singular المُفرَد

Singular nouns are marked by an absence of dual or plural suffixes. The following are examples of indefinite masculine and feminine nouns in the singular:

Masculine:

رَجُل	a man
مُمَثِّل	an actor
إبن	a son
كِتاب	a book

Feminine:

إمرأة	a woman
بِنت	a girl/daughter
مُمَثِّلة	an actress
طاوِلة	a table
مَكتَبة	a bookstore/library

Exercise: singular الـمُفرَد

Exercise 2

Read the phrases below. Each one comprises a noun followed by an adjective. Draw a line under the adjectives in the singular form.

a) مُتَرجِمون يابانيّون
b) مُتَرجِمات يابانيّات
c) مُدُن يابانية
d) سيارات يابانية
e) لُغات أوروبيّة
f) مُتَرجِمون عَرَب

Dual المُثَنّى

Dual nouns are marked by the compound dual suffixes انِ (aani) or يْنِ (ayni). It is important to note that the alif (ا) in the dual suffix انِ indicates that a dual noun is in the nominative (المرفوع) case, whereas a yaa' (ي) in the dual suffix ينِ indicates that a dual noun is in the accusative (الـمَنصوب) or the genitive (الـمَجرور) case (see Case). The following are the same singular nouns, as above, but in the dual:

Masculine:

	مَنصوب/مجرور	مرفوع
two men	رَجُلَيْنِ	رَجُلانِ
two actors	مُمَثِّلَيْنِ	مُمَثِّلانِ
two sons	اِبنَينِ	اِبنانِ
two books	كِتابَيْنِ	كِتابانِ

Feminine:

	مَنصوب/مجرور	مرفوع
two women	اِمرأتَيْنِ	اِمرأتانِ
two girls/daughters	بِنتَيْنِ	بِنتانِ
two actresses	مُمَثِّلَتَيْنِ	مُمَثِّلاتانِ
two tables	طاوِلَتَيْنِ	طاوِلَتَانِ
two bookstores/libraries	مَكتَبَتَيْنِ	مَكتَبَتانِ

Exercises: dual المُثَنّى

Exercise 3

Change the following duals to their singular forms. Write the singular forms in the blank spaces below. For this exercise, diacritic case markings may be left out of the answers.

Dual	Singular
رَجُلانِ	________
رَجُلَيْنِ	________
مُمَثِّلَيْنِ	________
كِتابانِ	________
اِبنَينِ	________
مَكتَبَتَيْنِ	________
مَكتَبَتانِ	________
مُمَثِّلاتانِ	________
بِنتانِ	________
اِمرأتَيْنِ	________

Exercise 4

Fill in the blanks in the table below.

Dual (مُثَنَّى)		*Singular* (مُفرد)			
مَنصوب/مجرور	مرفوع	مَنصوب/مجرور	مرفوع		
عربيَّيْنِ	______	______	عربيٌّ	Indefinite (نكرة)	Masculine
______	______	______	______	Definite (معرفة)	(مذكّر)
______	______	______	______	Indefinite (نكرة)	Feminine
______	______	______	______	Definite (معرفة)	(مؤنّث)

Plural الجَمع

Plural nouns are of two kinds: **sound plurals** and **broken plurals.**

Nouns that *happen to fall* in the category of sound plurals have predictable suffixes:

For masculine nouns, the plural suffix is either ون or ين
For feminine nouns, the plural suffix is ات

Nouns that *happen to fall* in the category of broken plurals are created by an internal shuffling of vowels. Broken plurals are not marked by a suffix.

Sound plurals جَمع السالم

Masculine sound plurals and feminine sound plurals behave predictably when transformed from their singular to plural forms.

Masculine sound plurals

Masculine sound plural nouns are marked by the compound plural suffixes ونَ (uuna) or ينَ (iina). It is important to note that the waaw (و) in the plural suffix ونَ indicates that a plural noun is in the nominative (المرفوع) case, whereas a yaa' (ي) in the plural suffix ينَ indicates that a plural noun is in the accusative (المَنصوب) or the genitive (المَجرور) case (see Case).

	مَنصوب/مَجرور	مَرفوع
actors	مُمَثِّلين	مُمَثِّلون

Feminine sound plurals

Feminine sound plural nouns are marked by the plural suffixes اتٌ (aatun) in the nominative (المرفوع) case, or اتٍ (aatin) in the accusative (المَنصوب) or the genitive (المَجرور) case (see Case). As is usual, the case markers are often not shown.

Examples:

plural	meaning
مُمَثِّلات	actresses
طاوِلات	tables
مَكتَبات	bookstores/libraries

Exercises: sound plurals جَمع السالم

Exercise 5

Change the following sound plurals to their singular forms. Write the singular forms in the blank spaces below.

Plural	Singular
a) مُمَثِّلات	__________
b) طاوِلات	__________
c) مَكتَبات	__________
d) مُمَثِّلين	__________
e) مُمَثِّلون	__________

Exercise 6

Once you have changed the sound plurals to their singular form, put them in four very simple sentences. Refer to the glossary below for help.

Glossary

a) مُمَثِّلات	actresses (female actors)
b) طاوِلات	tables
c) مَكتَبات	bookstores/libraries
d) مُمَثِّلون	actors (male actors)

Below are four blank spaces for four simple sentences.

a) ______________________________

b) ______________________________

c) ______________________________

d) ______________________________

Broken plurals جمع التَّكسير

Broken plurals are created by internal shuffling of vowels of the singular form of the noun. Unlike sound plurals, broken plurals are not marked by a predictable suffix.

Masculine broken plurals

Examples:

plural	meaning
رِجال	men
أبناء	sons
كُتُب	books

Gender النوع/الجِنس

No neutral

As noted above, gender is either masculine or feminine. There is no neutral category.

Feminine

Singular feminine

In the singular, feminine nouns are often marked by a taa' marbuta, whose shape is:

1) ة when unjoined to the preceding letter

Example:

اِمرأة	a woman

2) ـــة when joined to the preceding letter

Example:

مَكتَبة	a bookstore/library

3) ـــت if the feminine noun is the first term in an 'idafa phrase where the pronoun is suffixed to the noun.

Examples:

مَكتَبَـــتـــه	his bookstore/library
مَكتَبَـــتـــها	her bookstore/library

Not all singular feminine nouns have an overt feminine marker.

Examples:

شَمس	sun
الشمس	the sun
أرض	ground, floor, land
الأرض	the ground, the floor, the earth

Dual feminine

In the dual, the taa' marbuta at the end of the noun changes to a regular ـت, and is followed by the dual suffixes انِ (aani) or يْنِ (ayni).

Examples:

singular	dual	meaning
اِمرأتانِ	اِمرأتَيْنِ	two women
بِنتانِ	بِنتَيْنِ	two girls
مُمَثِّلتانِ	مُمَثِّلَتَيْنِ	two actresses
طاوِلتَانِ	طاوِلَتَيْنِ	two tables
مَكتَبَتانِ	مَكتَبَتَيْنِ	two bookstores/libraries

Similarly, in the case of a dual feminine noun being the first term of an 'idafa, the taa' marbuta at the end of the noun changes to a regular ت, and is followed by the dual suffix.

Examples:

singular	dual	meaning
مَكتبَتيْهِ –	مَكتَبَتاهُ	his two bookstores/libraries
مَكتبَتَيْها –	مَكتَبَتاها	her two bookstores/libraries

Note the obligatory deletion of the ن of the first term of the 'idafa in the dual.

Plural feminine

In the plural feminine, the taa' marbuta at the end of feminine singular noun often changes to the plural feminine marker ات.

Examples:

singular	plural	meaning
مُمَثِّلة	مُمَثِّلات	actresses
طاوِلة	طاوِلات	tables
مَكتَبة	مَكتَبات	bookstores/libraries

However, it should be noted that not all singular feminine nouns ending in taa' marbuuta automatically have sound feminine plural forms.

Example:

singular	plural	meaning
اِمرأة	نِساء	women

Not all plural feminine nouns have an overt feminine marker.

Examples:

singular	plural	meaning
الشمس	الشُموس	the suns
الأرض	الأراضي	the lands

Summary: feminine

Feminine nouns are marked by the suffix ة, the dual suffix تانِ or تَيْنِ, the sound plural feminine suffix ات. Some feminine nouns are not marked by any suffix:

Plural	*Dual*	*Singular*
نِساء	اِمرأتانِ – اِمرأتَيْنِ	اِمرأة
بَنات	بِنتانِ – بِنتَيْنِ	بِنت
مُمَثِّلات	مُمَثِّلتانِ – مُمَثِّلَتَيْنِ	مُمَثِّلة
طاوِلات	طاوِلتانِ – طاوِلَتَيْنِ	طاوِلة
مَكتَبات	مَكتَبتانِ – مَكتَبَتَيْنِ	مَكتَبة

Masculine

Like feminine dual suffixes, masculine dual suffixes are انِ (aani) or يْنِ (ayni). Masculine sound plural nouns are marked by the compound plural suffixes ونَ (uuna) or ينَ (iina).

Broken plural masculine

Broken plural masculine nouns are not marked by any suffix:

رَجُل، رَجُلانِ – رَجُلَيْنِ، رِجال

مُمَثِّل، مُمَثِّلانِ – مُمَثِّلَيْنِ، مُمَثِّلون – مُمَثِّلين

كِتاب، كِتابانِ – كِتابَيْنِ، كُتُب

Case الحالة and case markings (diacritics and letters)

Nominative case مَرفوع

A noun in the nominative (مَرفوع) case may be given the following case markers:

ضَمّة, تنوين ضَم, ان, and ون.

a) تنوين ضَم (a diacritic):

رَجُلٌ، مُمَثِّلٌ، كِتابٌ، اِمرأةٌ،

مُمَثِّلةٌ، طاوِلةٌ، مَكتَبةٌ

رِجالٌ، كُتُبٌ، نِساءٌ،

مُمَثِّلاتٌ، طاوِلاتٌ، مَكتَباتٌ

b) ضَمة (a diacritic):

الرَجُلُ، المـُمَثِّلُ،الكِتابُ، المرأةُ،
المـُمَثِّلةُ، الطاوِلةُ، المَكتَبةُ
الرجالُ، الكُتُبُ، النِساءُ،
المـُمَثِّلاتُ، الطاوِلاتُ، المَكتَباتُ

c) The letter ا in the dual ending انِ (a letter):

رَجُلانِ، مُمَثِّلانِ، كِتابانِ، امرأتانِ،
مُمَثِّلَتانِ، طاوِلتانِ، مَكتَبتانِ
الرَجُلانِ، المـُمَثِّلانِ، الكِتابانِ، المرأتانِ،
المـُمَثِّلَتانِ، الطاوِلتانِ، لمَكتَبتانِ

d) The letter و in the plural ending ونَ (a letter):

مُمَثِّلون، فَنّانون (artists) اِقتصاديّون (economists)
لُبنانيّون (Lebanese) سوريّون (Syrians) عِراقيّون (Iraqis)

Notes about the different markers of the مَرفوع case:

تنوين ضم marks indefinite nouns:

رَجُلٌ، مُمَثِّلٌ، كِتابٌ، اِمرأةٌ، مُمَثِّلةٌ، طاوِلةٌ، مَكتَبةٌ
رِجالٌ، كُتُبٌ، نِساءٌ، مُمَثِّلاتٌ، طاوِلاتٌ، مَكتَباتٌ

انِ marks duals:

رَجُلانِ، مُمَثِّلانِ، كِتابانِ، امرأتانِ، مُمَثِّلَتانِ، طاوِلتانِ، مَكتَبتانِ
الرَجُلانِ، المـُمَثِّلانِ، الكِتابانِ، المرأتانِ، المـُمَثِّلَتانِ، الطاوِلتانِ،
المَكتَبتانِ

ون marks sound masculine plurals:

مُمَثِّلون، المـُمَثِّلون

Accusative case مَنصوب

A noun in the accusative case – المَنصوب – may be given the following case markers: فتحة ,تنوين فتح ,ا+تنوين فتح, ى، كسرة

a) فتحة (diacritic) for definite nouns (except feminine sound plural nouns).
المهندسَ، المهندسةَ

b) تنوين فتح (diacritic) for indefinite feminine nouns (except feminine sound plural nouns)

مهندسةً

c) ا+تنوين فتح (letter and diacritic) for a singular masculine indefinite noun

مهندسًا

d) ى (letter) for dual nouns ending in يْنِ and sound plural masculine nouns ending in ينَ

المهندسَتَيْنِ، مهندسَتَيْنِ، المهندسَيْنِ، مهندسَيْن
مهندسينَ، المهندسينَ

e) كسرة only for feminine sound plural definite nouns

السياراتِ

f) تنوين كسرة only for feminine sound plural indefinite nouns

سياراتٍ

Genitive case مَجرور

A noun is recognized as being in the genitive case – المَجرور – by the following case markers: كسرة, تنوين كسر, ى

a) كسرة for a definite noun

المهندسِ، المهندسةِ، المهندساتِ

b) تنوين كسر for an indefinite noun

مهندسٍ، مهندسةٍ، مهندساتٍ

c) ى (letter) for dual nouns ending in يْنِ and sound plural masculine nouns ending in ينَ

المهندسَتَيْنِ، مهندسَتَيْنِ، المهندسَيْن، مهندسَيْن
مهندسينَ، المهندسينَ

Definiteness التَعريف والتنكير

Arabic nouns are either indefinite or definite.
When is a noun definite? A noun is definite when it:

has the prefix ال
is a مُضاف (i.e. the first term of an إضافة)
is a proper name

Indefinite nouns, (نكِرة),

may not have a definite article prefix ال
may not be the first term of an 'idafa (إضافة)
may have تنوين as a case marker

Examples:

رَجُلٌ، مُمَثِّلٌ، ابنٌ	(s., m., human)
كِتابٌ	(s., m., non-human)
مرأةٌ، مُمَثِّلةً	(s., f., human)
طاوِلةً، مَكتبةٌ	(s., f., non-human)

A noun is definite (مَعرِفة)

if it has the definite article prefix ال

Examples:

الرَجُل، المُمَثِّل، الابن	(s., m., human)
الكِتاب	(s., m., non-human)
المرأة، المُمَثِّلة	(s., f., human)
الطاوِلة، المكتبة	(s., f., non-human)

if it is the first term in an إضافة:

كِتابُه	his book
كِتاب مُحمد	Mohamed's book
كتاب الرجُل	the man's book
مَكتَبتُه	his bookstore/library
مَكتَبَة الرجُل	the man's bookstore/library

if it included a possessive pronoun suffix to express possession:

كِتابُه	his book
مَكتَبتُه	his bookstore/library

For definite nouns, a case-marking diacritic, if present, cannot have tanween (تَنوين)

Exercise: definiteness

Exercise 7

The simple sentences below are written in English from least to most specific. Fill in the blank spaces below with the Arabic version of the simple sentences that are relatively more specific (i.e. that contains the definite version of the noun).

a) This is a Sudanese song — هذه غنوة سودانية

This is the Sudanese song — ________________

b) This is an Egyptian song — هذه غنوة مصرية

This is the Egyptian song — ________________

c) This is a Sudanese Muhammad — هذا محمد سوداني

This is the Sudanese Muhammad — ________________

d) This is an Egyptian Muhammad — هذا محمد مصري

This is the Egyptian Muhammad — ________________

Exercises: summary of noun attributes

Exercise 8

Complete the table below by making all necessary changes to the singular form of the noun أمريكيٌّ (an American).

مفرد *(Singular)*		مجرور *(Genitive)*	منصوب *(Accusative)*	مرفوع *(Nominative)*
نكرة	مذكر (m.)	______	______	أمريكيٌّ
(Indefinite)	مؤنّث (f.)	______	______	______
معرفة	مذكر (m.)	______	______	______
(Definite)	مؤنّث (f.)	______	______	______

Exercise 9

Complete the table below by making all necessary changes to the dual form of the noun أمريكيٌّ (an American).

مُثَنّى *(Dual)*		مجرور *(Genitive)*	منصوب *(Accusative)*	مرفوع *(Nominative)*
نكرة	(m.) مذكر	______	______	______
(Indefinite)	(f.) مؤنّث	______	______	______
معرفة	(m.) مذكر	______	______	______
(Definite)	(f.) مؤنّث	______	______	______

Exercise 10

Complete the table below by making all necessary changes to the plural form of the noun أمريكيٌّ (an American).

جَمع *(Plural)*		مجرور *(Genitive)*	منصوب *(Accusative)*	مرفوع *(Nominative)*
نكرة	(m.) مذكر	______	______	______
(Indefinite)	(f.) مؤنّث	______	______	______
معرفة	(m.) مذكر	______	______	______
(Definite)	(f.) مؤنّث	______	______	______

UNIT 17
Numbers and counting الأعداد و المعدود

In dealing with numbers, the following are important terms:

العدد	the number
المعدود	the counted noun

Number of المعدود

A. For 1 and 2, the numbers are not listed, only the counted noun (المعدود) is listed in the singular or dual form.

Examples:

	Correct	Incorrect
One book	كتاب	واحد كتاب
Two books	كتابانِ/كتابَيْن	اثنين كتاب

B. For the range 3–10, the numbers are listed and the counted noun (المعدود) is in the plural form.

Examples:

3 cars	3 سيارات
10 women	10 نساء

C. For anything greater than 3 – 10, the numbers are listed and the counted noun (المعدود) is in the singular form.

Examples:

1000 nights	1000 ليلة
50 eye doctors	50 طبيب عُيون

Numbers أرقام

one	واحِد
two	اِثنان
three	ثلاثة
four	أربعة
five	خَمسَة
six	سِتّة
seven	سَبعَة
eight	ثمانية
nine	تِسعة
ten	عشرة

UNIT 18
The sentence الجُملَة – the basics

In Modern Standard Arabic (MSA) there are two sentence types: the verbal sentence (الجُملةُ الفِعليّة) and the nominal sentence (الجُملةُ الإسميّة). Each type of sentence consists of two parts.

Constituents of a basic sentence

A verbal sentence has 1) a verb and 2) a subject.

A nominal sentence has 1) a subject (المُبتَدأ) and 2) a predicate (الخَبَر).

The following summary illustrates each of the two clause types, their constituents, and the relative ordering of the constituents:

constituents		clause type
الفاعل (the subject)	الفِعل	الجملة الفعلية
الـخَـبَر	الـمُبتَدأ (the subject)	الجملة الاسمية

Exercises: constituents of a basic sentence

Exercise 1

Name the constituents of a verbal clause (جُملة فِعليّة). Write the correct answer in the blank spaces.

a) ______________________________

b) ______________________________

Exercise 2

Name the constituents of a nominal clause (جُملة إسميّة). Write the correct answer in the blank spaces.

a) ____________________

b) ____________________

Subject of a verbal and a nominal sentence

Arab grammarians differentiate between the "subject" of a verbal sentence and the "subject" of a nominal sentence:

The "subject" of a verbal sentence is called الفاعِل.

The "subject" of a nominal sentence is called الـمُبتَدأ.

Thus, it is important to keep in mind that the term "subject" is either going to mean فاعِل or مُبتَدأ depending on whether the sentence is a جملة فعلية or a جملة إسمية respectively.

Exercises: subject of a verbal and a nominal sentence

Exercise 3

What is the sentence type of each of these sentences? Choose the correct answer.

1) أَلَّفَ مَحمودٌ رِوايةً — Mahmoud wrote a novel.
   a) Verbal sentence
   b) Nominal sentence

2) مؤَلِّف الرِواية محمود — The author of the novel is Mahmoud.
   a) Verbal sentence
   b) Nominal sentence

3) محمود مؤلِّف الرِواية — Mahmoud is the author of the novel.
   a) Verbal sentence
   b) Nominal sentence

4) لا! الرواية مؤلِّفها محمود — No! the novel's author is Mahmoud.
   a) Verbal sentence
   b) Nominal sentence

Exercise 4

Study the following sentence:

أنتَ تَكَلَّمتَ You (2nd p. masc. sing.) spoke.

Rewrite the sentence above by replacing the subject with each of the following:

Subject

a) محمد
b) الرَجُلُ
c) ليلى
d) أنا
e) نحن
f) أنتُما
g) ليلى وسميرة
h) مُصطفى ومحمود وعائلاتُهم

a) ______
b) ______
c) ______
d) ______
e) ______
f) ______
g) ______
h) ______

Exercise 5

Study the following sentence:

أنتَ تَتَكَلَّمُ You (2nd p. masc. sing.) speak/are speaking.

Rewrite the sentence above by replacing the subject with each of the following:

Subject

a) الحَرامي
b) الشُرطِيّة
c) أنا

d) نحن
e) المُمَرِّضَتانِ
f) الطبيباتُ
g) الأَطِبّاءُ

a) ____________________
b) ____________________
c) ____________________
d) ____________________
e) ____________________
f) ____________________
g) ____________________

Syntax: the position of the subject in a sentence

One important difference between the verbal and nominal sentence is the position of the subject.

> الفاعِل (the subject) never comes before the verb in a جُملة فِعليّة (verbal sentence).
> المُبتَدأ (the subject) most often comes before the predicate (الخَبَر) in a إسمية جملة (nominal sentence).

The basic verbal sentence الجُملة الفِعليّة

In its most basic form, a verbal clause consists of a verb (فِعل) and an implied subject indicated by an embedded subject marker. If necessary, an explicit standalone subject (فاعِل) follows the verb and its embedded subject marker.

No Arabic verb exists without a subject. Thus any instance of a verb marks a verbal clause. The subject of a verb is either embedded, or else it follows the verb as an overt subject (فاعِل).

Exercises: basic verbal sentence

Exercise 6

Study the following sentence that starts with a perfect verb. What type of sentence is it? Choose the correct answer.

تَكَلَّمَت المَرأةُ The woman spoke

a) جُملة فِعليّة

b) جملة إسمية

Exercise 7

Copy the sentence above that starts with a perfect verb and identify the the subject (الفاعل) by drawing a line under the correct word. Write your answer in the blank space.

تَكَلَّمَت المَرأةُ The woman spoke

____

Exercise 8

Copy the sentence above which starts with a perfect verb by replacing the subject (الفاعل) with each of the common nouns below. Write the correct answers in the blank spaces.

Glossary

الرجُل	the man
الرَجُلانِ	the two men
المَرأتانِ	the two women
الرجالُ	the men
النِساءُ	the women

a) ________________

b) ________________

c) ________________

d) ________________

e) ________________

Exercise 9

Copy the sentences above and then identify the verb by drawing a line under the correct word. Write your answers in the blank spaces.

a) ________________

b) ________________

c) ______________________________

d) ______________________________

e) ______________________________

Exercise 10

Study the following sentence that starts with an imperfect verb. What type of sentence is it? Choose the correct answer.

يُسافِرُ الرجُلُ The man travels/is travelling.

a) جُملة فِعليّة

b) جملة إسمية

Exercise 11

Copy the sentence above which starts with an imperfect verb and then identify the the subject (الفاعل) by drawing a line under the correct word. Write your answer in the blank space.

يُسافِرُ الرجُلُ The man travels/is travelling.

____

Exercise 12

Study the following sentence.

يُسافِرُ الرجُلُ

Rewrite the sentence by replacing the subject (الفاعل) with each of the common nouns below. Write the correct answers in the blank spaces.

Glossary

محمد	Mohamed (singular m. proper noun)
ليلى	Laila (singular f. proper noun)
ليلى وسميرة	Laila and Samira (two singular f. proper nouns)
مُصطفى ومحمود وعائلاتُهم	Mostafa and Mahmood (two singular m. proper nouns) and their familiars

a) ____________________

b) ____________________

c) ____________________

d) ____________________

Exercise 13

Study the sentences below. Draw a line under the verb in each sentence. Write the verbs in the blank spaces.

a) يُسافِرُ محمد

b) تُسافِرُ ليلى

c) تُسافِرُ ليلى وسميرة

d) يُسافِرُ مُصطفى ومحمود وعائلاتُهم

a) ____________________

b) ____________________

c) ____________________

d) ____________________

Basic nominal sentence الجُملةُ الإسميّة

Arrangement of the basic nominal sentence

As noted above, in a nominal clause, the subject (المُبتَدأ) usually precedes the predicate (الخَبَر).

Examples:	الخَبَر	المُبتَدأ
I am Waheed	وحيد	أنا
Maha is Egyptian	مِصريّة	مها
New York is a large city	مدينة كبيرة	نيويورك

There is a special case where this order is obligatorily inverted and الخَبَر precedes the المُبتَدأ. This inversion occurs when 1) the subject (المُبتَدأ) is indefinite and 2) the predicate (الخَبَر) is a prepositional or adverbial phrase.

Examples: المُبتَدأ in the sentences below is underlined twice.

لي سَيّارةٌ	I have a car.
عِندَها صُداعٌ	She has a headache.

Types of headwords of nominal sentences

Proper nouns

الـمُديرةُ سميرةُ	The director is Samira.
هو مُحمّدٌ	He is Mohammed.

Common nouns

هذا بابٌ	This is a door.
هذه شَجَرَةٌ	This is a tree.
ليلى أُمٌّ	Laila is a mother.
مصطفى أبٌ	Mustafa is a father.

Adjectival nouns

سميرةُ مُديرةٌ	Samira is a director/manager.
سَميرٌ مُديرٌ	Samir is a director/manager.
الطريقُ طويلٌ	The road is long.
الطريقةُ مُعَقَّدةٌ	The method is complex.
الوَردُ جميلٌ	Roses are beautiful.
اللاعِبُ مُستَعِدٌّ	The player (m. s.) is ready.
اللاعِبةُ مُستَعِدّةٌ	The player (f. s.) is ready.
اللاعِبون مُستعِدّون	The players (m. pl.) are ready.
اللاعِبات مُستَعِدّاتٌ	The players (f. pl.) are ready.
الشُقَقُ غاليةٌ	Apartments/flats are expensive.

Temporal or locative adverbial nouns

الحَفلةُ بَعدَ العَشاء	The party is after dinner.
العَشاءُ بَعدَ الثامِنةِ	Supper is after eight.
الـمَطعَمُ قَبلَ الـمَكتَبةِ	The restaurant is before the bookstore.
أنتَ بَعدي	You are after me.
عَزّةُ تَحتَ السَريرِ	Azza is under the bed.

أنا تَحتَ السَريرِ	I am under the bed.
الحِذاءُ تَحتَ السريرِ	The shoe is under the bed.
الحلَويّاتُ فوقَ الثلاجةِ	The candy is on top of the refrigerator.
الصيدليةُ وَراءَ البيتِ	The pharmacy is behind the house.
السيارةُ أمامَ بيتٍ رماديٍّ	The car is in front of a grey house.
القِطّةُ فَوقَ شَجَرةٍ	The cat's on a tree.
الأوراق فوقَ مَكتَبٍ	The papers are on top of a desk.

Gerund مَصدَر

النَتيجةُ خَسارةٌ	The outcome is a loss.
التَطَوُّرُ الجَديدُ مَكسَبٌ لَنا	The new development is a gain for us.
الموسيقى الحديثةُ نَشازٌ	Modern music is discordant.

Exercises: basic nominal sentence

Exercise 14

Write the sentences below in Arabic. Use the glossary if necessary. Remember to add the correct preposition based on the context and intended meaning.

Glossary

Hoda	هُدى
the car	السيارةِ
the file	الـملَفُّ
the secretary's desk	مَكتَبِ السكرتيرِ
Barbara	باربارة
Nashville	ناشفيل
prize	جائزةُ
design	تصميم

a) Hoda is in the car.

____

b) The file is on the secretary's desk.

____

c) Barbara is from Nashville.

____

d) Magda is with Mounir.

____

e) The prize is for the best design.

____

Exercise 15

What type of sentence is each of the sentences below? Choose the correct answer.

a) هُدى في السيّارةِ
   i) جُملة فِعليّة
   ii) جملة إسمية
b) الـملَفُّ على مَكتَبِ السكرتيرِ
   i) جُملة فِعليّة
   ii) جملة إسمية
c) باربارة مِن ناشڤيل
   i) جُملة فِعليّة
   ii) جملة إسمية
d) ماجدةُ مَعَ مُنير
   i) جُملة فِعليّة
   ii) جملة إسمية
e) الجائزةُ لأحسن تصميم
   i) جُملة فِعليّة
   ii) جملة إسمية

Exercise 16

Copy the nominal sentences above and then identify the predicate (الخَبَر) by drawing a line under the word(s).

a) _______________________________

b) _______________________________

c) _______________________________

d) _______________________________

e) _______________________________

Exercise 17

Fill in the blanks using the words provided on the left. Please make all necessary changes to ensure agreement.

أوروبّا	a) الإيطالية والإسبانية والفرنسية لُغات ______
رَجُل	b) مُحَمَّد وعَلي وسَعيد ______ يَمَنيّون
سيّارة	c) هوندا وإيسوزو وتويوتا ______ يابانية
وِلاية	d) فيرمونت ونيو هامشير وكونيتيكت ______ أمريكية
صغير	e) منهاتن وبروكلين وبرونكس مَناطِق ______ في نيويورك
مدينة	f) بيروت ودِمشق والقاهرة ______ عربية

Exercise 18

Study each of the sentences above that start with a noun. Determine what type of sentence each one is. Write the correct answer in the blank space.

جملة إسمية or جُملة فِعليّة

a) ______
b) ______
c) ______
d) ______
e) ______

Exercise 19

Copy the sentences above and then identify the subject (الـمُبتَدأ) by drawing a line under the correct word. Write your answer in the blank space.

a) ______
b) ______
c) ______
d) ______
e) ______

UNIT 19
The noun–adjective phrases

Definition and form

A noun–adjective phrase, which occurs very frequently in Arabic, consists of a noun followed by one or more adjectives.

Order

In a noun–adjective phrase the adjective *follows* the noun. This order is the opposite of English; thus the English adjectival phrase 'the *white* house' is rendered in Arabic as البيت الأبيض, with the adjective الأبيض following the noun البيت.

Agreement

In a noun–adjective phrase, such as the expression البيت الأبيض, the adjective الأبيض agrees with the noun that it qualifies in four respects:

Number (i.e. singular, dual, or plural)

البيت is singular, thus the adjective must also be singular.

Gender (i.e. masculine, or feminine)

البيت is masculine (هو), thus the adjective must also be masculine (هو).

Definiteness (i.e. definite or indefinite)

البيت is definite (الـ), thus the adjective must also be definite.

Case (i.e. nominative, accusative, or genitive)

The adjective الأبيض must be in the same case as the noun, whatever that may be (مرفوع منصوب - مجرور):

البَيتُ الأبيضُ مَرفوع (nominative)

البيتَ الأبيضَ مَنصوب (accusative)

البيتِ الأبيضِ مَجرور (genitive)

Before a more detailed exposition of adjectival agreement with nouns, it is necessary to look at the following topics:

Noun types: not all nouns can function as adjectives (see Adjectival nouns, under Noun Types).

Human vs non-human classification of nouns: the classification of a noun as human or non-human affects its gender and number (see human vs "non-human classification of nouns).

Noun: number, gender, definiteness, case.

UNIT 20

Adjectives: agreement with nouns

Adjectives: agreement with nouns in the singular

In the singular, there's agreement between the noun and the adjective in all respects: number, gender, definiteness, and case – whether a noun is human or non-human.

Masculine indefinite

Human

Meaning	مَجرور	مَنصوب	مَرفوع
a big man	رَجُلٍ كبيرٍ	رَجُلاً كبيراً	رَجُلٌ كبيرٌ
a famous actor	مُمَثِّلٍ مَشهورٍ	مُمَثِّلاً مَشهوراً	مُمَثِّلٌ مَشهورٌ

Non-human

Meaning	مَجرور	مَنصوب	مَرفوع
a big book	كِتابٍ كبيرٍ	كِتاباً كبيراً	كِتابٌ كبيرٌ
a famous book	كِتابٍ مَشهورٍ	كِتاباً مَشهوراً	كِتابٌ مَشهورٌ

Number: the adjective is singular because the noun is singular.

Gender: the adjective is masculine because the noun is masculine.

Definiteness: the adjective is indefinite because the noun is indefinite.

Case: see case marking by diacritics.

The adjective is مَرفوع because the noun is مَرفوع; so marked by a تنوين ضَم.

The adjective is مَنصوب because the noun is مَنصوب; so marked by the letter تنوين فتح + ا, as with all masculine indefinite nouns.

The adjective is مَجرور because the noun is مَجرور; so marked by a تنوين كسر.

Feminine indefinite

Human

Meaning	مَجرور	مَنصوب	مَرفوع
a big woman	امرأةٍ كبيرةٍ	امرأةً كبيرةً	اِمرأةٌ كبيرةٌ
a famous actress	مُمَثِّلةٍ مَشهورةٍ	مُمَثِّلةً مَشهورةً	مُمَثِّلةٌ مَشهورةٌ

Non-human

Meaning	مَجرور	مَنصوب	مَرفوع
a big table	طاوِلةٍ كبيرةٍ	طاوِلةً كبيرةً	طاوِلةٌ كبيرةٌ
a famous bookstore	مَكتَبةٍ مَشهورةٍ	مَكتَبةً مَشهورةً	مَكتَبةٌ مَشهورةٌ

Number: the adjective is singular because the noun is singular.

Gender: the adjective is feminine because the noun is feminine; so marked by the feminine marker ة, ta' marbuta.

Definiteness: the adjective is indefinite because the noun is indefinite.

Case: see case marking by diacritics.

The adjective is مَرفوع when the noun is مَرفوع; so marked by a تنوين ضَم.

The adjective is مَنصوب when the noun is مَنصوب; so marked by a تنوين فتح.

The adjective is مَجرور when the noun is مَجرور; so marked by a تنوين كسر.

Masculine definite

Human

Meaning	مَجرور	مَنصوب	مَرفوع
the big man	الرَجُلِ الكبيرِ	الرَجُلَ الكبيرَ	الرَجُلُ الكبيرُ
the famous actor	المُمَثِّلِ المَشهورِ	المُمَثِّلَ المَشهورَ	المُمَثِّلُ المَشهورُ
her elder son	اِبنِها الكَبيرِ	اِبنَها الكَبيرَ	ابنُها الكَبيرُ

Non-human

Meaning	مَجرور	مَنصوب	مَرفوع
the big book	الكِتابِ الكبيرِ	الكِتابَ الكبيرَ	الكِتابُ الكبيرُ
the famous book	الكِتابِ المَشهورِ	الكِتابَ المَشهورَ	الكِتابُ المَشهورُ
his famous book	كِتابِهِ المَشهورِ	كِتابَهُ المَشهورَ	كِتابُهُ المَشهورُ

Number: the adjective is singular because the noun is singular.

Gender: the adjective is masculine because the noun is masculine.

Definiteness: the adjective is definite because the noun is definite, so marked by a definite article ال, or by being a first term of 'idafa.

Case: (see case marking by diacritics)

The adjective is مَرفوع when the noun is مَرفوع; so marked by a ضَمّة.

The adjective is مَنصوب when the noun is مَنصوب; so marked by a فتحة.

The adjective is مَجرور when the noun is مَجرور; so marked by a كسرة.

Feminine definite

Human

Meaning	مَجرور	مَنصوب	مَرفوع
the big woman	المرأةِ الكبيرةِ	المرأةَ الكبيرةَ	المرأةُ الكبيرةُ
the famous actress	المُمَثِّلةِ المَشهورةِ	المُمَثِّلةَ المَشهورةَ	المُمَثِّلةُ المَشهورةُ
his elder daughter	ابنَتِهِ الكَبيرةِ	ابنَتَهُ الكَبيرةَ	ابنَتُهُ الكَبيرةُ

Non-human

Meaning	مَجرور	مَنصوب	مَرفوع
the big table	الطاولةِ الكبيرةِ	الطاولةَ الكبيرةَ	الطاولةُ الكبيرةُ
the famous bookstore	المَكتَبةِ المَشهورةِ	المَكتَبةَ المَشهورةَ	المَكتَبةُ المَشهورةُ
his famous bookstore	مَكتَبتِهِ المَشهورةِ	مَكتَبتَهُ المَشهورةَ	مَكتَبتُهُ المَشهورةُ

Number: the adjective is singular because the noun is singular.

Gender: the adjective is feminine because the noun is feminine; so marked by the feminine marker ة, ta' marbuta.

Definiteness: the adjective is definite because the noun is definite; so marked by a definite article ال, or by being a first term of 'idafa.

Case: (see case marking by diacritics)

The adjective is مَرفوع when the noun is مَرفوع; so marked by a ضَمّة.
The adjective is مَنصوب when the noun is مَنصوب; so marked by a فتحة.
The adjective is مَجرور when the noun is مَجرور; so marked by a كسرة.

Summary of adjectival agreement in the singular

In the singular, irrespective of whether the noun is human or non-human, the adjective agrees with the noun in all respects:

Number: the adjective is the same number as the noun.

Gender: the adjective is the same gender as the noun, either masculine or feminine.

Definiteness: the adjective is the same as the noun, either definite or indefinite.

Case: the adjective is the same as the noun, either مَنصوب ,مَرفوع, or مَجرور

Indefinite masculine singular human and non-human

Number: the adjective is singular because the noun is singular.

Gender: the adjective is masculine because the noun is masculine.

Definiteness: the adjective is indefinite because the noun is indefinite.

Case: see case marking by diacritics.

The adjective is مَرفوع because the noun is مَرفوع; so marked by a تنوين ضَم.

The adjective is مَنصوب because the noun is مَنصوب; so marked by the letter ا + تنوين فتح, as with all masculine indefinite nouns.

The adjective is مَجرور because then noun is مَجرور; so marked by a تنوين كسر.

Indefinite feminine singular human and non-human

Number: the adjective is singular because the noun is singular.

Gender: the adjective is feminine because the noun is feminine; so marked by the feminine marker ة, ta' marbuta.

Definiteness: the adjective is indefinite because the noun is indefinite.

Case: see case marking by diacritics.

The adjective is مَرفوع when the noun is مَرفوع; so marked by a تنوين ضَم.

The adjective is مَنصوب when the noun is مَنصوب; so marked by a تنوين فتح.

The adjective is مَجرور when the noun is مَجرور; so marked by a تنوين كسر.

Definite masculine singular human and non-human

Number: the adjective is singular because the noun is singular.

Gender: the adjective is masculine because the noun is masculine.

Definiteness: the adjective is definite because the noun is definite, so marked by a definite article ال, or by being a first term of 'idafa.

Case: (see case marking by diacritics)

The adjective is مَرفوع when the noun is مَرفوع; so marked by a ضَمّة.

The adjective is مَنصوب when the noun is مَنصوب; so marked by a فتحة.

The adjective is مَجرور when the noun is مَجرور; so marked by a كسرة.

Definite feminine singular human and non-human

Number: the adjective is singular because the noun is singular.

Gender: the adjective is feminine because the noun is feminine; so marked by the feminine marker ة, ta' marbuta.

Definiteness: the adjective is definite because the noun is definite; so marked by a definite article ال, or by being a first term of 'idafa.

Case: (see case marking by diacritics)
The adjective is مَرفوع when the noun is مَرفوع; so marked by a ضَمّة.
The adjective is مَنصوب when the noun is مَنصوب; so marked by a فتحة.
The adjective is مَجرور when the noun is مَجرور; so marked by a كسرة.

Exercise: adjectival agreement with nouns in the singular

Exercise 1

Fill in the blanks. Please make all necessary changes to ensure agreement. The first one is completed for reference.

Glossary

قَوِيّ الشَخصيّة	strong-willed (s., m.)
رَجُلٌ	a man
اِمرأةٌ	a woman

a) رَجُلٌ ______ الشَخصيّةِ — a strong-willed man
رَجُلٌ قَوِيٌّ الشَخصيّةِ
b) الرَجُلُ ______ الشَخصيّةِ — the strong-willed man
c) اِمرأةٌ ______ الشَخصيّةِ — a strong-willed woman
d) المَرأةُ ______ الشَخصيّةِ — the strong-willed woman

Adjectives: agreement with nouns in the dual

In the dual, as in the singular, there's agreement between the noun and the adjective in number, gender, definiteness, and case whether a noun is human or non-human.

Masculine indefinite

Human

Meaning	مَنصوب/مَجرور	مَرفوع
two big men	رَجُلَيْنِ كبيرَيْنِ	رَجُلانِ كبيرانِ
two famous actors	مُمَثِّلَيْنِ مَشهورَيْنِ	مُمَثِّلانِ مَشهورانِ

Non-human

Meaning	مَنصوب/مَجرور	مَرفوع
two big books	كِتابَيْنِ كبيرَيْنِ	كِتابانِ كبيرانِ
two famous books	كِتابَيْنِ مَشهورَيْنِ	كِتابانِ مَشهورانِ

Number: the adjective is dual because the noun is dual.

Gender: the adjective is masculine because the noun is masculine.

Definiteness: the adjective is indefinite because the noun is indefinite.

Case: in the dual, there is no distinction in case marking between the مَنصوب, and the مَجرور. See Case marking by letters.

The adjective is مَرفوع when the noun is مَرفوع; so marked by the letter ا in the dual suffix ان.

The adjective is مَنصوب when the noun is مَنصوب; so marked by the letter ي in the dual suffix ين.

The adjective is مَجرور when the noun is مَجرور; so marked by the letter ي in the dual suffix ين.

Feminine indefinite

Human

Meaning	مَنصوب/مَجرور	مَرفوع
two big women	امرأتَيْنِ كبيرتَيْنِ	امرأتانِ كبيرتانِ
two famous actresses	مُمَثِّلَتَيْنِ مَشهورتَيْنِ	مُمَثِّلَتانِ مَشهورتانِ

Non-human

Meaning	مَنصوب/مَجرور	مَرفوع
two big tables	طاوِلَتَيْنِ كبيرتَيْنِ	طاوِلَتانِ كبيرتانِ
two famous bookstores	مَكتَبَتَيْنِ مَشهورتَيْنِ	مَكتَبتانِ مَشهورتانِ

Number: the adjective is dual because the noun is dual.

Gender: the adjective is feminine because the noun is feminine; so marked by the feminine marker ت.

Definiteness: the adjective is indefinite because the noun is indefinite.

Case: in the dual, there is no distinction in case marking between the مَنصوب, and the مَجرور. See Case marking by letters.

The adjective is مَرفوع when the noun is مَرفوع; so marked by the letter ا in the dual suffix ان.

The adjective is مَنصوب when the noun is مَنصوب; so marked by the letter ي in the dual suffix ين.

The adjective is مَجرور when the noun is مَجرور; so marked by the letter ي in the dual suffix ين.

Masculine definite

Human

Meaning	مَنصوب/مَجرور	مَرفوع
two big men	الرَجُلَيْنِ الكبيرَيْنِ	الرَجُلانِ الكبيرانِ
two famous actors	الـمُمَثِّلَيْنِ الـمَشهورَيْنِ	الـمُمَثِّلانِ الـمَشهورانِ
its two famous actors	مُمَثِّلَيْهِ الـمَشهورَيْنِ	مُمَثِّلاهُ الـمَشهورانِ

Non-human

Meaning	مَنصوب/مَجرور	مَرفوع
two big books	الكِتابَيْنِ الكبيرَيْنِ	الكِتابانِ الكبيرانِ
two famous books	الكِتابَيْنِ المَشهورَيْنِ	الكِتابانِ المَشهورانِ
his two famous books	كِتابَيْهِ المَشهورَيْنِ	كِتاباهُ المَشهورانِ

Number: the adjective is dual because the noun is dual.

Gender: the adjective is masculine because the noun is masculine.

Definiteness: the adjective is definite because the noun is definite, so marked by a definite article ال, or by being the first term of an 'idafa. In an 'idafa, the ن of the dual suffix ان or ين is dropped.

Case: in the dual, there is no distinction in case marking between the مَنصوب, and the مَجرور. See Case marking by letters.

The adjective is مَرفوع when the noun is مَرفوع; so marked by the letter ا in the dual suffix ان.

The adjective is مَنصوب when the noun is مَنصوب; so marked by the letter ي in the dual suffix ين.

The adjective is مَجرور when the noun is مَجرور; so marked by the letter ي in the dual suffix ين.

Feminine definite

Human

Meaning	مَنصوب/مَجرور	مَرفوع
the two large women	المرأتَيْنِ الكبيرتَيْنِ	المرأتانِ الكبيرتانِ
the two famous actresses	المُمَثِّلَتَيْنِ المَشهورتَيْنِ	المُمَثِّلَتانِ المَشهورتانِ
his two famous actresses	مُمَثِّلَتَيْهِ المَشهورتَيْنِ	مُمَثِّلَتاهُ المَشهورتانِ

Non-human

Meaning	مَنصوب/مَجرور	مَرفوع
the two big tables	الطاوِلتَيْنِ الكبيرتَيْنِ	الطاوِلتانِ الكبيرتانِ
the two famous bookstores	المَكتَبتَيْنِ المَشهورتَيْنِ	المَكتَبتانِ المَشهورتانِ
his two famous bookstores	مَكتَبتَيْهِ المَشهورتَيْنِ	مَكتَبتاهُ المَشهورتانِ

Number: the adjective is dual because the noun is dual.

Gender: the adjective is feminine because the noun is feminine; so marked by the feminine marker ت.

Definiteness: the adjective is definite because the noun is definite; so marked by a definite article ال, or by being a first term of an 'idafa. In an 'idafa, the ن of the dual suffix ان or ين is dropped.

Case: in the dual, there is no distinction in case marking between the مَنصوب, and the مَجرور. See Case marking by letters.

The adjective is مَرفوع when the noun is مَرفوع; so marked by the letter ا in the dual suffix ان.

The adjective is مَنصوب when the noun is مَنصوب; so marked by the letter ي in the dual suffix ين.

The adjective is مَجرور when the noun is مَجرور; so marked by the letter ي in the dual suffix ين.

Summary of adjectival agreement in the dual

In the dual, irrespective of whether the noun is human or non-human, the adjective agrees with the noun in number, definiteness, gender, and case.

Indefinite masculine dual: human and non-human

Number: the adjective is dual because the noun is dual.

Gender: the adjective is masculine because the noun is masculine.

Definiteness: the adjective is indefinite because the noun is indefinite.

Case: in the dual, there is no distinction in case marking between the مَنصوب, and the مَجرور. See Case marking by letters.

The adjective is مَرفوع when the noun is مَرفوع; so marked by the letter ا in the dual suffix ان.

The adjective is مَنصوب when the noun is مَنصوب; so marked by the letter ي in the dual suffix ين.

The adjective is مَجرور when the noun is مَجرور; so marked by the letter ي in the dual suffix ين.

Indefinite feminine dual: human and non-human

Number: the adjective is dual because the noun is dual.

Gender: the adjective is feminine because the noun is feminine; so marked by the feminine marker ت.

Definiteness: the adjective is indefinite because the noun is indefinite.

Case: in the dual, there is no distinction in case marking between the مَنصوب, and the مَجرور. See Case marking by letters.

The adjective is مَرفوع when the noun is مَرفوع; so marked by the letter ا in the dual suffix ان.

The adjective is مَنصوب when the noun is مَنصوب; so marked by the letter ي in the dual suffix ين.

The adjective is مَجرور when the noun is مَجرور; so marked by the letter ي in the dual suffix ين.

Definite masculine dual: human and non-human

The adjective agrees with the noun in number, definiteness, gender, and case.

Number: the adjective is dual because the noun is dual.

Gender: the adjective is masculine because the noun is masculine.

Definiteness: the adjective is definite because the noun is definite, so marked by a definite article ال, or by being the first term of an ’idafa. In an ’idafa, the ن of the dual suffix ان or ين is dropped.

Case: in the dual, there is no distinction in case marking between the مَنصوب, and the مَجرور. See Case marking by letters.

The adjective is مَرفوع when the noun is مَرفوع; so marked by the letter ا in the dual suffix ان.

The adjective is مَنصوب when the noun is مَنصوب; so marked by the letter ي in the dual suffix ين.

The adjective is مَجرور when the noun is مَجرور; so marked by the letter ي in the dual suffix ين.

Definite feminine dual: human and non-human

Number: the adjective is dual because the noun is dual.

Gender: the adjective is feminine because the noun is feminine; so marked by the feminine marker ت.

Definiteness: the adjective is definite because the noun is definite; so marked by a definite article ال, or by being a first term of an 'idafa. In an 'idafa, the ن of the dual suffix ان or ين is dropped.

Case: in the dual, there is no distinction in case marking between the مَنصوب, and the مَجرور. See Case marking by letters.

The adjective is مَرفوع when the noun is مَرفوع; so marked by the letter ا in the dual suffix ان.

The adjective is مَنصوب when the noun is مَنصوب; so marked by the letter ي in the dual suffix ين.

The adjective is مَجرور when the noun is مَجرور; so marked by the letter ي in the dual suffix ين.

Adjectives: agreement with nouns in the plural

In the plural, there's agreement between a human noun and the adjective in all respects: number, gender, definiteness, and case.

In the case of plural non-human nouns, however, an adjective only agrees in two respects – definiteness and case – but must be singular and feminine.

Masculine indefinite

Human

Meaning	مَجرور	مَنصوب	مَرفوع
big men	رِجالٍ كِبارٍ	رِجالاً كِباراً	رِجالٌ كِبارٌ
famous actors	مُمَثِّلينَ مَشهورينَ	مُمَثِّلينَ مَشهورينَ	مُمَثِّلون مَشهورونَ

Non-human

Meaning	مَجرور	مَنصوب	مَرفوع
big books	كُتُبٍ كَبيرةٍ	كُتُباً كَبيرةً	كُتُبٌ كَبيرةٌ
famous books	كُتُبٍ مَشهورةٍ	كُتُباً مَشهورةً	كُتُبٌ مَشهورةٌ

Number:

Human: the adjective is plural because the noun is plural.

Non-human: the adjective is singular and feminine because plural non-human nouns take feminine singular adjectives.

Gender:

Human: the adjective is masculine because the noun is masculine.

Non-human: the adjective is feminine and singular because plural non-human nouns take feminine singular adjectives.

Definiteness: the adjective is indefinite because the noun is indefinite.

Case: see case marking by diacritics and Case marking by letters.

The adjective is مَرفوع when the noun is مَرفوع; so marked by an appropriate مَرفوع marker as follows:

For broken plurals, the marker is تنوين ضَم.

For sound masculine plurals, i.e. with the suffix ون, the marker is و.

The adjective is مَنصوب when the noun is مَنصوب; so marked by the appropriate مَنصوب marker as follows:

For broken masculine plurals, the marker is by the letter تنوين فتح + ا.

For sound masculine plurals, i.e. with the suffix ين, the marker is ي.

The adjective is مَجرور when the noun is مَجرور; so marked by the appropriate مَجرور marker as follows:

For broken plurals, the marker is تنوين كسر.

For sound masculine plurals, i.e. with the suffix ين, the marker is ي.

For sound masculine plurals there's no distinction in case marking between مَجرور and مَنصوب.

Feminine indefinite

Human

Meaning	مَنصوب/مَجرور	مَرفوع
big women	نِساءٍ كبيراتٍ	نِساءٌ كبيراتٌ
famous actresses	مُمَثِّلاتٍ مَشهوراتٍ	مُمَثِّلاتٌ مَشهوراتٌ

Non-human

Meaning	مَجرور	مَنصوب	مَرفوع
big tables	طاوِلاتٍ كَبيرةٍ	طاوِلاتٍ كَبيرةً	طاوِلاتٌ كَبيرةٌ
famous bookstores	مَكتَباتٍ مَشهورةٍ	مَكتَباتٍ مَشهورةً	مَكتَباتٌ مَشهورةٌ

Number:

Human: the adjective is plural because the noun is plural.

Non-human: the adjective is singular (and feminine) because plural non-human nouns take singular feminine adjectives.

Gender: the adjective is feminine because the noun is feminine.

Definiteness: the adjective is indefinite because the noun is indefinite.

Case: see case marking by diacritics.

The adjective is مَرفوع when the noun is مَرفوع; so marked by تنوين ضَمّ.

The adjective is مَنصوب when the noun is مَنصوب; so marked by تنوين كَسر. For sound feminine plurals, there is no distinction in case marking between the مَنصوب, and the مَجرور.

The adjective is مَجرور when the noun is مَجرور; so marked by تنوين كَسر. For sound feminine plurals, there is no distinction in case marking between the مَنصوب, and the مَجرور.

Masculine definite

Human

Meaning	مَجرور	مَنصوب	مَرفوع
the big men	الرِجالِ الكِبارِ	الرِجالَ الكِبارَ	الرِجالُ الكِبارُ
the famous actors	المُمَثِّلينَ المَشهورينَ	المُمَثِّلينَ المَشهورينَ	المُمَثِّلونَ المَشهورونَ
its famous actors	مُمَثِّليهِ المَشهورينَ	مُمَثِّليهِ المَشهورينَ	مُمَثِّلوهُ المَشهورونَ

Non-human

Meaning	مَجرور	مَنصوب	مَرفوع
the big books	الكُتُبِ الكَبيرةِ	الكُتُبَ الكَبيرةَ	الكُتُبُ الكَبيرةُ
the famous books	الكُتُبِ المَشهورةِ	الكُتُبَ المَشهورةَ	الكُتُبُ المَشهورةُ
his famous books	كُتُبِهِ المَشهورةِ	كُتُبَهُ المَشهورةَ	كُتُبُهُ المَشهورةُ

Number:

Human: the adjective is plural because the noun is plural.

Non-human: the adjective is singular because plural non-human nouns take singular feminine adjectives.

Gender:

Human: the adjective is masculine because the noun is masculine.

Non-human: the adjective is feminine because plural non-human nouns take feminine singular adjectives.

Definiteness: the adjective is definite because the noun is definite, so marked by a definite article ال, or by being the first term of an 'idafa. In an 'idafa, the ن of the sound masculine suffix ون or ين is dropped.

Case: with the sound masculine plural there is no distinction in case marking between the مَنصوب and the مَجرور. See Case marking by diacritics and Case marking by letters.

The adjective is مَرفوع when the noun is مَرفوع; so marked by the appropriate مَرفوع marker as follows:

For broken plurals, the marker is ضَمّة.

For sound masculine plurals, the marker is the letter و in the suffix ون.

The adjective is مَنصوب when the noun is مَنصوب; so marked by the appropriate مَنصوب marker as follows:

For broken plurals, the marker is فَتحة.

For sound masculine plurals, the marker is the letter ي in the suffix ين.

The adjective is مَجرور when the noun is مَجرور; so marked by the appropriate مَجرور marker as follows:

For broken plurals, the marker is كَسرة.

For sound masculine plurals, the marker is the letter ي in the suffix ين.
For broken plurals, the marker is كَسرة.

Feminine definite

Human

Meaning	مَنصوب/مَجرور	مَرفوع
the big women	النِساءِ الكبيراتِ	النِساءُ الكبيراتُ
the famous actresses	المُمَثِّلاتِ المَشهوراتِ	المُمَثِّلاتُ المَشهوراتُ
its famous actresses	مُمَثِّلاتِه المَشهوراتِ	مُمَثِّلاتُه المَشهوراتُ

Non-human

Meaning	مَجرور	مَنصوب	مَرفوع
the big tables	الطاوِلاتِ الكَبيرةِ	الطاوِلاتِ الكَبيرةَ	الطاوِلاتُ الكَبيرةُ
the famous bookstores	المَكتَباتِ المَشهورةِ	المَكتَباتِ المَشهورةَ	المَكتَباتُ المَشهورةُ
his famous bookstores	مَكتَباتِهِ المَشهورةِ	مَكتَباتِهِ المَشهورةَ	مَكتَباتُهُ المَشهورةُ

Number:

Human: the adjective is plural because the noun is plural.
Non-human: the adjective is singular because plural non-human nouns take singular feminine adjectives.

Gender: the adjective is feminine because the noun is feminine.

Definiteness: the adjective is definite because the noun is definite, so marked by a definite article ال, or by being the first term of an 'idafa.

Case: for sound feminine plurals, there is no distinction in case marking between the مَنصوب and the مَجرور. See Case marking by diacritics.

The adjective is مَرفوع when the noun is مَرفوع, so marked by a ضَمّة.

The adjective is مَنصوب when the noun مَنصوب. The noun is a sound feminine plural which receives a كسرة in the مَنصوب.

The adjective is مَجرور, when the noun is مَجرور.

Summary of adjectival agreement in the plural

In the plural, adjectival agreement depends on whether the noun is human or non-human.

With human nouns:

Number: the adjective agrees with the noun.

Gender: the adjective agrees with the noun.

Definiteness: the adjective agrees with the noun.

Case: the adjective agrees with the noun.

With non-human nouns:

Number: the adjective is singular.

Gender: the adjective is feminine.

Definiteness: the adjective agrees with the noun.

Case: the adjective agrees with the noun.

Indefinite masculine plural: human and non-human

Number:

Human: the adjective is plural because the noun is plural.

Non-human: the adjective is singular and feminine because plural non-human nouns take feminine singular adjectives.

Gender:

Human: the adjective is masculine because the noun is masculine.

Non-human: the adjective is feminine and singular because plural non-numan nouns take feminine singular adjectives.

Definiteness: the adjective is indefinite because the noun is indefinite.

Case: see case marking by diacritics and Case marking by letters.

The adjective is مَرفوع when the noun is مَرفوع; so marked by an appropriate مَرفوع marker as follows:

For broken plurals, the marker is تنوين ضَم.

For sound masculine plurals, i.e. with the suffix ون, the marker is و.

The adjective is مَنصوب when the noun is مَنصوب; so marked by the appropriate مَنصوب marker as follows:

For broken masculine plurals, the marker is the letter تنوين فتح + ا.

For sound masculine plurals, i.e.with the suffix ين, the marker is ي.

The adjective is مَجرور when the noun is مَجرور; so marked by the appropriate مَجرور marker as follows:

For broken plurals, the marker is تنوين كسر.

For sound masculine plurals, i.e. with the suffix ين, the marker is ي.

For sound masculine plurals there's no distinction in case marking between مَنصوب and مَجرور.

Indefinite feminine plural: human and non-human

Number:

Human: the adjective is plural because the noun is plural.

Non-human: the adjective is singular (and feminine) because plural non-human nouns take singular feminine adjectives.

Gender: the adjective is feminine because the noun is feminine.

Definiteness: the adjective is indefinite because the noun is indefinite.

Case: for sound feminine plurals, there is no distinction in case marking between the مَنصوب, and the مَجرور. See Case marking by diacritics.

The adjective is مَرفوع when the noun is مَرفوع; so marked by تنوين ضَمّ.

The adjective is مَنصوب when the noun is مَنصوب; so marked by تنوين كسر.

The adjective is مَجرور when the noun is مَجرور; so marked by تنوين كَسر.

For sound feminine plurals, there is no distinction in case marking between the مَنصوب, and the مَجرور.

Definite masculine plural: human and non-human

Number:

Human: the adjective is plural because the noun is plural.

Non-human: the adjective is singular because plural non-human nouns take singular feminine adjectives.

Gender:

Human: the adjective is masculine because the noun is masculine.

Non-human: the adjective is feminine because plural non-human nouns take feminine singular adjectives.

Definiteness: the adjective is definite because the noun is definite, so marked by a definite article ال, or by being the first term of an 'idafa. In an 'idafa, the ن of the sound masculine suffix ون or ين is dropped.

Case: with the sound masculine plural there is no distinction in case marking between the مَنصوب and the مَجرور. See Case marking by diacritics and Case marking by letters.

The adjective is مَرفوع when the noun is مَرفوع; so marked by the appropriate مَرفوع marker as follows:

For broken plurals, the marker is ضَمّة.

For sound masculine plurals, the marker is the letter و in the suffix ون.

The adjective is مَنصوب when the noun is مَنصوب; so marked by the appropriate مَنصوب marker as follows:

For broken plurals, the marker is فَتحة.

For sound masculine plurals, the marker is the letter ي in the suffix ين.

The adjective is مَجرور when the noun is مَجرور; so marked by the appropriate مَجرور marker as follows:

For broken plurals, the marker is كَسرة.

For sound masculine plurals, the marker is the letter ي in the suffix ين.

For broken plurals, the marker is كَسرة.

Definite feminine plural: human and non-human

Number:

Human: the adjective is plural because the noun is plural.

Non-human: the adjective is singular because plural non-human nouns take singular feminine adjectives.

Gender: the adjective is feminine because the noun is feminine.

Definiteness: the adjective is definite because the noun is definite, so marked by a definite article ال, or by being the first term of an 'idafa.

Case: for sound feminine plurals, there is no distinction in case marking between the مَنصوب and the مَجرور. See Case marking by diacritics.

The adjective is مَرفوع when the noun is مَرفوع, so marked by a ضَمّة.

The adjective is مَنصوب when the noun مَنصوب. The noun is a sound feminine plural which receives a كَسرة in the مَنصوب.

The adjective is مَجرور, when the noun is مَجرور.

UNIT 21

The ’idafa phrase الإضافة

The إضافة, is a sequence of two adjacent nouns (or a noun and a pronoun suffix). For example in *Cairo University,* Cairo and University are both nouns, and they are adjacent.

One noun is made more specific by the other. For example, “University” is made specific by “Cairo”. In other words, “university” is any university, but “university” in “Cairo University” is a specific university.

The first term is المُضاف and is followed by المُضاف إليه. The مُضاف, the first term, is a definite noun.

الإضافة is often considered to have six types.

I Identity: مدينة دمشق, فريضة الحجّ

II Partitive/quantitative: فنجال قهوة, طلائع الثورة.

III Possession: سيارة المدير

IV Agent relationship: وصول الملك

V Object relationship: إعدام المجرم

VI Limitation of first term by second: بعيد المَدى

The إضافة may express possession, either overtly or implicitly. Possession is clear in examples like “Maha’s car” or “Maha’s book”. Possession is not really semantical possession but grammatical possession (i.e. implicit) in examples like “the front of the house” or “the city of New York”.

Definition and form

One very basic and high-frequency Arabic noun phrase/adverbial phrase is known by the name ’idafa (إضافة). Syntactically, the إضافة comprises two adjacent terms. Morphologically, the first term is usually a (substantive) noun, a gerund, a temporal or locative adverbial noun, or – less commonly – an adjectival noun. The second term is usually a (substantive) noun, a gerund, or a pronoun suffix (see Pronouns). The second term provides information, or specificity, about the first. Neither of the terms is an adjective.

Schematically:

noun or adverbial + noun or pronoun suffix
noun + noun
noun + pronoun suffix
adverbial noun + noun
adverbial noun + pronoun suffix:

The following are some examples:

noun + noun

جامعة القاهرة	Cairo University
سيارة مها	Maha's car

noun + pronoun suffix

سيارتها	her car
بيتي	my house
صديقنا	our friend
بيوتنا	our houses

adverbial noun + noun

بعد الظهر	afternoon
أمام البيت	in front of the house

adverbial noun + pronoun suffix:

فوقه	on top of it
تحتها	under it

Rules:

The first term is a noun (includes locative and temporal adverbs)
The first term does not have the definite article ال.
The two terms are always adjacent; nothing can come between them.

The second term is in the genitive case (see Case).

It is helpful to remember that none of the nouns in such a sequential arrangement is an adjective.

The first noun is made more specific by the second one.

Meaning

The second term gives the first a measure of specificity. Thus, in سيارة مها (Maha's car), the first term – سيارة – is made specific by the second term مها; it's not any car, but Maha's car. Similarly, the noun كِتاب (an indefinite unspecified book) is any book in the universe of books; however, in the following two إضافة phrases, كِتاب مها (Maha's book) or كتابها (her book), the first term كتاب is no longer any book in the universe of books, but a specific one كِتاب.

The four examples below show a noun ranging from an unspecified noun, to not unspecified, to specified, as the second term adds specificity to the first term:

1 an unspecified door, any door باب
2 a house door (not any door) باب بيتٍ
3 a door of a house (not any door) باب بيتٍ
4 the door of the house (a specific door) باب البيتِ

In 1 above, the term باب refers to *any* door; it is an unspecified door. However in 2 and 3, the first term باب is more specific than in 1; it is no longer *any* door; it gains specificity and becomes a door in the universe of doors of houses. Finally, in 4 above, when the second term has the definite article, البيت, the first term باب is even more specific.

An إضافة can be used to express possession, as in:

my house بيتي
her car سيارتها
Maha's car سيارة مها
our houses بيوتنا

An إضافة can also be used to express grammatical possession (i.e. *x of y*), such as in the following English examples where the apostrophe + s ('s) is not used:

in front *of* the house أمام البيت
the city *of* New York مدينة نيويورك
the House *of* Representatives مجلس النوّاب
the irony *of* fate سُخرية القَدَر

In addition, an إضافة is also used in phrases where the apostrophe + s ('s) occurs but does not literally indicate possession, as in:

the teacher's wife	زوجة المدرّس
your friend	صديقك

Finally, an إضافة is also used in contexts with English phrases expressing relative location but without "of":

under the table	تحت الطاولة
over the city	فوق المدينة
near the restaurant	قُرب المطعم

Order (syntax)

English has similar arrangements, but in comparison with Arabic the order of this arrangement in English is inverted.

English examples: the first term amplifies the second one. That is, contrary to Arabic, the second noun is made more specific by the preceding one.

1 Without "the" or "of" or "'s"

Examples:

Metro Airport, China syndrome, Buffalo wings, cylinder head,
Starbucks café, software design, dining room, gas station, . . .

2 With "'s"

Examples:

cat's meow, day's end, . . .

3 With gerunds

Examples:

reading books, understanding things,
hearing voices, eating pie, . . .

Opposite of English

In an English expression such as: "a summer night", the amplifying or specifying term "summer" precedes the substantive noun "night".

The equivalent إضافة expression in Arabic is ليلة صيف. In this إضافة phrase, the order is the opposite of that in English: the substantive noun, ليلة, precedes the amplifying or specifying term, صيف. In the case of these English expressions with the structure [noun + noun], where the order is substantive noun then amplifying or specifying term, the order of the Arabic expressions is consistently switched to amplifying or specifying term then substantive noun.

Examples:

English

1st term	2nd term (amplifying term + substantive noun)
Oxford	University
Heathrow	Airport
bus	station

Arabic

2nd term	1st term (noun + amplifying term)
أُكسفورد	جامعة
هيثرو	مطار
الحافلاتِ	محطة

Similarly, in English expressions such as "Kathy's sister", the amplifying or specifying term, Kathy, precedes the substantive noun, sister. The equivalent إضافة expression in Arabic is "أخت كاثي." In this إضافة phrase, the substantive noun, أخت, precedes the amplifying or specifying term, كاثي.

In the case of these English expressions with the structure [noun + 's + noun] where the order is amplifying or specifying term then substantive noun, the order of their Arabic expressions is consistently switched to substantive noun then amplifying or specifying term.

Examples:

English

1st term	2nd term (amplifying or specifying term then noun)
a cat's	tail
a winter's	tale

Arabic

2nd term	1st term (noun then amplifying or specifying term)
قطةٍ	ذيل
شتاءٍ	قصّة

Same as English

In English expressions such as "University of Michigan", the substantive noun, "University", precedes the amplifying or specifying term, "Michigan". The equivalent إضافة expression in Arabic is جامعة ميشيجان. The order in this إضافة phrase is as follows: the substantive noun, جامعة, precedes the amplifying or specifying term, ميشيجان. The order of these English expressions with the structure [*x* of *y*] mirrors the إضافة phrase.

Examples:

English

1st term	2nd term (substantive noun then amplifying or specifying term)
a cup of	tea

Arabic

2nd term	1st term (substantive noun then amplifying or specifying term)
شاي	فنجان

In this إضافة phrase, the order mirrors the order of the English expression.

In the case of these English expressions with the structure [*x* of *y*], such as: *University of Michigan*, or *cup of tea*, the order of terms in the إضافة mirrors the order of the English expression "the University of Michigan", جامعة ميشيجان, and "a cup of tea", فنجان شاي.

Here are some further examples. Imagine them with the question "what . . .?":

What airport? Metro Airport.

What syndrome? China syndrome.

What wings? Buffalo wings.

What head? Cylinder head.

What design? Software design.

What room? Dining room.

What station? Gas station.

What university? Michigan University.

Same as English

The following slightly varying types of English phrases are all rendered as Arabic إضافة phrases:

Example 1:

English noun phrase: possessive pronoun + noun (expressing ownership)

(indefinite noun + pronoun suffix)

بيتي my house

صديقي my friend

Example 2:

English noun phrase: possessive pronoun + noun (not expressing ownership)

(indefinite noun + pronoun suffix)

بنتي my daughter

تَنَفُّسك your breathing

جامعتها her university

Example 3:

English noun phrase: noun + 's + noun (expressing ownership)

(indefinite noun + def. or indef. noun)

سيارة وحيدٍ Waheed's car

شنطة طالبٍ a student's bag

شنطة الطالبِ the student's bag,

Example 4:

English noun phrase: noun + 's + noun (not expressing ownership)

(indefinite noun + def. or indef. noun)

أخ محمد Mohamed's (m.s.) brother

Example 5:

English noun phrase: noun + of + noun (expressing ownership)

(indefinite noun + def. or indef. noun)

قصر أرستُقراطي	a palace of an aristocrat
بيت محمد	the house of Mohamed
بيت المُحامي	the house of the lawyer

Example 6:

English noun phrase: noun + of + noun (not expressing ownership)

(indefinite noun + def. or indef. noun)

جامعة ميشيجان	The University of Michigan
صُندوق بيرةٍ	a case of beer
غرفة الطعام	the dining room

Example 7:

English noun phrase: noun + noun (amplification or specification)

(indefinite noun + def. or indef. noun)

غرفة طعامٍ	dining room
قسم التاريخِ	the History department
مكتب التذاكر	the ticket office

Example 8:

English noun phrase: gerund + noun (amplification or specification) (see gerund, in About Arabic noun forms)

(indefinite noun + def. or indef. noun)

قراءة كُتُبٍ	reading books
فَهْم الأشياءِ	understanding things
سَماع أصواتٍ	hearing voices
أكْل اللحمِ	eating meat

Same as English

Example 9:

English adverb phrase: locative adverbial noun + noun, amplification or specification

(indefinite adverbial + def. or indef. noun)

فوق التلفزيون above the TV
تحت طاولةٍ under a table

Example 10:

English prepositional phrase: preposition + noun, amplification or specification

(indefinite adverbial + def. or indef. noun)

بعد ساعةٍ after an hour
بعد اليومِ after today

Example 11:

English noun phrase: (partitive) noun + of + noun, specification

(indefinite noun + def. or indef. noun)

بعض الوقتِ some of the time
مُعظم اليومِ most of the day

'Idafa sequences (1st 'idafa + 2nd 'idafa + 3rd 'idafa + . . .)

An idafa phrase can be longer than two terms.

Examples

سيارة صديقِ محمد Mohamed's friend's car
سيارة صديقِ محمد the car of the friend of Mohamed

In fact there is no grammatical constraint on how long an إضافة can be. In 'idafa sequences, the second term of the first 'idafa is itself the first term of the second 'idafa, and the second term of the second 'idafa is the first term of the third 'idafa and so on. The table below offers two examples of idafa phrases with more than two terms: أخت صديقي and حذاء كرة القدم. The table illustrates how the second term of the first 'idafa can itself be the first term of the second 'idafa.

Second term	First term	Second term	First term	'idafa phrase
ي	صديق	صديق	أخت	اخت صديقي
القدم	كرة	كرة	حذاء	حذاء كرة القدم

Exercises: The 'idafa phrase الإضافة

Exercise 1

Turn each of the following English phrases into an Arabic إضافة phrase with a possessive pronoun suffix. Write the إضافة phrases in the blanks below. The first example is answered for reference.

Glossary

بيت	house	خاتم	ring
قلم	pen	أرض	land
سيارة	car	أفكار	ideas
ساعة	watch	رأي	opinion

1 my house ____________

بيتي

2 your (m. s.) pen ____________

3 Your (f. s.) car ____________

4 his watch ____________

5 her ring ____________

6 our land ____________

7 their (m. pl.) opinion ____________

8 your (m. s.) ideas ____________

Exercise 2

Turn each of the following English phrases into an Arabic إضافة phrase with a second term that is a noun, definite or indefinite. Write the إضافة phrases in the blanks below. The first example is answered for reference.

Glossary

حِذاء	shoe	بِداية	beginning
لاَعِب	player	عام/سن	year
قميص	shirt	قِط	cat
صفّارة	whistle	نهاية	end
مُدرّب	trainer	يومِ	day
خطيبة	fiancée	صديق	friend
شارع	street	أخت	sister

1 Omar's shirt ________ ________

قميص عمر

2 a player's shoe ________ ________

3 the trainer's whistle ________ ________

4 the cat's meow ________ ________

5 the day's end ________ ________

6 my friend's (m.) sister ________ ________

7 Salma's street ________ ________

8 Mahmoud's fiancée ________ ________

9 the beginning of the year ________ ________

Exercise 3

Turn each of the following English phrases into an Arabic إضافة phrase "x *of* y" to express ownership. Write the إضافة phrases in the blanks below. The first example is answered for reference.

Glossary

قصر	palace	آلة	an instrument
أرستُقراطي	an aristocrat	مَلِك	king
موسيقار	a musician		

1 a palace of an aristocrat ________ ________

أرستُقراطي قصر

2 an instrument of a musician ________ ________

3 the palace of the king ________ ________

Exercise 4

Turn each of the following English phrases into an Arabic إضافة phrase "x *of* y" that does not express ownership. Write the إضافة phrases in the blanks below. The first example is answered for reference.

Glossary

زجاجة	bottle	فنجان	(coffee) cup
اِستقلال	independence	قهوة	coffee
مياه	water	طَعم	taste
صُندوق	a case	الحِساب	reckoning (the day of, religious)
بيرةٍ	beer		
عام	year	عَسَل	honey

1 a case of beer ________ ________

صُندوق ‏ بيرةٍ

2 the bottle of water ________ ________

3 the year of independence ________ ________

4 a cup of coffee ________ ________

5 the taste of honey ________ ________

Exercise 5

Turn each of the following English phrases into an Arabic إضافة phrase with a second noun offering amplification or specification to the first noun, with no overt expression of ownership. Write the إضافة phrases in the blanks below. The first example is answered for reference.

Glossary

مطار	Cairo	مقهى	café
القاهرة	airport	البرامجِ	software
ستاربَكس	Starbucks	تصميم	design

1 Cairo Airport ________ ________

مطار ‏ القاهرة

2 Starbucks café ________ ________

3 software design ________ ________

4 gas station ________ ________

5 the history department ________ ________

6 the ticket office ________ ________

7 football shoes ________ ________

Exercise 6

Turn each of the following into an Arabic إضافة phrase. Write the answers in the blank spaces below. The first phrase is given for reference.

Glossary

جهاز	machine/unit	زيت	oil
فاكس	fax	خـزّان	tank
تـكييف	air conditioning	بنزين/وقود	gas
تـكييف	building	طبيب	physician
مدخل	entrance	جامعة	university
عمارة/مَبنى	building	غرُفة	room
فِلتَر/مُرَشِّح	filter	اِجتماع	meeting

1 a fax machine ________ ________

جهاز فاكس

2 the air conditioning unit ________ ________

3 the building entrance ________ ________

4 an oil filter ________ ________

5 the gas tank ________ ________

6 the university physician ________ ________

7 a meeting room ________ ________

Exercise 7

Answer the questions below with a second noun that adds a measure of specificity to the first noun. Place the correct responses in the blank spaces below. Recall that the first term does not have the definite article ال. The first example is answered for reference.

Glossary

عائلة	family
شيكاغو	Chicago
فرجينيا	Virginia
الشرق الأوسط	the Middle East region
عمّ	uncle (father's brother)
بِنت	girl/daughter
خالة	aunt (mother's sister)
مَكتَب القُبول	the office of admissions
داليا	Dalia

1	What picture?	أيّ صورة؟
	The family picture	صورة ________
		صورة العائلة
2	What city?	أيّ مَدينة؟
	The city of Chicago	مدينة ________
3	What state?	أيّ وِلاية؟
	The state of Virginia	ولاية ________
4	What region?	أيّ منطقة؟
	The Middle East region	منطقة ________
5	Whose son?	اِبن مَن؟
	My uncle's son	اِبن ________
6	Whose address?	عُنوان مَن؟
	The girl's address	عنوان ________
7	Whose husband?	زَوج مَن؟
	My aunt's husband	زوج ________
8	Which office?	أيّ مَكتَب؟
	The office of admissions	مَكتَب ________
9	Whose room?	غرفة مَن؟
	Dalia's room	غُرفة ________

UNIT 22

The 'idafa-adjective phrase

Definition and form

An 'idafa-adjective phrase comprises three terms:

1st term of 'idafa + 2nd term of 'idafa + adjective

The adjective, which can modify either term of the 'idafa, must come after the 'idafa.

Consider these two examples:

1 The big girl's dress فُستانُ البنتِ الكبيرةِ
2 The girl's big dress فُستانُ البنتِ الكبيرُ

In example 1, the adjective "big" qualifies the noun "girl" (البنت in Arabic). The adjective must therefore agree with the noun, البنت, in number, gender, definiteness, and case (see The noun-adjective phrase). The adjective is therefore singular, feminine, and definite (as well as being in the genitive case): الكبيرةِ.

However in example 2, where the adjective "big" qualifies the noun "dress", it would not be possible to place the adjective immediately after the noun فُستان because فُستان البنت is an 'idafa. Recall the إضافة comprises two adjacent terms (see The 'idafa phrase).

Therefore, in example 2, the adjective qualifying the noun فُستان is placed after the 'idafa (فُستان البنت). The adjective must follow the فُستان in number, gender, definiteness, and case. The adjective is therefore singular, masculine, and definite (as well as being in the nominative case): الكبيرُ.

Why is the adjective definite (الكبير, with the definite article ال)? Because in the 'idafa expression فُستان البنت, the first term فُستان is made specific because the second term of that 'idafa is definite (see The 'idafa phrase). Thus فُستان is not any فُستان; rather it is the girl's فُستان.

Exercise: The 'idafa-adjective phrase

Exercise 1

Express the following in Arabic using an 'idafa-adjective phrase:

Hameeda, her hearing is weak ______________________

Glossary

her hearing	سَمَعها
weak	ضَعيف

Reading old books ______________________

Glossary

reading	قِراءة
books	كُتُب
old	قديم (m.) قديمة (f.)

Reading the books is boring ______________________

Glossary

reading	قِراءة
books	كُتُب
boring	مُمِلّة

UNIT 23

The definite article ال

Definiteness of nouns and adjectives

A noun that is deemed specific takes ال.

An adjective with a noun that is specific takes ال.

The first term in an إضافة does not take ال.

Example:

Incorrect	Correct
التاريخ الوجود الفرنسيّ	تاريخ الوجود الفرنسيّ

Some sentences comprise a sequence of two nouns where the first noun has ال and the second does not.

Examples:

the revolution is industrial	الثورة صناعية
the industrial revolution	الثورة الصناعية

UNIT 24
Prepositions

Definition

Arabic prepositions comprise a small closed class of words that receive no case.

Syntax

Prepositions can take pronoun suffixes (see Pronominal suffixation), and can be followed by nouns; however, they are not immediately followed by verbs.

In the case of intransitive verbs – in particular – prepositions constitute an important aspect of meaning, grammar, and usage. Thus, when consulting a dictionary, careful attention should be paid to prepositions that are used with verbs (see Transitive vs intransitive verbs).

Meaning

Prepositions provide the following kind of information: temporal and locative, participatory (with someone), agency (by means of), ownership (have a house), relationship (have a cousin), as well as adverbial information (the manner of occurrence of an event). See also Adverbials.

The sections which follow offer a detailed account of the context in which the following prepositions are used and their meaning:

في، على، مِن، إلى، بِـ، ل، مَع

Meanings

In: temporal
In: locative

At: locative
On: locative

Examples

In: temporal (time required)

أصل إلى مكتبي في حوالي ٧ دقائق
I get to my office in about 7 minutes.

تُسلَق البيضة في ٥ دقائق
An egg is boiled in 5 minutes.

In: locative

ليس المفتاح في جيبي
The key is not in my pocket.

قرأت مجلّةً في الطائرة
I read the magazine in the aeroplane.

نسيت تليفوني في التاكسي
I forgot my telephone in the taxi.

At: locative

الكتاب في البيت
The book is at home.

المسرحية في الجامعة
The play is at the university.

الموناليزا في متحف اللوڤر
The Mona Lisa is at the Louvre museum.

On: locative

قرأت مجلّةً في الطائرة
I read the magazine on the aeroplane.

هو في مهمّة رسمية
He's on an official assignment.

Pronunciation

cvv
fii في
fii 'il maadii في إلماضي

على

Meanings

On: locative
In: form, shape
In: stages, degrees

Examples

On: locative

الجريدة على الطاولة The newspaper is on the table

In: form, shape

ماعِزة على شكل دجاجة
a sheep in the shape of a chicken

بيتزا على شكل مستطيل
a pizza in the shape of a rectangle

وبيتسا على شكل دائري
and a pizza in a circular shape

منزل ٤٠ متر٢ على شكل دائري
a home, 40 square metres, circular in shape

In: stages, degrees

أكملت المشروع على مراحل
I completed the project in stages

تعلّمت الطبيخ على مراحل
I learned to cook in stages

مِن

Meanings

From: direction
From: location
From: someone
By: cause
By: because of, by reason of
Of: material
One of: an instance

Examples

From: direction

من اليمين	from the right
من الجنوب	from the south

From: location

من مصر	from Egypt

From: someone

من بابانويل	from Santa
من حبيبتي	from my love

By: cause

محروق من الشمس	burned by the sun

By: because of, by reason of

من شِدّة الحَرّ
because of the extreme heat

كاد يموت من البرد
He almost died because of the cold

أُغمِيَ عليها من المُفاجأة
She fainted because of the surprise

Of: material

من قطن	of cotton
من ذهب	of gold

One of: an instance,

من أعزّ أصدقائي
one of my best friends

زُحَل" من أكبر الكواكب في المجموعة الشمسية"
Saturn is one of the largest planets in the planetary system

إلى

Meanings

To: direction
To: location
To: someone

Examples

To: direction

from up to down — من فوق إلى تحت

To: location

I will travel to Alexandria — سأسافر إلى الإسكندرية

To: someone

This ring is from me to you my darling
هذا الخاتم مِنّي إليكِ يا حبيبتي

He gave the diamond to the woman he loves

أعطى الماسة إلى حبيبته

Pronunciation

’ilaa إلى
albayt البيت
’ilalbayt إلى البيت

بِـ

Meanings

By: means, way
With: means, tool
With In: means contents, constituents
In: terms, units
-ly: manner

Examples

By: means

I go to work by car sometimes

أذهب إلى العمل بِالسيارة أحيانا

and by bus other times

وبِالأتوبيس أحياناً أخرى

and by bicycle sometimes

وبالعَجَلة أحيانا

With: means

Light the fire with a match

ولّع النار بـِكبريت

Pound this nail with a heavy hammer

دُقّ هذا المسمار بـِشاكوش ثقيل

With: contents, constituents

I drink tea with sugar and with a bit of milk

أشرب الشاي بالسكّر وبقليل مِن الحَليب

They have an excellent pie with nuts

عِندَهُم فطيرة بِالمكسّرات مُمتازة

In: means

Write in ink

أُكتُب بِـالحِبر

Speaking in English is forbidden

الكلام بِـالإنجليزية ممنوع

In: terms

السعر بالجُنيه المصري

The price is in Egyptian Pounds

الوزن بِـالكيلوجرام

The weight is in kilograms

والمَسافة بِـالكيلومتر

and the distance is in kilometres

-ly: manner

يمشي بِـسرعة

He walks/is walking quickly

يتكلّم بِـغَضَب

He talks/is talking angrily

تَكَلّمي بِـبُطء من فضلك

Speak slowly please

Meanings

(See: To have)
Have: relationship
Have: ownership

Examples

Have: relationship (see To have)

ل	+	ى
(preposition for to have a relationship)		(1st p. singular pronoun suffix me/my)

لـي بِنت
I have a daughter

ليلى لـها صديقة تعيش معها
Layla has a friend living with her

Have: ownership (see To Have)

لـه بيتٌ كبير في الريف
He has a big house in the countryside

لـها سيارة حمراء
She has a red car

مَع

Meaning

With: accompaniment
With: on possession (See: To Have)

Examples

With: accompaniment

Do you want to have lunch with me?	هل تريدين أن تتغدّي مَعـي؟
I'm going with him to the movies	سأذهب مَعَـه إلى السينما

With: on possession

Do you have a lighter with you?	مَعَك ولاّعة؟
Do you have any change with you?	مَعَك فَكّة؟
Do you have a car with you?	مَعَك سَيّارة؟

UNIT 25
Adverbials

Definition

Arabic adverbials comprise a closed class of words. Although some of them may appear similar to English prepositions, Arabic adverbials comprise a class that is distinct from prepositions. A key difference is that adverbials receive case and prepositions do not.

Meaning

Adverbials provide information about time and location (see also Prepositions).

Adverbials also play a major role in expressing various meanings of "to have", such as ownership, availability, disease, time, have in the mind, have an inclination, have an aptitude, have a skill, have difficulty, have problems, and others (see: To have).

Syntax

An adverbial often occurs as a first term of an 'idafa. In such cases, the term that immediately follows – the second term of the 'idafa – is *either* a noun or a pronoun suffix (see Pronominal suffixation).

A verb never immediately follows an adverbial.

The subordinating conjunctions أَنْ or ما can immediately follow an adverbial, instead of a noun or pronoun. These coordinating conjunctions permit a subordinate verb clause to follow an adverbial.

Meanings

At: locative

At: temporal

On: temporal
When: temporal
Has: (See: To have)

Syntax

عِندَ often occurs as a first term of an 'idafa. The immediately following second term of an 'idafa is a noun or a pronoun suffix.

عِندَ is not immediately followed by a verb.

ما can immediately follow عِندَ to introduce a verb clause.

Examples

At: locative, someone's place, similar to French *chez*

Followed by the second term of the 'idafa, i.e. a noun or pronoun suffix:

الحَفلةُ الليلة عِندَ بَيّومي.
The party tonight is at Bayyoumy's (house).

الأوراقُ عِندَ المُحامي.
The papers are at the lawyer's (office).

سَمِعتُ شَيئاً عَجيباً عِندَ الحلاّق.
I heard a strange thing at the barber's.

مَن عِندَهُم؟
Who's at their place?

At: locative

Followed by the second term of the 'idafa, i.e. a noun or pronoun suffix:

تَعالَ نَتَقابَلُ عِندَ تقاطُعِ الطُرُق.
Let's meet at the intersection

تَقابَلا عِند الباب.
They met at the door

تَقابَلا عِندَه.
They met there; they met at his place

At: temporal

Followed by the second term of the 'idafa, i.e. a noun or pronoun suffix:

تَقابَلا عِندَ الفجر.	They met at dawn
يَبكي الطِفلُ عِندَ الوِلادة.	A child cries at birth

On: temporal

Followed by the second term of the 'idafa, i.e. a noun or pronoun suffix:

عِندَ الوُصول	on arrival, upon arrival
عِندَ الخُروج	on exiting or going out
عِندَ الدُخول	on entering or going in

When: temporal

Followed by ما + verb clause:

سَنَخرُجُ عِندَما يأتي المساء
We will go out when evening falls (comes)

يَسعَدُ السَفّاحُ عِندَما يَغيبُ القَمَر
The serial killer is happy when the moon is away

قالَت شَهرَزاد:
وعِندَما فَتَحَ المَلِكُ الباب وَجَدَ زَوجَتَهُ في حُضنِ رَجُل.
Scheherazade said: . . . and when the king opened the door, he found his wife in the arms of a man.

Has: (See: To have)

I have an aeroplane	عندي طَيّارة
I have 3 cameras	عندي ٣ كاميرات
I have two houses	عندي بيتين

بَعدَ

Meanings

After: temporal
After: locative

Syntax

بَعدَ often occurs as a first term of an 'idafa. The immediately following second term of the 'idafa is a noun or a pronoun suffix.

بَعدَ is not immediately followed by a verb.

Either أنْ or ما can immediately follow بَعدَ to introduce a verb clause. For example:

اشتريتُ الكتاب بَعدَ أنْ سمعتك تتكلّم عنه.

I bought the book after I heard you talk about it.

اشتريتُ الكتاب بَعدَ ما سمعتك تتكلّم عنه.

I bought the book after I heard you talk about it.

The preposition بـِ is used to provide specific temporal or locative quantifying information. For example:

سافرَتْ بَعدَ زوجها بِأسبوع.

Literally: She travelled after her husband by a week.

Note that the quantifying information expressed by the prepositional phrase بـِ does not come before the adverbial, as it does in English (She travelled one week after her husband); rather, the quantifying information follows the second term of the 'idafa (زوجها): (She travelled after her husband by a week).

Examples

After: temporal

Followed by the second term of the 'idafa, i.e. a noun or pronoun suffix:

سنذهب إلى السينما بَعدَ العَشاء.

We'll go to the movies after supper.

سنخرج بَعدَهم.

We'll go out after them.

With بـِ providing specific temporal information, after the second term of the 'idafa (my mother):

تُوُفِّي أبي بَعدَ أمّي بِعَشَرِ سنوات.

My father died ten years after my mother.

Followed by أنْ + verb clause:

تَغَيَّرَ بَعدَ أنْ تَزَوّج.
He changed after he married.

يَتَغَيَّرُ الرجُلُ بَعدَ أنْ يَتَزَوّج.
A man changes after marrying.

سأعطيك رأيي بَعدَ أنْ أقرأ الكتاب.
I'll give you my opinion after I read the book.

Followed by ما + verb clause (perhaps less frequent than أن):

ماذا عَمِلتُم بَعدَ ما أكَلتُم؟
What did you do after you ate?

ماذا تَعمَلون بَعدَ ما تأكُلون؟
What do you do after you eat?

After: locative

Followed by the second term of 'idafa, i.e. a noun or pronoun suffix:

المكتبة بَعدَ البقّال
The bookstore is after the grocer.

With بِـ providing specific locative information, after the second term of the 'idafa (the station):

بيتُها بَعدَ المحطّة بِشارِعَين
Her house is two streets after the station.

قَبلَ

Meanings

Before: temporal

Before: locative

Syntax

قَبلَ often occurs as a first term of the 'idafa. The immediately following second term of the 'idafa is a noun or a pronoun suffix.

قَبلَ is not immediately followed by a verb.

Either أنْ or ما can immediately follow قَبلَ to introduce a verb clause. For example:

أفطُر في البيت قَبلَ أنْ أذهَبَ إلى الجامعة.
I have breakfast at home before going to the university.

فَطَرتُ في البيت قَبلَ أنْ أذهَبَ إلى الجامعة.
I had breakfast at home before going to the university.

As the two examples immediately above illustrate, قبل أنْ is not followed by a verb in the perfect tense.

The preposition بـ is used to provide specific temporal or locative information. For example:

سافرَتْ قَبلَ زوجها بِأسبوع.
She travelled one week before her husband.

Note that the quantifying information expressed by the prepositional phrase بـ does not come before the adverbial, as it does in English (She travelled one week before her husband); rather, the quantifying information follows the second term of the 'idafa (زوجها): (She travelled before her husband by a week).

Examples

Before: temporal

Followed by the second term of the 'idafa, i.e. a noun or pronoun suffix:

I'll see you before the lecture.
سأراكِ قَبلَ المُحاضرةِ.

With بـ providing specific temporal information:

We went to the airport two hours before departure time.
ذهبنا إلى المطار قَبلَ السفر بِساعَتين.

Followed by أنْ + verb clause *and* with بـ providing specific temporal information:

She called her friend five minutes before going down.

اِتّصلت بصديقتها قبل أنْ تنزل بِخمس دقائق.

Before: locative

Followed by the second term of the 'idafa, i.e. a noun or pronoun suffix:

المطعم قبل المكتبة.

The restaurant is before the bookstore.

With بِـ providing specific locative information:

بيتُها قَبلَ إشارة المُرور بِشارعين.

Her house is two streets before the traffic light.

Followed by أنْ + verb clause *and* with بِـ providing specific locative information:

سترى الخليج والفندق قبل أنْ تصل بِعِدّة كيلومترات.

You'll see the bay and the hotel several kilometres before you arrive.

أمامَ

Meaning

In front of: locative

Syntax

أمامَ often occurs as a first term of an 'idafa. The immediately following second term of the 'idafa is a noun or a pronoun suffix.

أمامَ is not immediately followed by a verb.

The preposition بِـ is used to provide specific temporal or locative information. For example:

أمامَ الباب بِـعِدّة أمتار.

several metres in front of the door

Note that the quantifying information expressed by the prepositional phrase بِـ does not come before the adverbial, as it does in English (several metres in front of the door); rather, the quantifying information follows the second term of the 'idafa (الباب): (in front of the door by several metres).

Examples

In front of: locative

Followed by the second term of the 'idafa, i.e. a noun or pronoun suffix:

كانوا يتقابلون أمامَ المطعم.
They used to meet in front of the restaurant.

أمامَ البيتِ شجرةٌ كبيرة.
In front of the house is a big tree.

وَراءَ

Meaning

Behind: locative

Syntax

وَراءَ often occurs as the first term of an 'idafa. The second term of the 'idafa can be a pronoun suffix (see Pronominal suffixation) or a noun.

وَراءَ is not immediately followed by a verb.

When quantifying information is provided a prepositional phrase is required; the preposition بِـ is used. For example:

وَراءَ البيتِ بِعِدَّة شوارِع.
several streets behind the house

Note that the quantifying information expressed by the prepositional phrase بِـ does not come before the adverbial, as it does in English (She travelled several streets behind the house); rather, the quantifying information follows the second term of the 'idafa (البيت): (behind the house by several streets).

Examples

Behind: locative

Followed by the second term of the 'idafa, i.e. a noun or pronoun suffix:

كانا يتقابلان وراءَ ظَهرِها.
They used to meet behind her back.

وراءَ البيتِ شجرةٌ كبيرة.

Behind the school is a big tree.

With بِـ providing specific locative information:

Her house is five kilometres behind the station.

بيتُها وراءَ المحطّة بِخمسة كيلومتر.

فَوق

Meanings

On top of, above: locative

Syntax

فَوق often occurs as a first term of an 'idafa. The second term of the 'idafa can be a pronoun suffix (see Pronominal suffixation) or a noun.

فَوق is not immediately followed by a verb.

When quantifying information is provided a prepositional phrase is required; the preposition بِـ is used. For example:

تسكن فوقي بِعِدَّة طَوابِق.

She lives several floors above me

Note that the quantifying information expressed by the prepositional phrase بِـ does not come before the adverbial, as it does in English (She lives several floors above me); rather, the quantifying information follows the second term of the 'idafa (ي): (She lives above me by several floors).

Examples

On top of, above: locative

Followed by the second term of the 'idafa, i.e. a noun or pronoun suffix:

تَرَكتُ المِفتاحَ فوقَ الكُتُب.

I left the key on top of the books.

كانت الطائرة فوق السحاب، فَلَم نُشاهِد النَهر.

The aeroplane was above the clouds, so we didn't see the river.

تَحتَ

Meanings

Below, under, underneath: locative

Syntax

تَحتَ often occurs as a first term of an 'idafa. The second term of the 'idafa can be a pronoun suffix (see Pronominal suffixation) or a noun.

تَحتَ is not immediately followed by a verb.

When quantifying information is provided a prepositional phrase is required; the preposition بِـ is used. For example:

تَحتَ الأرض بِعِدَّة أمتار
several metres below the ground

Note that the quantifying information expressed by the prepositional phrase بِـ does not come before the adverbial, as it does in English (several metres under the ground); rather, the quantifying information follows the second term of the 'idafa (الأرض): (under the ground by several metres).

قُربَ

Meanings

Near: locative or temporal

Syntax

قُربَ often occurs as a first term of an 'idafa. The second term of the 'idafa can be a pronoun suffix (see Pronominal suffixation) or a noun.

قُربَ is not immediately followed by a verb.

جانِبَ

Meanings

Next to, beside: locative

Syntax

جانِبَ often occurs as a first term of an 'idafa. The second term of the 'idafa can be a pronoun suffix (see Pronominal suffixation) or a noun.

جانِبَ is not immediately followed by a verb.

وَقتَ

Meanings

At the time of, when: temporal

Syntax

وَقتَ often occurs as a first term of an 'idafa. The second term of the 'idafa can be a pronoun suffix (see Pronominal suffixation) or a noun.

وَقتَ is not immediately followed by a verb.

أنْ immediately follows وقتَ to introduce a verb clause. For example:

قابَلتُها في المَطار وَقتَ أن وصلَت طائرتُها.

I met her at the airport when her aeroplane arrived.

سأُقابِلُك وَقتَ أنْ تَكوني جاهِزة.

I'll meet you when you are ready.

ساعةً

Meanings

At the time of: temporal.[1]

Syntax

ساعةً often occurs as a first term of an 'idafa. The second term of the 'idafa can be a pronoun suffix (see Pronominal suffixation) or a noun.

ساعةً is not immediately followed by a verb.

أنْ immediately follows ساعةً to introduce a verb clause. For example:

اشتريتُ السيارة ساعة أنْ كانت النقود معي.

I bought the car when I had the money with me.

Note

1. Similar to ساعةً are the following words:
ثانية، دقيقة، يوم، نهار، ليلة، أسبوع، شهر، سنة

UNIT 26

To have عِندَ، لِ، مَع، في

Meaning

The expression "to have" in English comprises a broad range of meanings such as to have ownership, availability, disease, time, in the mind, an inclination, an aptitude, a skill, difficulty, problems, and others. Depending on the English meaning of "to have", equivalent Arabic meanings can be expressed with the adverbial عِندَ, and with the prepositions مَع, لِ, and في. The following four examples illustrate:

عندي عربية.	I have a car.
لِمحمد أختان.	Mohamed has two sisters.
معك ولاّعة؟	Do you have a lighter (with you)?
البيت فيه تكييف جيد.	The house has good air-conditioning.

English meanings of "have" that are not possible in Arabic

The following are expressions of "to have" in English for which Arabic equivalents **do not** include the "to have" meaning:

- To declare or state (e.g. so gossip *has* it)
- To bear or beget (offspring)
- To cause to have (e.g. *have* them walk home)
- To cause to be (e.g. *have* this done first)
- To permit; tolerate (e.g. I will not *have* this nonsense)
- To hold at a disadvantage or to overcome (e.g. I *have* my opponent now!)
- To deceive; take in; cheat (e.g. they were *had* in that business deal
- To have sexual relations with

Adverbials and prepositions expressing "to have"

The following sections describe in detail certain adverbials and prepositions used for expressions of "to have": عِندَ، لِ، مَع، في.

Meaning

Aside from its locative and temporal meanings, as noted earlier, عِندَ is also used to communicate "to have."

Context of usage

عِندَ, meaning "to have", is used to show that humans have something. For contexts requiring non-humans having please see لِ and في.

Syntax

عِندَ occurs as the first term of an 'idafa.
The second term of the 'idafa is a pronoun suffix:

ᶜinda + pronoun suffix

عِندَه سَيّارة	he has a car

In instances where a proper noun – instead of a pronoun – is used, such as "Mohamed has a car", the preferred syntax is:

محمد عِندَه سيارة
Mohamed he has a car

Have: ownership

Followed by the second term of an 'idafa, specifically a pronoun suffix:

عِندي سيارة.	I have a car.
ماري عِندَها سيارة سوداء.	Mary has a black car.
لورا عِندَها سيارة خَضراء.	Laura has a green car.
سميرة عِندَها بيتان.	Samira has two houses.
ليس عِندي مُمتَلَكات.	I have no possessions.

Have: relationship, friend, not ownership

They have 5 boys and 7 girls. عندُهُم ٥ وِلاد و٧ بَنات
She has a ballet trainer. عندها مُدَرِّب باليه
We have many friends. عندنا أصحاب كتير
I have a friend from Mars. عندي صديق مِن المَرّيخ

Have: available

عِندَكُم كمبيوترات؟ Do you have any computers?
ليس عِندَهم ما نريد. They don't have what we want.

Have: condition, disease, illness

عِندَه مَرَض. He has a disease.
سُعاد عندها بَرد. Suad has a cold.

Have: time

ليس عِندَه وقت لِلكلام معي.
He has no time to talk to me.

لورا ليس عِندَها وقتٌ لي. Laura has no time for me.

Have: in the mind

ليس عِندَهُم أيّ فكرة إطلاقاً.
They have absolutely no idea.

كان عِندَها إحساس غريب.
She had a strange feeling.

Have: inclination

عِندَه قابلية
عِندَه مُيول عُدوانية He has hostile tendencies

Have: aptitude, skill, ability

عِندَه نَظَر
عِندَه مقدرة
عِندَه قابلية

Have: a difficulty, problem

عِندَها مشاكل كثيرة She has many problems

لِ

My house has a door, my car has a wheel.

In such instances, the preposition ل or في is used:

My house has a door
بيتي له باب، بيتي فيه باب

My car has a wheel سيارتي لها عجلة، سيارتي فيهاعجلة

Have: relationship, friend, not ownership

He has 3 sisters لُه ٣ إخوات بَنات

مَع

Have: not permanent, temporary

Do you have a lighter with you? مَعَك ولاّعة؟
Do you have any change with you? مَعَك فَكّة؟
Do you have a car with you? مَعَك سَيّارة؟

في

Have: contents

My house has a door, my car has a wheel

In such instances, the preposition ل or في is used:

بيتي له باب، بيتي فيه باب
My house has a door

سيارتي لها عجلة، سيارتي فيها عجلة
My car has a wheel

Exercises: to have عِندَ، لِ، مَع، في

Exercise 1

Study the phrases below, all of which convey the following meanings: to hold in the hand or in control, to own, to possess (e.g. to have wealth). Fill in the blank spaces below with the appropriate preposition and pronoun suffix. Refer to the list of pronoun suffixes below for assistance. The first answer is given as an example.
Pronoun suffixes attached to prepositions:

ـي، ـكَ، ـكِ، ـهُ، ـها، ـكما، ـهما، ـنا، ـكم، ـكُنَّ، ـهُم، ـهُنَّ

A He has half the land.

______ نصف الأرض
لَ + هو (he) = لَه
لَه نصف الأرض

B She only has her house.

ليس ______ إلا بيتها

C If you have to sell land, you (2nd p. s. m.) have your father's land.

إذا كان لازم تبيع أرض ______ أرض أبوك

D He has tons of money. (Note: قارون is a historic figure who was exceptionally wealthy.)

______ مال قارون

E In the countryside, people used to give the merchant some of their produce if they wanted to buy something and did not have money.

في الريف كان الناسُ يُعطون التاجر شيئاً مِن إنتاجهم
الزراعي إذا أرادوا شراء شيءٍ ولم يكُن ______ مال

Exercise 2

Study the phrases below, all of which convey the following meanings: to possess or contain as a part, a characteristic or attribute (e.g. she has blue eyes). Fill in each blank space below with the appropriate preposition and pronoun suffix or noun and pronoun suffix or preposition and noun and pronoun suffix. Refer to the list of pronoun suffixes below for assistance. The first answer is given as an example. Pronoun suffixes attached to prepositions:

ـي، ـكَ، ـكِ، ـهُ، ـها، ـكُما،
ـهُما، ـنا، ـكُم، ـكُنَّ، ـهُم، ـهُنَّ

A She has a beautiful smile.

____ ابتسامة جَميلة
لَ + هي (she) = لَها
لَها ابتسامة جَميلة

B Rooms that have high windows.

غُرَف ____ شبابيك عالية

C It (non-human) has no effect on him.

لا أثرَ ____ عليه

D He said that his country has youth who are very understanding.

Glossary

بلاد country

قال إنّ ____ شبابًا يتحلّون بتفهّم واسع

Exercise 3

Fill in the blanks below with the appropriate 1) prepositions that convey the meaning "to possess by way of experience", "experience", "undergo" (e.g. "have a good time") and 2) pronoun suffixes attached to these prepositions. The first answer is given as an example.

a) God has his own plans for mankind.

لِله في خلقه شؤون.

b) I have an idea.

____ فكرة.

c) She has aspirations.

____ طموحات.

d) He has a view.

____ رؤية.

Exercise 4

Fill in the blank space below with the appropriate 1) preposition that conveys the meaning "to perform", "carry on", "engage in something" (e.g. "to *have* an argument") and 2) pronoun suffixes attached to these prepositions.

She had a meeting.

كان ــــــ اجتماع.
كان عِندَها اجتماع.

Exercise 5

Fill in the blanks below with the appropriate 1) prepositions that convey the meaning to have a certain relation with someone (e.g. to *have* brothers and sisters) and 2) noun or pronoun suffixes attached to these prepositions. The first answer is given as an example.

a) Baher bek only had one son. (باهر)

ولم يكن ــــــ بك غير ابن واحد.
ولم يكن لِباهر بك غير ابن واحد.

b) We have no enemies.

ليس ــــــ أعداء

c) He has three daughters.

ــــــــــــــــــ ثلاث بنات

d) She has a pretty daughter.

ــــــــــــــــــ بنت حلوة

e) Denmark has a soldier in the peace-keeping forces. (دنمارك)

ــــــــــــــــــ جندي ضمن قوات حفظ السلام

UNIT 27
Questions

Interrogative particles are placed before the question. Here are some examples.

Yes/no questions are asked with هَل

Examples:

Is Maha American?	هَل مها أمريكية؟
Are you a father?	هل انتَ أب؟
Are you a mother?	هل انتِ أُمّ؟

What? (in questions without verbs) ما

Examples:

What is your name?	ما اِسمُكَ؟
What is this (m. s.)?	ما هذا؟

What? (in questions with verbs) ماذا

Examples:

What are you studying?	ماذا تَدرُس؟
What is he doing?	ماذا يَفعل؟

How? كيف

Example:

How did you know?	كيف عَرَفت؟

Which? أي

Examples:

Which book (m. s.)?	أي كِتاب؟
Which car (f. s.)?	أي سيّارة؟
Which student (f. s.)?	أي طالِبة؟

Who? مَن

Examples:

Who is he?	مَن هو؟
Who is Maha?	مَن مَها؟

Where? أينَ

Examples:

Where do you (m.) live?	أينَ تَسكُن؟
Where do you (f.) live?	أينَ تَسكُنينَ؟

How much? بِكَم

Examples:

How much is your new car?	بِكَم سيارتَك الجديدة؟
How much is the cheeseburger?	بِكَم الهامبورجَر بالجِبنة؟

The following prepositions are sometimes used with interrogatives:

مَع	with
في	in
مِن	from

Examples:

Where from? مِن أين؟
With whom? مَع مَن؟
In which? في أي؟

How many? كَم

كَم is followed by a singular indefinite noun in the مَنصوب (accusative) case.

Examples:

How many students? كَم طالِبةً؟
How many students? كَم طالِباً؟
How many cars? كَم سيارةً؟

Exercises: Questions

Exercise 1

Fill in the blanks with the correct prepositions and interrogative participles.

1 With whom do you (m.) live? ________ تَسكُن؟
2 In which university? ________ جامعة؟
3 Where are you (f.) from? ________ أنتِ؟
4 How much is this dress? ________ هذا الفُستان؟
5 How much is a kilo of potatoes? ________ كيلو البطاطس؟

Exercise 2

Translate the following from English to Arabic. Use the vocabulary in the glossary below to identify the appropriate interrogative articles and nouns. Write the answers in the blank spaces below. The first answer is given as an example.

Glossary

how many? كَم؟
time مَرّة
day (m. s.) يَوم

week (m. s.)	أُسبوع
American (m.)	أمريكيّ
American (f.)?	أمريكيّة
idea? (f.)	فِكرَة

1 How many times? ____________

How many times? كَم مَرّةً؟

(Note: the تنوين فَتح diacritic case marking is added to the end of the noun مَرّة)

2 How many days? ____________

3 How many weeks? ____________

4 How many Americans (m.)? ____________

5 How many Americans (f.)? ____________

6 How many ideas? ____________

Exercise 3

The following seven items each represent a question followed by an answer. Write the appropriate question word in the blank.

1 Where are you from, Magda? I am from Lebanon.

_____ أنتِ يا ماجدة؟

أنا مِن لُبنان

2 Are you (f.) Syrian? No, I am Lebanese.

____ انتِ سوريّة؟

لا أنا لُبنانيّة

3 Where is the University of Michigan? In the city of Ann Arbor.

_____جامعة ميشيجان؟

في مدينة آن آربور

4 Who is she? The new professor

_______ هي؟

الأستاذة الجديدة

5 What do you study at University? Spanish literature.

_______ تَدرُس في الجامعة؟

الأدب الأسباني

6 <u>What</u> is this? Coffee.

_____ هذِهِ؟

قهوة

7 How do we say bathroom in Arabic? حَمّام

_______ نَقول "bathroom" بالعربية؟

حَمّام

UNIT 28
Negation

A present tense sentence is negated by using the word لا.

The لا comes before the verb being negated: لا يفعل

A past tense sentence may be negated in two ways:

ما + perfect verb: ما فعل
لَمْ + imperfect verb in jussive: لم يفعل

Nominal sentences are negated using the verb ليس in the present.
Adjectives may be negated with غَيْر

Examples:

I did not claim to be innocent	ما ادّعيتُ أنّي بريئة
She does not like flowers.	لا تُحِبّ الورد
Mahmoud is not happy	ليس مُحَمّدٌ سعيداً
This number is not correct	هذا الرقم غير صحيح

UNIT 29
About the Arabic verb الفِعل

Apart from its meaning, an Arabic verb has attributes carried in seven bits of information which are contained in seven (morphological) inflections laid out below:

Tense: indicates time

Perfect tense (الماضي)
Imperfect tense (المُضارِع)
Imperative (الأمر)

Person: indicates subject

First person (المُتكلِّم)
Second person (المُخاطَب)
Third person (الغائب)

Gender: indicates subject

Masculine (مذكّر)
Feminine (مؤنّث)

Number: indicates subject

Singular (مُفرَد)
Dual (مُثَنّى)
Plural (جَمع)

Voice: active or passive

Pattern (وزن): plays a role in indicating meaning

(See Verb and noun paradigm chart)

Mood: (الحالة الإعرابية) indicative, subjunctive or jussive – indicates aspects of an event, such as that it is an actual occurrence, a desire, or hypothetical.

The following sections first provide a broad overview of the preceding verbal attributes. Following the overview is a detailed treatment.

Tense

In morphological terms, there are three verb tenses in Arabic. These are called الفِعل الماضي, often referred to as the perfect tense, الفعل الـمُضارع, often referred to as the imperfect tense, and فِعل الأمر, often referred to as the imperative tense.

Subject marker of the verb: person, gender and number

An Arabic verb cannot exist without a subject marker (an inflection showing person, gender, and number). In this respect – subject marking – Arabic differs from English verbs, where for example the verb "played" is the same word for all subjects, with subject marking being by independent subject pronouns.

The following three tables show an Arabic perfect tense verb with the 13 conjugation possibilities, each being a standalone verb – without any need for an independent subject pronoun.

The first table shows the verb conjugated for the singular.

English		*Arabic*
I played	I played (1st p. s.)	لَعِبتُ
you played	you played (2nd p. m. s.)	لَعِبتَ
you played	you played (2nd p. f. s.)	لَعِبتِ
he played	he played (3rd p. m. s.)	لَعِبَ
she played	she played (3rd p. m. s.)	لَعِبَتْ
it played	(neutral)	لَعِبَتْ

The second table shows the verb conjugated for the dual.

English		*Arabic*
-----	we played (1st p. d.)	لَعِبنا
-----	you played (2nd p. m. & f. d.)	لَعِبتُما
-----	they played (3rd p. m. d.)	لَعِبا
-----	they played (3rd p. f. d.)	لَعِبَتا

The third table shows the verb conjugated for the plural.

English		*Arabic*
we played	we played (1st p. pl.)	لَعِبنا
you played	you played (2nd p. m. pl.)	لَعِبتُم
you played	you played (2nd p. f. pl.)	لَعِبتُنَّ
they played	they played (3rd p. m. pl.)	لَعِبوا
they played	they played (3rd p. f. pl.)	لَعِبنَ

Note about the neutral

Arabic has no neutral "it". Everything is either he (m.) or she (f.); لَعِبَ or لَعِبَتَ above.

Voice

Arabic verbs are changed from the active to the passive by internal vowel changes (see Passive voice).

Pattern

The majority of Arabic verbs are called tri-literal because they are derived from three consonants, called a root. Some verbs are derived from four consonants; such verbs are called quadri-literal. Deriving verbs from their roots follows set patterns (see Verb patterns).

Definition

In Modern Standard Arabic (MSA) there are 10 common tri-literal verb forms. These forms are designated I through X (see Verb and noun paradigm chart). Below are the ten forms in the perfect tense along with an example for each form.

The table illustrates how verbs may be derived by substituting ف ع ل with root radicals of verbs such as د ر س.

Example	Form	
دَرَسَ	فَعَلَ	I
دَرَّسَ	فَعَّلَ	II
شاهَدَ	فاعَلَ	III

أقبَلَ	أَفعَلَ	IV
تَحَدَّثَ	تَفَعَّلَ	V
تَراسَلَ	تَفاعَلَ	VI
اِنقَلَبَ	اِنفَعَلَ	VII
اِرتَفَعَ	اِفتَعَلَ	VIII
اِحمَرَّ	اِفعَلَّ	IX
اِستَخدَمَ	اِستَفعَلَ	X

Mood

What are verb moods?

One way to think of an event is to consider whether it is actual or not. In the following three examples, consider the action "watching":

		Actual or not?
تُشاهدين المُسَلسَل	You watch the serial. You are watching the serial.	"Watching" actually occurs.
تريدينَ أنْ تُشاهدي المُسَلسَل	You want to watch the serial.	"Watching" not an actuality, but it is a desire.
شاهدي المُسَلسَل	Watch the serial!	"Watching" not an actuality, but is considered a necessity.

There is an overarching distinction between the first example in the table and the two that follow it because whereas in the first example "watching" falls within the realm of the actually occuring, the other two examples fall outside that realm.

In Arabic, the indicative mood (المرفوع) is used for events that are actual. The other two, the subjunctive (المَنصوب), and the jussive (المَجزوم) broadly speaking, are used for events that are not actual.

What verb tenses have moods?

The imperfect (المُضارع) and imperative (الأمر) are the two tenses that have moods. The perfect (الماضي) does not. Therefore, there are no case endings for past tense.

UNIT 30

Conjugating the perfect تصريف الماضي

The perfect tense verb (الماضي), mostly used to express past time, does not exist without a subject marker (person, gender, and number; see About the Arabic verb). In the case of the perfect (الماضي), the subject marker is **suffixed** to the verb.

In the singular there are five possibilities, in the dual there are three, and in the plural there are five. The total number is therefore 13. In the following these subject markers are detailed, first for the singular, then the dual, and finally the plural.

Subject-marker suffixes of the perfect verb in the singular

Below is an overall view of the subject markers for the perfect verb in the singular. Each of these subject markers is suffixed to a verb stem. As illustrated, for the singular there are five distinct subject markers. The first person, ـتُ (tu), makes no distinction between masculine and feminine.

First person	ـتُ

Second person	
Masculine	ـتَ
Feminine	ـتِ

Finally, the third person also has two subject markers: one for the masculine, which is just a فتحة (a), and one for the feminine, ـَتْ (at).

Third person	
Masculine	...َ
Feminine	ـَتْ

Subject-marker suffixes of the perfect verb in the dual

Below is an overall view of the subject markers for the perfect verb in the dual. Each of these subject markers is suffixed to a verb stem. As illustrated, for the dual there are **only three** distinct subject markers.

There is no first person dual, for which the first person plural subject-marker suffix is used. The second person has one subject marker, تُما (tumā), with no distinction between the masculine and feminine.

Second person	
Masculine	تُما
Feminine	تُما

Finally, the third person has two subject markers: one for the masculine, ا (ā) and one for the feminine, تا (atā).

Third person	
Masculine	ا
Feminine	تا

Subject-marker suffixes of the perfect verb in the plural

Below is an overall view of the subject markers for the perfect verb in the plural. Each of these subject markers is suffixed to a verb stem. As illustrated, for the plural there are five distinct subject markers.

The first person marker, نا (nā), makes no distinction between masculine and feminine, and is also used if the subject is dual.

First person	نا

The second person has two subject markers: one for the masculine, تُم (tum), and one for the feminine, تُنَّ (tunna).

Second person	
Masculine	تُم
Feminine	تُنَّ

Finally, the third person also has two subject markers: one for the masculine, وا (ū), (where the final ا, alif, is not pronounced) and one for the feminine, نَ (na).

Third person	
Masculine	وا
Feminine	نَ

The table below, a conjugation of the verb "write" for the perfect verb, is an example showing subject marking.

In the stem column is the verb stem, كَتَبـ, which is unchanged for all subject markers.

The following column, subject marker, shows the 13 subject-marker suffixes outlined above.

The third column shows the verb as it is actually written or uttered, which consists of the stem with the subject-marker suffix, as represented in the right-most column, stem – subject marker.

Stem	*Subject marker*	*Verb*	*Person*	*Meaning*	*Stem – subject marker*
كَتَبـ	ـتُ	كَتَبْتُ	1 s.	I wrote	stem-**tu**
كَتَبـ	ـتَ	كَتَبْتَ	2 m. s.	you wrote	stem-**ta**
كَتَبـ	ـتِ	كَتَبْتِ	2 f. s.	you wrote	stem-**ti**
كَتَب	...َ	كَتَبَ	3 m. s.	he wrote	stem-**a**
كَتَبـ	ـَتْ	كَتَبَتْ	3 f. s.	she wrote	stem-**at**
كَتَبـ	ـتُما	كَتَبْتُما	2 d.	you wrote	stem-**tumā**
كَتَبـ	ـا	كَتَبا	3 m. d.	they wrote	stem-**ā**
كَتَبـ	ـَتا	كَتَبَتا	3 f. d.	they wrote	stem-**atā**
كَتَبـ	ـنا	كَتَبْنا	1 pl.	we wrote	stem-**nā**
كَتَبـ	ـتُم	كَتَبْتُم	2 m. pl.	you wrote	stem-**tum**
كَتَبـ	ـتُنَّ	كَتَبْتُنَّ	2 f. pl.	you wrote	stem-**tunna**
كَتَبـ	ـوا	كَتَبوا	3 m. pl.	they wrote	stem-**ū**
كَتَبـ	ـنَ	كَتَبْنَ	3 f. pl.	they wrote	stem-**na**

About Arabic dictionaries

Traditionally, a verb entry in an Arabic dictionary is presented in its shortest form, which is the third person masculine singular. You might not see the subject marker, the فتحة (a), because it is understood to be there.

Exercise: conjugating the perfect verb

Exercise 1

Conjugate the following two perfect verb stems by suffixing all possible subject markers to them:

Stem	*Meaning*	
ذَهَب	dhahab	past of: to go
تَكَلَّم	takallam	past of: to speak

UNIT 31

Conjugating the imperfect تصريف المُضارع

The imperfect tense verb (المُضارع) is often used to express present time. Like any Arabic verb, the imperfect tense does not exist without a subject marker (person, gender, and number; see About the Arabic verb).

Subject markers of the imperfect verb

An imperfect verb always has a subject marker **prefix**, but certain conjugation forms have an additional subject marker, so they have two subject markers.

There are a total of 11 distinct forms of the subject marker of the imperfect verb.

In the singular there are four possibilities. Only four distinct forms exist in the singular because the second person masculine and the third person feminine are identical.

In the dual there are two possibilities. There are only two distinct forms. No first person form exists, and there is no distinction between masculine and feminine for the second person. Additionally, there is one form for the third person feminine and the second person masculine and feminine.

In the plural there are five distinct forms of the subject marker for the imperfect verb.

The following sections detail these subject markers, first for the singular, then the dual, and finally the plural.

Subject markers of the imperfect verb in the singular

Below is an overall view of the subject markers for the imperfect verb in the singular. As illustrated, for the singular there are four distinct subject markers.

The first person, ا (a), makes no distinction between masculine and feminine.

The second person distinguishes between the masculine and the feminine. The masculine has one subject marker, a prefix تَ (t), and the feminine has two, تِ (t), and ي (y).

Finally, the third person also has two subject markers: one for the masculine, which is just a فتحة (a), and one for the feminine, تَ (at):

First person		
Subject marker$_2$	Stem	Subject marker$_1$
(none)	. . .	أ

Second person			
Gender	Subject marker$_2$	Stem	Subject marker$_1$
Masculine	(none)	. . .	تـ
Feminine	ـي	. . .	تـ

Third person			
Gender	Subject marker$_2$	Stem	Subject marker$_1$
Masculine	(none)	. . .	يـ
Feminine	(none)	. . .	تـ

Exercise: subject markers of the imperfect verb in the singular

Exercise 1

How many distinct forms of the singular subject marker exist for an imperfect verb? Choose the correct answer:

a) 2
b) 4
c) 5
d) 11
e) 13

Subject markers of the imperfect verb in the dual

Second person			
Gender	Subject marker$_2$	Stem	Subject marker$_1$
Masculine	ا	. . .	تـ
Feminine	ا	. . .	تـ

Third person			
Gender	Subject marker$_2$	Stem	Subject marker$_1$
Masculine	ا	. . .	يـ
Feminine	ا	. . .	تـ

Exercise: subject markers of the imperfect verb in the dual

Exercise 2

How many distinct forms of the dual subject marker exist for an imperfect verb? Choose the correct answer:

a) 2
b) 4
c) 5
d) 11
e) 13

Subject markers of the imperfect verb in the plural

First person		
Subject marker$_2$	Stem	Subject marker$_1$
(none)	. . .	نـ

Second person			
Gender	Subject marker$_2$	Stem	Subject marker$_1$
Masculine	. . .و	. . .	تـ
Feminine	. . .نَ	. . .	تـ

Third person			
Gender	Subject marker$_2$	Stem	Subject marker$_1$
Masculine	. . .و	. . .	يـ
Feminine	. . .نَ	. . .	يـ

Exercise: subject markers of the imperfect verb in the plural

Exercise 3

How many distinct forms of the plural subject marker exist for an imperfect verb? Choose the correct answer:

a) 2
b) 4
c) 5
d) 11
e) 13

Exercises: conjugating the imperfect verb

Exercise 4

Conjugate the following verb stem by suffixing all possible subject markers.

	stem	v	meaning
قابِل	qaabil	/u/	present of: to meet

Exercise 5

Conjugate the following verb stem by suffixing all possible subject markers.

	stem	v	meaning
سمَع	sma^{c}	/a/	present of: to hear

Exercise 6

Fill in the blanks by conjugating the two verbs for the second person singular masculine and the second person singular feminine.

أنا	أسكُن	أدرُس	
هُوَ	___	___	يَعمَل
هِيَ	___	___	تَعمَل

UNIT 32

Subject and mood markers of the imperfect verb

Like any Arabic verb, the imperfect tense does not exist without a subject marker (person, gender, and number; see About the Arabic verb).

A subject marker either consist of one part, a prefix, in the first position or, two parts, a prefix and a second marker after the stem. Following the initial subject marker is a vowel v, which is either /a/ or /u/. Following the vowel is the stem. Following the stem, where applicable, is the second part of the subject marker.

Finally, except for the feminine plural, there is a mood marker.

The following schematic includes the fully conjugated verb كتب (to write); the table breaks down the verb's constituents (subject marker + v + stem + {subject marker}2 + mood) with the focus on subject marker:

Meaning	*Subject marker(s)*	*Constituents*	*Subject*	*Verb*
I write/am writing	أ . . .	'a + v + stem + mood	1st p. s.	أكتُبُ
you write/are writing	تـ . . .	t + v + stem + mood	2nd p. s.	تَكتُبُ
you write/are writing	تـ . . . يـ	t + v + stem + ii + mood	2nd p. s. f.	تَكتُبِينَ
he writes/is writing	يـ . . .	y + v + stem + mood	3rd p. m. sing.	يَكتُبُ
she writes/is writing	تـ . . .	t + v + stem + mood	3rd p. f. sing.	تَكتُبُ
you write/are writing	تـ . . . ا	t + v + stem + aa + mood	2nd p. f. + m. dual.	تَكتُبانِ
they write/are writing	يـ . . . ا	y + v + stem + aa + mood	3rd p. m. dual	يَكتُبانِ
they write/are writing	تـ . . . ا	t + v + stem + aa + mood	3rd p. f. dual	تَكتُبانِ

(*Continued*)

Meaning	*Subject marker(s)*	*Constituents*	*Subject*	*Verb*
we write/are writing	نـ . . .	n + v + stem + mood	1st p. pl.	نَـكْتُبُ
you write/are writing	تـ . . . و	t + v + stem + uu + mood	2nd p. m. pl.	تَـكْتُبونَ
you write/are writing	تـ . . . نَ	t + v + stem + na	2nd p. f. pl.	تَـكْتُبـنَ
they write/are writing	يـ . . . و	y + v + stem + uu + mood	3rd p. m. pl.	يَـكْتُبونَ
they write/are writing	يـ . . . نَ	y + v + stem + na	3rd p. f. pl.	يَـكْتُبـنَ

Subject marker

As illustrated above, the imperfect tense verb (الفعل المُضارِع) either has a single subject marker or a two-part split one.

The single subject marker is in the first person singular and plural, third person masculine and feminine, and second person masculine. The two-part split subject marker is in the second person feminine singular, all duals, and all plurals except the first person.

The single subject marker is a consonant located in first position (followed by the diacritic /a/ or /u/), before the stem. In the case of the two-part split subject marker, the second part is located in the penultimate position before the mood marker.

Stem

Verb stems vary according to the verb form. However, the relative location of verb constituents – subject markers, stem, and mood marker – is not affected by stem variation.

Mood

When present, the mood marker (see Mood markers) usually occupies the final position in the imperfect tense verb.

Plural feminine verbs: no mood markers.

One-part mood marker verbs: mood marker occupies final position in the imperfect tense verb. In the illustration with the verb "write" above, the mood marker is the diacritic u:ُ

Two-part mood marker verbs: the mood marker occupies final position in the imperfect tense verb. In the illustration with the verb "write" above, the mood marker is the letter: ن

The third person masculine singular form of the verb, comprises the subject marker prefix يـ /y/, followed by a diacritic vowel v (either /a/ or /u/), followed by the stem. The diacritic vowel may not be there because it is understood. To isolate the verb stem, strip the subject marker away from the front of the verb and the vowel /a/ or /u/, if present.

Mood names

There are three moods for Arabic verbs. Their Arabic names are followed by English equivalents:

المرفوع, the indicative (e.g. يقومُ)
المَنصوب, the subjunctive (e.g. لن يقومَ) and
المَجزوم, the jussive (e.g. لم يَقُمْ)

Mood marking

As with nouns, which are marked to show what case they are in, verbs are also marked for mood. Arabic imperfect verbs may be grouped into three categories for the purposes of mood marking:

1 Verbs marked by the addition of diacritics (فَتحة, ضَمّة, and سُكون) immediately following the last radical; this group includes weak radical verbs that are marked by the loss of the medial or final vowel; for example:

يقومُ – مرفوع
لن يقومَ – منصوب
لم يَقُمْ – مَجزوم

2 Verbs that are marked by the addition or loss of the letter ن at the end of the word, after the subject marker; for example

أنتما تَكتُبان – مَرفو
حتّى تَكتُبا – مَنصوب
لم تَكتُبا – مَجزوم

3 Verbs that accept no overt mood markings.

أنتُنَّ تَكتُبنَ – مَرفوع
حتّى تَكتُبنَ – مَنصوب
لم تَكتُبنَ – مَجزوم

	علامة الرفع	علامة النصب	علامة الجزم
أنا	ـُ (ضَمّة)	ـَ (فَتحة)	ـْ (سُكون)
أنتَ	ـُ (ضَمّة)	ـَ (فَتحة)	ـْ (سُكون)
أنتِ	نَ		
هو	ـُ (ضَمّة)	ـَ (فَتحة)	ـْ (سُكون)
هي	ـُ (ضَمّة)	ـَ (فَتحة)	ـْ (سُكون)
أنتما	نِ		
هُما	نِ		
هُما	ن		
نحن	ـُ (ضَمّة)	ـَ (فَتحة)	ـْ (سُكون)
أنتُم	نَ		
أنتُنّ			
هُم	نَ		
هُنَّ			

UNIT 33
Verb patterns أوزان الفعل

Derivational system of Arabic verbs

The majority of Arabic verbs are called tri-literal because they are derived from three consonants, called a root. Some verbs are derived from four consonants; such verbs are called quadri-literal. Deriving verbs from their roots follows set patterns.

Root

By convention, the triliteral verb is derived from a tri-consonantal root wherein the first root consonant is represented by "f" (ف), the second by "c" (ع), and the third by "l" (ل).

Root + form الوزن + الجذر	الماضي	المُضارِع	المصدر
فَعل + ت ب ع	تَبِع	يَتبَعُ	تَبَعِيّة
فَعل + ج م ع	جَمَعَ	يَجمَعُ	جَمْع
فَعل + ص ن ع	صَنَعَ	يَصنَعُ	صِناعَة
فَعل + ض ر ب	ضَرَبَ	يَضرِبُ	ضَرْب
فَعل + م ض ي	مَضَى	يَمضي	مُضِيٌّ
فَعل + ن ق ل	نَقَلَ	يَنقُلُ	نَقْل
فَعل + و ض ع	وَضَعَ	يَضَعُ	وَضْع
فَعَّل + ح د ث	حَدَّثَ	يُحَدِّثُ	تَحديث
فَعَّل + ح ض ر	حَضَّرَ	يُحَضِّرُ	تَحضير
فَعَّل + ز ي ن	زَيَّنَ	يُزَيِّنُ	تَزيين
فَعَّل + ص ل و	صَلَّى	يُصَلِّي	صلاة

(*Continued*)

Root + form الوزن + الجذر	الماضي	المُضارِع	المصدر
فاعَل + ش ر ك	شارَك	يُشارِكُ	مُشارَكَة
فاعَل + ن د و	نادَى	يُنادي	مُناداةٌ
أفْعَل + ف ط ر	أفطَرَ	يُفطِرُ	إفطار
أفْعَل + ق و م	أقامَ	يُقيمُ	إقامَة
تَفَعَّل + ج م ع	تَجَمَّعَ	يَتَجَمَّعُ	تَجَمُّع
اِفتَعَل + ح ف ل	اِحتَفَلَ	يَحتَفِلُ	اِحتِفال
اِفتَعَل + ن ظ ر	اِنتظر	يَنتَظر	اِنتِظار

Forms أوزان

In Modern Standard Arabic (MSA) there are 10 common tri-literal verb forms. These forms are designated I through X (see Verb and noun paradigm chart).

One difference between the verb forms is in the stem constituent of each. Again, the tri-literal verb is derived from a tri-consonantal root wherein the first root consonant is represented by "f" (ف), the second by "c" (ع), and the third by "l" (ل). Interleaved between the stem consonants are stem vowels.

Short vowels, /a/ (فتحة), /u/ (ضَمّة), and /i/ (كسرة), do not always appear in print; however, they are shown below.

The two verb columns below الماضي and المُضارِع only show the conjugation of the third person masculine, which is the form the dictionary lists (for the full conjugation, see Conjugating the perfect, and Conjugating the imperfect). Form I is marked by a question mark (?) below because it behaves unpredictably. Specifically, the diacritic following the second radical, ع, can be فَتحة, ضَمّة, or كَسرة.

	الماضى	المضارع
I	فَعـ؟ـلَ	يَفعـ؟ـلُ
II	فَعّلَ	يُفَعّلُ
III	فاعَلَ	يُفاعِلُ
IV	أفعَلَ	يُفعِلُ
V	تَفَعّلَ	يَتَفَعّلُ

VI	تَفاعَلَ	يَتَفاعَلُ
VII	اِنفَعَلَ	يَنفَعِلُ
VIII	اِفتَعَلَ	يَفتَعِلُ
IX	اِفعَلَّ	يَفعَلّ
X	اِستَفعَلَ	يِستَفعِلُ

To acquire colours (ألوان) Form IX

Each of the following seven roots refers to a colour.

ح م ر – خ ض ر – ز ر ق – ص ف ر
س و د – ب ي ض – س م ر

When combined with the pattern for Form IX, each root generates a verb that refers to the acquisition of one of the seven colours.

Example:

اِحمَرَّ	To become red
اِخضَرَّ	To become green

The table below shows perfect and imperfect verbs in Form IX for the seven roots listed above.

The root الأصل	*The perfect* الماضي	*The imperfect* المُضارِع
ح م ر	اِحمَرَّ	يَحمَرُّ
خ ض ر	اِخضَرَّ	يَخضَرُّ
ز ر ق	اِزرَقَّ	يَزرَقُّ
ص ف ر	اِصفَرَّ	يَصفَرُّ
س و د	اِسوَدَّ	يَسوَدُّ
ب ي ض	اِبيَضَّ	يَبيَضُّ
س م ر	اِسمَرَّ	يَسمَرُّ

Exercise: verb patterns

Exercise 1

Use the chart below to help you replace ف ع ل with the roots ق ب ل (from right to left):

الماضي	المُضارع
فَعَّل	يُفَعِّل
أَفعَل	يُفعِل
تَفَعَّل	يَتَفَعَّل
اِستَفعَل	يَستَفعِلُ
اِستَفعَل	يَستَفعِل

Below are two charts showing an overview of the 10 forms, first in the perfect, followed by the imperfect. The subject-marker location is shown, but the subject markers themselves are not. Only the Form I stem – unlike the others – is unpredictable in this way where v_2 can be any of /a/, /u/, or /i/.

Perfect الماضي

Form	*Stem*	*Subject marker*
I	f + v_1 + ᶜ + v_2 + l	
a	{faᶜal}	فَعَل
b	{faᶜul}	فَعُل
c	{faᶜil}	فَعِل
II	faᶜᶜal	فَعَّل
III	faaᶜal	فاعَل
IV	'afᶜal	أَفعَل
V	tafaᶜᶜal	تَفَعَّل
VI	tafaaᶜal	تَفاعَل
VII	infaᶜal	اِنفَعَ
VIII	iftaᶜal	اِفتَعَل
IX	ifᶜall	اِفعَلَّ
X	istafᶜal	اِستَفعَل

Exercises: verb patterns, الماضي, Forms I–X

Exercise 2

Write the perfect form stems I–X in Arabic, replacing the consonant “f” with “ف”, “c” with “ع”, and “l” with “ل”; and the vowels /a/ with a فتحة, /u/ with a ضمة, and /i/ with a كسرة. For example, Form VII would be written like this: اِنفَعَلَ. When done, you should have the 10 forms – without the subject marker – written in Arabic.

	Perfect (الماضي)	Arabic
Form I stem:	fa^{c}vl	
	{fa^{c}al}	____________
	{fa^{c}ul}	____________
	{fa^{c}il}	____________
Form II stem:	fa^{cc}al	____________
Form III stem:	faa^{c}al	____________
Form IV stem:	'af^{c}al	____________
Form V stem:	tafa^{cc}al	____________
Form VI stem:	tafa^{ac}al	____________
Form VII stem:	infa^{c}al	____________
Form VIII stem:	ifta^{c}al	____________
Form IX stem:	if^{c}all	____________
Form X stem:	istaf^{c}al	____________

Exercise 3

Conjugate the perfect Form II by adding the appropriate subject markers. Use the following root radicals to conjugate Form II in the perfect:

ف for the first radical,

ك for the second, and

ر for the third.

Imperfect المُضارِع

Form	*Subject marker 1*	*Subject marker vowel*	*Imperfect stem*	*Subject marker 2*
I		a	$f + {}^{c} + v_2 + l$	
		a	{f^cal}	
		a	{f^cul}	
		a	{f^cil}	
II		u	fa^{cc}il	
III		u	faa^cil	
IV		u	f^cil	
V		a	ta fa^{cc}al	
VI		a	tafaa^cal	
VII		a	nfa^cil	
VIII		a	fta^cil	
IX		a	f^call	
X		a	staf^cil	

Only the Form I stem – unlike the others – is unpredictable in this way where v_2 can be any of /a/, /u/, or /i/.

Note that the subject marker of Forms II, III, and IV of المُضارِع are all followed by a ضَمّة. In all the remaining forms a فتحة follows the subject marker.

Exercise: verb patterns, المُضارِع, Forms I–X

Exercise 4

Write the imperfect form stems I–X replacing the consonants “f” with “ف”, “c” with “ع”, and “l” with “ل”; and the vowels /a/ with a فتحة, /u/ with a ضمة, and /i/ with a كسرة. For example, Form VII would be written like this, نفَعِل, without the subject marker. When done, you should have the 10 forms, without the subject marker, written in Arabic.

	Imperfect (المُضارِع)	Arabic
Form I stem:	f^{c}vl	
	{f^{c}al}	____________
	{f^{c}ul}	____________
	{f^{c}il}	____________
Form II stem:	fa^{cc}il	____________
Form III stem:	faa^{c}il	____________
Form IV stem:	f^{c}il	____________
Form V stem:	tafa^{cc}al	____________
Form VI stem:	tafaa^{c}al	____________
Form VII stem:	nfa^{c}il	____________
Form VIII stem:	fta^{c}il	____________
Form IX stem:	f^{c}all	____________
Form X stem:	staf^{c}il	____________

UNIT 34
The perfect, Form I فَعَل

Definition and form

Form I is the most common. The perfect tense of Form I is made up of the root, comprising three consonants c_1, c_2, and c_3. Interleaved between the consonants are two vowels v_1 and v_2. The sequence is as follows:

$$c_1 + v_1 + c_2 + v_2 + c_3$$

By convention the three consonants, c_1, c_2, and c_3, are respectively represented as f, ^{c}, and l.

$$f v_1 {}^c v_2 l = (f + v_1 + {}^c + v_2 + l)$$

Unless the verb is in the passive voice (see Passive voice) the first vowel, v_1, is always /a/. In contrast, the second vowel, v_2, can be /a/, /u/, or /i/:

fa^{c}al	فَعَل
fa^{c}ul	فَعُل
fa^{c}il	فَعِل

Form I examples:

Form	Perfect (الماضي)	Meaning
fa^{c}al	فَتَح	(to open)
fa^{c}ul	كَبُر	(to grow)
fa^{c}il	سَمِع	(to hear)

Exercises: the perfect, Form I فَعَل

Exercise 1

Conjugate the perfect Form I verb فَتَحَ for all possible 13 subjects. Write down all 13 possibilities in the blank spaces below. See Conjugating the perfect if necessary.

______________________	1st person singular
______________________	2nd person masculine singular
______________________	2nd person feminine singular
______________________	3rd person masculine singular
______________________	3rd person feminine singular
______________________	2nd person dual
______________________	3rd person masculine dual
______________________	3rd person feminine dual
______________________	1st person plural
______________________	2nd person masculine plural
______________________	2nd person feminine plural
______________________	3rd person masculine plural
______________________	3rd person feminine plural

Exercise 2

Conjugate the perfect Form I verb كَبُرَ for all possible 13 subjects. Write down all 13 possibilities in the blank spaces below. See Conjugating the perfect if necessary.

____________________ 1st person singular

____________________ 2nd person masculine singular

____________________ 2nd person feminine singular

____________________ 3rd person masculine singular

____________________ 3rd person feminine singular

____________________ 2nd person dual

____________________ 3rd person masculine dual

____________________ 3rd person feminine dual

____________________ 1st person plural

____________________ 2nd person masculine plural

____________________ 2nd person feminine plural

____________________ 3rd person masculine plural

____________________ 3rd person feminine plural

Exercise 3

Conjugate the perfect Form I verb سَمِع for all possible 13 subjects. Write down all 13 possibilities in the blank spaces below. See Conjugating the perfect if necessary.

____________________ 1st person singular

____________________ 2nd person masculine singular

____________________ 2nd person feminine singular

____________________ 3rd person masculine singular

____________________ 3rd person feminine singular

____________________ 2nd person dual

____________________ 3rd person masculine dual

____________________ 3rd person feminine dual

____________________ 1st person plural

____________________ 2nd person masculine plural

____________________ 2nd person feminine plural

____________________ 3rd person masculine plural

____________________ 3rd person feminine plural

UNIT 35

The perfect, Form II فَعَّلَ

Definition and form

The perfect tense of Form II is made up of the root, comprising three consonants: c_1, c_2, and c_3. The middle c_2 consonant is geminated (doubled): interleaved between the consonants are two vowels v_1 and v_2. Unless the verb is in the passive voice, (see Passive voice), the first and second vowels, v_1 and v_2, are always /a/. The sequence is as follows:

fa^{cc}al = (f + a + ^{c} + ^{c} + a + l)

Form II examples:

نَوَّرَت المَدخَل	She turned on the entrance lights
ولَّعتُ النار في البيت	I set the house on fire
كَسَّرنا الأطباق	We smashed the dishes

Exercises: the perfect, Form II فَعَّلَ

Exercise 1

Conjugate the perfect Form II verb نَوَّر for all possible 13 subjects. See Conjugating the Perfect if necessary.

Form II	Perfect (الماضي)	Meaning
fa^{cc}al	نَوَّر	to turn (lights) on

Exercise 2

Conjugate the perfect Form II verb وَلَّع for all possible 13 subjects. See Conjugating the Perfect if necessary.

Form II	Perfect (الماضي)	Meaning
fa^{cc}al	وَلَّع	to set fire to

Exercise 3

Conjugate the Perfect Form II verb كَسَّر for all possible 13 subjects. See Conjugating the Perfect if necessary.

Form II	Perfect (الماضي)	Meaning
fa^{cc}al	كَسَّر	to smash

UNIT 36

The perfect, Form III فاعَل

Definition and form

The perfect tense of Form III is made up of the root, comprising three consonants: c_1, c_2, and c_3. Interleaved between the consonants are vowels v_1, a long /a:/, and v_2, /a/. Unless the verb is in the passive voice (see Passive voice), the first and second vowels, v_1 and v_2, are always respectively /a:/ and /a/. The sequence is as follows:

faa^c^al = (f + a + a + ^c^ + a + l)

Form III examples:

ناوَلتُ البِنتَ المُسَدّس	I handed the girl the pistol
حاوَلنا أنْ نَفهم	We tried to understand
قاوَمَ الرَغبة	He resisted the desire

Exercises: the perfect, Form III فاعَل

Exercise 1

Conjugate the perfect Form III verb ناوَل for all possible 13 subjects. Write down all 13 possibilities in the blank spaces below. See Conjugating the Perfect if necessary.

Form III	Perfect (الماضي)	Meaning
faa^c^al	ناوَل	to hand (something to someone)

______________________ 1st person singular

______________________ 2nd person masculine singular

______________________ 2nd person feminine singular

______________________ 3rd person masculine singular

______________________ 3rd person feminine singular

______________________ 2nd person dual

______________________ 3rd person masculine dual

______________________ 3rd person feminine dual

______________________ 1st person plural

______________________ 2nd person masculine plural

______________________ 2nd person feminine plural

______________________ 3rd person masculine plural

______________________ 3rd person feminine plural

Exercise 2

Conjugate the perfect Form III verb حاوَل (in حاوَل أنْ) for all possible 13 subjects. Write down all 13 possibilities in the blank spaces below. See Conjugating the perfect if necessary.

Form III	Perfect (الماضي)	Meaning
faa[c]al	حاوَل أنْ	to try to (do something)

______________________ 1st person singular

______________________ 2nd person masculine singular

______________________ 2nd person feminine singular

______________________ 3rd person masculine singular

______________________ 3rd person feminine singular

______________________ 2nd person dual

______________________ 3rd person masculine dual

_______________ 3rd person feminine dual

_______________ 1st person plural

_______________ 2nd person masculine plural

_______________ 2nd person feminine plural

_______________ 3rd person masculine plural

_______________ 3rd person feminine plural

Exercise 3

Conjugate the perfect Form III verb قاوَم for all possible 13 subjects. Write down all 13 possibilities in the blank spaces below. See Conjugating the perfect if necessary.

Form III	Perfect (الماضي)	Meaning
faaᶜal	قاوَم	to resist (someone or something)

_______________ 1st person singular

_______________ 2nd person masculine singular

_______________ 2nd person feminine singular

_______________ 3rd person masculine singular

_______________ 3rd person feminine singular

_______________ 2nd person dual

_______________ 3rd person masculine dual

_______________ 3rd person feminine dual

_______________ 1st person plural

_______________ 2nd person masculine plural

_______________ 2nd person feminine plural

_______________ 3rd person masculine plural

_______________ 3rd person feminine plural

UNIT 37

The perfect, Form IV أَفعَلَ

Definition and form

The perfect tense of Form IV is made up of the root, comprising three consonants: c_1, c_2, and c_3. Interleaved between the consonants are vowels v_1, /a/, and v_2, /a/. Unless the verb is in the passive voice (see Passive voice), the first and second vowels, v_1 and v_2, are always respectively /a:/ and /a/. The sequence is as follows:

'afʿal = (' + a + f + ᶜ + a + l)

Form IV examples:

أحضَرَ الكرة إليها
He brought back the ball to her

أخبَرَت زوجها عن الحادثة
She informed her husband about the accident

أجبَرا الطفل على أكل الخُضار
They forced (dual) the child to eat vegetables

Exercises: the perfect, Form IV أَفعَل

Exercise 1

Conjugate the perfect Form IV verb أحضَر for all possible 13 subjects. See Conjugating the perfect if necessary.

Form IV	Perfect (الماضي)	Meaning
'afʿal	أحضَر	to bring (someone or something)

____________________	1st person singular
____________________	2nd person masculine singular
____________________	2nd person feminine singular
____________________	3rd person masculine singular
____________________	3rd person feminine singular
____________________	2nd person dual
____________________	3rd person masculine dual
____________________	3rd person feminine dual
____________________	1st person plural
____________________	2nd person masculine plural
____________________	2nd person feminine plural
____________________	3rd person masculine plural
____________________	3rd person feminine plural

Exercise 2

Conjugate the perfect Form IV verb أخبَر for all possible 13 subjects. Write down all 13 possibilities in the blank spaces below. See Conjugating the perfect if necessary.

Form IV	Perfect (الماضي)	Meaning
'afʿal	أخبَر	to inform (someone about (عن) something)

______________	1st person singular
______________	2nd person masculine singular
______________	2nd person feminine singular
______________	3rd person masculine singular
______________	3rd person feminine singular
______________	2nd person dual
______________	3rd person masculine dual
______________	3rd person feminine dual
______________	1st person plural
______________	2nd person masculine plural
______________	2nd person feminine plural
______________	3rd person masculine plural
______________	3rd person feminine plural

Exercise 3

Conjugate the perfect Form IV verb أجبَر for all possible 13 subjects. Write down all 13 possibilities in the blank spaces below. See Conjugating the perfect if necessary.

Form IV	Perfect (الماضي)	Meaning
'afʿal	أجبَر	to force (someone into (على) doing something)

______________________	1st person singular
______________________	2nd person masculine singular
______________________	2nd person feminine singular
______________________	3rd person masculine singular
______________________	3rd person feminine singular
______________________	2nd person dual
______________________	3rd person masculine dual
______________________	3rd person feminine dual
______________________	1st person plural
______________________	2nd person masculine plural
______________________	2nd person feminine plural
______________________	3rd person masculine plural
______________________	3rd person feminine plural

UNIT 38
The perfect, Form V تَفَعّلَ

The sequence of consonants and vowels for the perfect tense verb Form V is as follows: tafa^{cc}al = (t+a+f+a+^{c}+^{c}+a+l)

Examples:

Form	Perfect (الماضي)	Meaning
tafa^{cc}al	تَجَمَّعَ	to congregate to gather together
tafa^{cc}al	تَحَدَّثَ	to speak
tafa^{cc}al	تَزَيَّنَ	got decorated

Exercise: the perfect, Form V تَفَعّلَ

Exercise 1

Conjugate the perfect Form V by adding the appropriate subject markers. Use the following root radicals to conjugate Form V in the perfect for all 13 possibilities. Write the answers in the blank spaces below.

ج for the first radical,

م for the second, and

ع for the third.

__________________	1st person singular
__________________	2nd person masculine singular
__________________	2nd person feminine singular
__________________	3rd person masculine singular
__________________	3rd person feminine singular

________________ 2nd person dual

________________ 3rd person masculine dual

________________ 3rd person feminine dual

________________ 1st person plural

________________ 2nd person masculine plural

________________ 2nd person feminine plural

________________ 3rd person masculine plural

________________ 3rd person feminine plural

UNIT 39
The perfect, Form VI تَفاعَلَ

The sequence of consonants and vowels for the perfect tense verb Form VI is as follows: tafaa^c^al = (t+a+f+a+a+^c^+a+l)

Examples:

Form	Perfect (الماضي)	Meaning
tafaa^c^al	تَراسَلَ	to send each other letters/correspond
tafaa^c^al	تَعامَلَ	to work with each other

Exercises: the perfect, Form VI تَفاعَلَ

Exercise 1

Conjugate the perfect Form VI by adding the appropriate subject markers. Use the following root radicals to conjugate Form VI in the perfect for all 13 possibilities. Write the answers in the blank spaces below.

س for the first radical,

ل for the second, and

م for the third.

____________________ 1st person singular

____________________ 2nd person masculine singular

____________________ 2nd person feminine singular

____________________ 3rd person masculine singular

____________________ 3rd person feminine singular

____________________ 2nd person dual

______________________ 3rd person masculine dual

______________________ 3rd person feminine dual

______________________ 1st person plural

______________________ 2nd person masculine plural

______________________ 2nd person feminine plural

______________________ 3rd person masculine plural

______________________ 3rd person feminine plural

UNIT 40

The perfect, Form VII اِنفَعَل

The sequence of consonants and vowels for the perfect tense verb Form VII is as follows: infaᶜal = (i+n+f+a+ᶜ+a+l)

Example:

Form VII	Perfect (الماضي)	Meaning
infaᶜal	انقطع	to be cut off (from)

Exercises: the perfect, Form VII اِنفَعَل

Exercise 1

Conjugate the perfect Form VII by adding the appropriate subject markers. Write the answers in the blank spaces below. Use the following root radicals to conjugate Form VII in the perfect for all 13 possibilities:

ح for the first radical,
ر for the second, and
ف for the third.

________________	1st person singular
________________	2nd person masculine singular
________________	2nd person feminine singular
________________	3rd person masculine singular
________________	3rd person feminine singular
________________	2nd person dual
________________	3rd person masculine dual
________________	3rd person feminine dual

__________ 1st person plural

__________ 2nd person masculine plural

__________ 2nd person feminine plural

__________ 3rd person masculine plural

__________ 3rd person feminine plural

Exercise 2

Conjugate the perfect Form VII by adding the appropriate subject markers. Write the answers in the blank spaces below. Use the following root radicals to conjugate Form VII in the perfect for all 13 possibilities:

ع for the first radical,
ك for the second, and
س for the third.

__________ 1st person singular

__________ 2nd person masculine singular

__________ 2nd person feminine singular

__________ 3rd person masculine singular

__________ 3rd person feminine singular

__________ 2nd person dual

__________ 3rd person masculine dual

__________ 3rd person feminine dual

__________ 1st person plural

__________ 2nd person masculine plural

__________ 2nd person feminine plural

__________ 3rd person masculine plural

__________ 3rd person feminine plural

UNIT 41
The perfect, Form VIII اِفْتَعَلَ

To generate the stem of Form VIII verbs in the perfect, an اِ is placed before (immediately to the right of) the first radical and a ـتَـ after (immediately to the left of) the first radical.

Examples

Form VIII	Perfect (الماضي)	Meaning
iftaᶜal	اِجتَمَع	to get together (in a group)
iftaᶜal	اِعتَقَد	to think something to be true, to be of the opinion that, to be under the impression that
iftaᶜal	اِعتَرَف	to confess

In some cases, such as when certain letters are the first radical, for example,

د, ز, ص, ض, ط

the ـتَـ is transformed into another letter, such as:

ط or د

Examples:

Form VIII	Perfect (الماضي)	Meaning
iftaᶜal	اِجتَمَع	to get together (in a group)

Exercises: the perfect, Form VIII اِفْتَعَلَ

Exercise 1

Conjugate the perfect Form VIII by adding the appropriate subject markers. Write the answers in the blank spaces below. Use the following root radicals to conjugate Form VIII in the perfect for all 13 possibilities:

ق for the first radical,
ن for the second, and
ع for the third.

________________	1st person singular
________________	2nd person masculine singular
________________	2nd person feminine singular
________________	3rd person masculine singular
________________	3rd person feminine singular
________________	2nd person dual
________________	3rd person masculine dual
________________	3rd person feminine dual
________________	1st person plural
________________	2nd person masculine plural
________________	2nd person feminine plural
________________	3rd person masculine plural
________________	3rd person feminine plural

Exercise 2

Conjugate the perfect Form VIII by adding the appropriate subject markers. Write the answers in the blank spaces below. Use the following root radicals to conjugate Form VIII in the perfect for all 13 possibilities:

ز for the first radical,

ح for the second, and

م for the third.

______________________	1st person singular
______________________	2nd person masculine singular
______________________	2nd person feminine singular
______________________	3rd person masculine singular
______________________	3rd person feminine singular
______________________	2nd person dual
______________________	3rd person masculine dual
______________________	3rd person feminine dual
______________________	1st person plural
______________________	2nd person masculine plural
______________________	2nd person feminine plural
______________________	3rd person masculine plural
______________________	3rd person feminine plural

Exercise 3

Conjugate the perfect Form VIII by adding the appropriate subject markers. Write the answers in the blank spaces below. Use the following root radicals to conjugate Form VIII in the perfect for all 13 possibilities:

ص for the first radical,
د for the second, and
م for the third.

______________________	1st person singular
______________________	2nd person masculine singular
______________________	2nd person feminine singular
______________________	3rd person masculine singular
______________________	3rd person feminine singular
______________________	2nd person dual
______________________	3rd person masculine dual
______________________	3rd person feminine dual
______________________	1st person plural
______________________	2nd person masculine plural
______________________	2nd person feminine plural
______________________	3rd person masculine plural
______________________	3rd person feminine plural

UNIT 42

The perfect, Form IX اِفعَلّ

The sequence of consonants and vowels for the perfect tense verb Form IX is as follows: ifᶜall = (i+f+ᶜ+a+l+l)

Some Form IX verbs refer to the acquisition of colour or physical defect.

Example:

Form	Perfect (الماضي)	Meaning
ifᶜall	اِحمَرّ	to become red

Exercise: the perfect, Form IX اِفعَلّ

Exercise 1

Find the perfect Form IX verb for the following three roots. Write down the verbs in the blanks spaces below.

The root (الأصل)	The perfect (الماضي)
a) خ ض ر	________________
b) ز ر ق	________________
c) ص ف ر	________________

UNIT 43
The perfect, Form X اِسْتَفْعَلَ

The sequence of consonants and vowels for the perfect tense verb Form X is as follows: istafᶜal = (i+s+t+a+f+ᶜ+a+l)

Examples:

Form	Perfect (الماضي)	Meaning
istafᶜal	استبعد	to consider far away or unlikely

Exercises: the perfect, Form X اِستَفعَلَ

Exercise 1

Conjugate the perfect Form X by adding the appropriate subject markers. Write down all 13 possibilities in the blank spaces below. Use the following root radicals to conjugate Form X in the perfect:

خ for the first radical,
د for the second, and
م for the third.

____________________ 1st person singular

____________________ 2nd person masculine singular

____________________ 2nd person feminine singular

____________________ 3rd person masculine singular

____________________ 3rd person feminine singular

____________________ 2nd person dual

____________________ 3rd person masculine dual

____________________ 3rd person feminine dual

_______________ 1st person plural

_______________ 2nd person masculine plural

_______________ 2nd person feminine plural

_______________ 3rd person masculine plural

_______________ 3rd person feminine plural

Exercise 2

Conjugate the perfect Form X by adding the appropriate subject markers. Use the following root radicals to conjugate Form X in the perfect. Write down all 13 possibilities in the blank spaces below.

ث for the first radical,

م for the second, and

ر for the third.

_______________ 1st person singular

_______________ 2nd person masculine singular

_______________ 2nd person feminine singular

_______________ 3rd person masculine singular

_______________ 3rd person feminine singular

_______________ 2nd person dual

_______________ 3rd person masculine dual

_______________ 3rd person feminine dual

_______________ 1st person plural

_______________ 2nd person masculine plural

_______________ 2nd person feminine plural

_______________ 3rd person masculine plural

_______________ 3rd person feminine plural

UNIT 44
Noun–verb paradigm chart

The schematic outline of the 10 tri-literal verb forms below comprises rows numbered I–X. The columns show that each row has two verbs (الـمَاضـي), followed by (الـمُضارع), one gerund (الـمَصدَر), and finally two participles (إسم الفاعِل), followed by (إسم الـمَفعول).

إسم الـمَفعول	إسم الفاعِل	الـمَصدَر	الـمُضارع	الماضِي	
مَفعول	فاعِل	؟	يَفعـ؟ل	فَعـ؟لَ	I
مُفَعَّل	مُفَعِّل	تَفعيل	يُفَعِّل	فَعَّلَ	II
مُفاعَل	مُفاعِل	مُفاعَلَة	يُفاعِل	فاعَلَ	III
مُفعَل	مُفعِل	إفعال	يُفعِل	أَفعَلَ	IV
مُتَفَعَّل	مُتَفَعِّل	تَفَعُّل	يَتَفَعَّل	تَفَعَّلَ	V
مُتَفاعَل	مُتَفاعِل	تَفاعُل	يَتَفاعَل	تَفاعَل	VI
مَنفَعَل	مُنفَعِل	إنفِعال	يَنفَعِل	اِنفَعَل	VII
مُفتَعَل	مُفتَعِل	إفتِعال	يَفتَعِل	اِفتَعَلَ	VIII
	مُفعِلّ	إفعِلال	يَفعَلّ	اِفعَلَّ	IX
مُستَفعَل	مُستَفعِل	اِستِفعال	يَستَفعِل	اِستَفعَلَ	X

Finding meaning in paradigm charts and tables

Given the central part played by the derivational system of Arabic, verbs are more efficiently dealt with in a tabular form exposition that shows meaningful differences between words.

While perhaps dry, these tables are in fact liberating; understanding how to use them is the key to unlocking the true meaning of concepts and information conveyed in an Arabic script. These tables empower readers to extrapolate meaning, even from words they've never seen before.

In addition, the Arabic dictionary does not list words in alphabetical order based on their spelling. Therefore, one cannot look up a word in the dictionary based on how it is spelled in the text in which the word is found. To find a word in an Arabic dictionary, one must be able to remove markings and suffixes (e.g. reduce a word from its plural to singular form, remove pronoun suffixes, remove subject markers) to arrive at the root radicals, most likely three consonants.

Analysing the paradigm chart

Each cell in the paradigm chart contains an entry showing variations on the tri-literal root radicals ف ع ل. Looking at column 1, الماضي, variation is introduced by interleaving the diacritics فتحة /i/, ضمّة /u/, and كسرة /u/ between the three radicals, as well as by a shadda (the consonant doubling diacritic), and by the letters.

The two verb columns الماضي and المُضارِع only show the conjugation of the third person masculine, which is the form the dictionary lists (for the full conjugation, see Conjugating the perfect and Conjugating the imperfect).

Note that the subject markers of Forms II, III, and IV of المُضارِع are all followed by a ضمّة. In all the remaining forms a فتحة follows the subject marker.

Only in Form IV, specifically in الماضي, and المَصدر is there a hamza written with the alif. Any other alifs found throughout the chart have no hamza.

For each of the Forms II–X, the paradigm of الفِعل المُضارِع can be used to generate the corresponding اسم الفاعِل and اسم المَفعول. Starting with الفِعل المُضارِع, replace the subject marker of the verb and its immediately following diacritic, i.e. يَـ or يُـ, with مُـ. The resulting word is اسم الفاعِل, To generate اسم المَفعول, replace the كسرة immediately following the ع radical with a فَتحة.

Form I is unpredictable in the first three cells: الفِعل, الفِعل الماضي المُضارِع, and المَصدر. The unpredictability is marked by the question mark (?). Specifically, for each different radical ف ع ل, the diacritic following the second radical, ع, can be فَتحة,ضمّة, or كسرة. Similarly, المَصدر is also unpredictable. The dictionary provides the unknown information.

Exercises: noun–verb paradigm chart

Exercise 1

For Form I, find the perfect – الماضي – and imperfect – المُضارِع – of the following six roots.

ف ت ح   ف ر ح
ن ص ر   ض ر ب
ح س ن   ح س ب

Exercise 2

For Form I, find the gerund – المصدر – of the following 12 roots.

خ ط ر	د ر س	ل غ ز
ش ع ر	خ ر ب	ن د م
ك ت ب	ط ل ع	ب ط ل
ل ق م	خ د م	غ س ل

Exercise 3

Fill in the blanks.

Gerund (المصدر)	*Imperfect* (المُضارع)	*Perfect* (الماضي)	*Form* (الوزن)
______	______	اِشتَهَر بِـ	______
______	يَهتَمُّ بِـ	______	______

Exercise 4

For Form IX, find the perfect and imperfect verbs, the gerund, and the active participle of the following seven roots. As mentioned above, these roots correspond to colours ألوان.

ص ف ر	ز ر ق	خ ض ر
ح م ر	س م ر	
ب ي ض	س و د	

UNIT 45
Time

The perfect tense verb, الماضي, is most often – but not exclusively – used to refer to (simple) past time. However, الماضي can, in certain environments, refer to other time contexts. For example, when preceded by certain conditional particles, such as إذا، إن، لو, the time reference is future.

The imperfect tense verb, المُضارِع, is most often – but not exclusively – used to refer to (simple) present time. However, المُضارِع can also refer to the future, for example with the future marker prefix, سَ, or when preceded by the future marker word, سَوف, or when preceded by the future negation particle لَن, or when preceded by conditional particles such as إن، مَهما, and others.

More detailed and elaborate temporal aspects are signalled by grouping sequences of word types including perfect verb, imperfect verb, adverbial and other elements.

Note that active participles (participles: adjectival forms) are also used as verbal elements (see Participles) signalling varying time contexts (past, present, and future).

Examples follow.

Past

جاء	he came
لم يأتِ	he has not/did not come
كِدتُ أسافر	I was about to leave, I almost left
ظللتُ أحاول	I continued to try, I kept on trying
كُنتُ هناك	I was there
كنتُ في البيت	I was at home
كنتُ قد تكلّمتُ	I had spoken

Present

يأتي	he comes
أنا في البيت	I am home
أنا هنا	I'm here
أنا وحيد	I am Waheed
أتكلّم الآن	I am speaking now

عادةً بحلول الصيف، أكون ناوياً أنْ أزورَ أصدقائي في مصر
By the summer time, I will usually be planning to visit my friends in Egypt.

Future

إذا جاء	if he comes
لن يأتيَ	he will not come
لن نذهب إلى البيت	we will not go home
إنْ يأتِ	if he comes
سيأتي	he will come
سأكون قد تكلَّمتُ	I will have spoken
سأكون في البيت	I will be at home
سأكون هناك	I will be there

UNIT 46
Verb–subject agreement

A verb is marked by number and gender when it follows its subject.

The students (female) went ذهبتِ الطالباتُ

A verb is marked only by gender when it comes before its subject.

The students (female) went الطالباتُ ذهبنَ

UNIT 47
Constituents of verb-type words

Typical arrangement of constituents of verb-type words

Verb stems vary according to the verb form (see Verb patterns). However, the relative location of key verb constituents – subject markers, stem, and mood marker – is not affected by stem variation. The following table also highlights the location of the object pronoun suffix relative to the other constituents.

Example:

Form II	فَعَّل	كَسَّرتُها	I broke it, I smashed it
Form I	يَفعَل	يَسمَعُها	He hears her

Object pronoun suffix	*Mood marker*	*Subject marker*	*Stem*	*Subject marker*	*Example*
ـها	none	ـتُ	كَسَّر		كَسَّرتُها
ـها	ُ		ـسمَعـ	يَـ	يَسمَعُها

Verbs with two objects

Some Arabic verbs (e.g. to give, to grant, to present, to think) take two objects.

Example:

The man gave his sweetheart a present. أعطَى الرَجُلُ حَبيبَتَهُ هديَّةً

UNIT 48

Verb types (sound, hamzated, doubled, weak radicalled)

Arabic verbs must conform with syllabic structure rules. The order of consonants, semi-vowels and vowels, as well as the existence of the hamza in the root of a verb may require morphological adjustments to the فعل paradigm to ensure the conjugated verb conforms with syllabic structure rules.

There are four types of verb; one type is conjugated predictably, following the فعل paradigm, and three follow different rules when conjugated. An overview follows with examples of the four types of verb:

1 Sound (السالم); this type of verb follows the فعل paradigm.
2 Doubled (المضعّف)

Examples:

ظنّ، مرّ، أحَبّ

3 'Hamzated' (المهموز)

Examples:

أَخَذ، سأل، قرأ

4 Weak radicalled (المعتلّ)

Examples:

وَعَد، نام، حكى

There are five types of weak radicalled verbs (المعتلّ):

a) Initial weak (المثال)

Examples:

وَعَدَ، وَصَفَ

b) Medial weak (الأجوف)

Examples:

كان، نام، صار

c) Final weak radicalled (الناقص)

Examples:

لقي، حكى، دعا

d) Initial and final weak (اللفيف المفروق)

Examples:

وَفِيَ، وَقِيَ، وَلِيَ

e) Medial and final weak (اللفيف المقرون)

Examples:

لَوَى، رَوَى

Exercises: verb types

Exercise 1

The following verb, أَحَبّ, is doubled (مضعّف). Conjugate the perfect and imperfect Form IV verb أَحَبّ for the subjects identified in the table below. The first answer is filled out as an example.

الضمير	الماضي	المُضارع		
		المرفوع	المنصوب	المجزوم
هو	أَحَبَّ	يُحِبُّ	لن يُحِبَّ	لم يُحِبَّ
هُم	______	______	لن ______	لم ______
هي	______	______	لن ______	لم ______
أنتَ	______	______	لن ______	لم ______
أنتُم	______	______	لن ______	لم ______
أنتِ	______	______	لن ______	لم ______
أنا	______	______	لن ______	لم ______

Exercise 2

The following verb, أعطى, is final weak radicalled (ناقص). Conjugate the perfect and imperfect Form IV verb أعطى for all possible 13 subjects.

الضمير	الماضي	المُضارع
1st person singular	______	______
2nd person masculine singular	______	______
2nd person feminine singular	______	______
3rd person masculine singular	______	______
3rd person feminine singular	______	______
2nd person dual	______	______
3rd person masculine dual	______	______
3rd person feminine dual	______	______
1st person plural	______	______
2nd person masculine plural	______	______
2nd person feminine plural	______	______
3rd person masculine plural	______	______
3rd person feminine plural	______	______

UNIT 49
Adverbs marked by the accusative case

The accusative case can be used on nouns and adjectives. The accusative case is often used as a common adverbial complement to verbs.

Examples:

always	دائماً
actually, really	فعلاً
also, too	أيضاً
a lot, often	كَثيراً
sometimes	أحياناً
very	جِدّاً
well	جَيِّداً
thank you, thanks	شُكراً
you are welcome	عَفواً

شُكراً and عَفواً go together. شُكراً is thanks; عَفواً is the response.

UNIT 50
The passive voice

Using the passive voice to give recipes

In giving recipes, English uses the imperative form (e.g. "put the meat in the pot") whereas Arabic uses the passive form (e.g. "the meat is placed in the pot").

Examples	Meaning
يوضَعُ	placed
يُغَطّى	covered
تُحَمَّرُ	fried
يُضافُ إلَيْهِ	added to it

Outline of the steps in passive transformation

Passive transformation requires performing the following actions:

- Delete the subject of the verb if it is an overt standalone noun.
- Make the direct object of the verb the new subject. In Arabic this new subject is called نائب الفاعِل.
- Inflect the verb for the passive voice (see Inflecting the verb for the passive voice, below).
- Make the verb agree with the new subject (نائب الفاعِل).

Example 1

The correspondent wrote the article.	كَتَبَ المراسلُ المقالةَ
Delete the subject of the verb:	كَتَبَ (~~المراسلُ~~) المقالةَ
Make the old object the new subject:	كَتَبَ المقالةُ
Inflect the verb for the passive voice:	كُتِبَ المقالةُ
Make the verb agree with the new subject:	كُتِبَت المقالة

Example 2

He wrote the the article.	كَتَبَ المقالةَ
There is no independent noun to delete:	كَتَبَ المقالةَ.
Make the old object the new subject:	كَتَبَ المقالةُ.
Inflect the verb for the passive voice:	كُتِبَ المقالةُ.
Make the verb agree with the new subject:	كُتِبَت المقالة.

Example 3

The author (f.) published the book.	نَشَرَت المؤلفةُ الكتابَ.
Delete the subject of the verb:	نَشَرَت (~~المؤلفةُ~~) الكتاب
Make the old object the new subject:	نَشَرَت الكتابُ
Inflect the verb for the passive voice:	نُشِرَت الكتابُ
Make the verb agree with the new subject:	نُشِرَ الكِتابُ.

Exercise: the passive voice

Exercise 1

Change the following from the active to the passive voice. Write the new sentences in the blank spaces below.

Reminder: when doing passive transformations remember the following:

- the subject of the original sentence is deleted
- the direct object becomes the new subject
- the verb in the passive agrees with the new subject

The following are the passives of the three verbs: تُرِك، كُتِب، سُجِّل

1 The father left the keys in the room on the table.

تَرَكَ الأبُ المفاتيح في الغُرفةِ على الطاولة

---

2 I wrote the report yesterday.

كَتَبْتُ التقريرَ أمس.

---

3 The team scored a goal in the fifth minute of the match/game.

سجَّلَ الفريق هدفاً في الدقيقة الخامسة مِن المُباراة.

UNIT 51
Inflecting the verb for the passive voice

The previous section outlined the steps of passive transformation without dealing with step 3: "Inflect the verb for the passive voice". This is done by changing the vowel quality of specific vowels in the verb. In other words, what distinguishes the active from the passive is internal vocalization of the verb.

Passive vocalization of the perfect tense verb

For the perfect form of the verb, the following are the relevant vowels:

v_0 = initial vowel, v_1 = the ف vowel, v_2 = the ع vowel
(Forms I, II, and III have no initial vowel v_0.)

Passive vocalization of the perfect:

If present, vowel v_0 has to be /**u**/
If present, vowel v_1 has to be /**u**/
Vowel v_2 has to be /**i**/

Vowel transformations to inflect active for passive

The following chart illustrates the vowel transformations necessary to inflect active perfect tense verbs for the passive voice:

Form		*Active*	*Transformation*	*Passive*	*Example*
I	$f + v_1 + {}^c + v_2 + l$	{fa^{c}al}	$v_1 \rightarrow u$, $v_2 \rightarrow i$	fu^{c}il	قُطِع
		{fa^{c}ul}	$v_1 \rightarrow u$, $v_2 \rightarrow i$	fu^{c}il	none
		{fa^{c}il}	$v_1 \rightarrow u$, $v_2 \rightarrow i$	fu^{c}il	فُهِم
II	$f + v_1 + {}^{cc} + v_2 + l$	fa^{cc}al	$v_1 \rightarrow u$, $v_2 \rightarrow i$	fu^{cc}il	كُسِّر

III	f + $\mathbf{v}_1$ + ^{c} + $\mathbf{v}_2$ + l	**faa^{c}al**	v_1 → u, v_2 → i	**fuu^{c}il**	لوحِظ
IV	' + $\mathbf{v}_0$ + f + ^{c} + $\mathbf{v}_2$ + l	**'af^{c}al**	v_0 → uu, v_2 → i	**'uf^{c}il**	أُخرِج
V	t + $\mathbf{v}_0$ + f + $\mathbf{v}_1$ + ^{cc} + $\mathbf{v}_2$ + l	**tafa^{cc}al**	v_0→u, v_1→ u, v_2→ i	rare **tufu^{cc}il**	تُقُبِّل
VI	t + $\mathbf{v}_0$ + f + $\mathbf{v}_1$ + ^{c} + $\mathbf{v}_2$ + l	tafaa^{c}al	v_0→u, v_1→ u, v_2→ i	rare **tufuu^{c}il**	تُنووِل
VII	' + $\mathbf{v}_0$ + n + f + $\mathbf{v}_1$ + ^{c} + $\mathbf{v}_2$ + l	infa^{c}al		none	
VIII	' + $\mathbf{v}_0$ + f + t + $\mathbf{v}_1$ + ^{c} + $\mathbf{v}_2$ + l	ifta^{c}al	v_0→ u, v_2→ i	iftu^{c}il	اِقتُرِح
IX	' + $\mathbf{v}_0$ + f + ^{c} + $\mathbf{v}_2$ + l + l	if^{c}all		none	
X	'ist + v_0 + f + ^{c} + $\mathbf{v}_2$ + l	istaf^{c}al	v_0→ u, v_2→ i	istuf^{c}il	اِستُقبِل

Generalizations about the perfect in the passive voice

If there is a v_0, the vowel quality is /u/.
If there is a v_1, the vowel quality is /u/.
The v_2 vowel quality is /i/.
Rare passives for forms V and VI.
No passives for forms VII and IX because they are reflexive in meaning.

Active and passive forms of the perfect tense

The following summary chart contrasts the perfect active and passive.

Form	Active	Passive
I	فَعَل	فُعِل
	فَعِل	
II	فَعَّل	فُعِّل
III	فاعَل	فوعِل
IV	أَفعَل	أُفعِل
V	تَفَعَّل	rare تُفوعِل
VI	تَفاعَل	rare تُفوعِل
VII	اِنفَعَل	none
VIII	اِفتَعَل	اِفتُعِل
IX	اِفعَلّ	none
X	اِستَفعَل	اِستُفعِل

Passive vocalization of the imperfect tense verb

For the imperfect form of the verb, the following are the relevant vowels:

v_s = subject marker vowel, v_2 = the ع vowel

Passive vocalization of the imperfect:

Vowel v_s has to be /**u**/.

Vowel v_2 has to be /**a**/.

Vowel transformations to inflect active imperfect for passive

The following chart illustrates the vowel transformations necessary to inflect active imperfect tense verbs for the passive voice:

Form		*Active*	*Transformation*	*Passive*	*Example*
I	$y + v_s + f + {}^c + v_2 + l$	{**ya**f^{c}al}	$v_s \rightarrow u$	{**yu**f^{c}al}	يُقطَع
		{**ya**f^c**u**l}	$v_s \rightarrow u$, $v_2 \rightarrow a$	{**yu**f^c**a**l}	
		{**ya**f^c**i**l}	$v_s \rightarrow u$, $v_2 \rightarrow a$	{**yu**f^c**a**l}	يُفهَم
II	$y + v_s + f + v_1 + {}^{cc} +$ $\mathbf{v_2} + l$	yufa^{cc}**i**l	$v_2 \rightarrow a$	yu fa^{cc}**a**l	يُكَسَّر
III	$y + v_s + f + v_1 + {}^c +$ $v^2 + l$	yufaa^c**i**l	$v_2 \rightarrow a$	yufaa^c**a**l	يُلاحَظ
IV	$y + v_s + f + {}^c + v_2 + l$	yuf^c**i**l	$v_2 \rightarrow a$	yuf^c**a**l	يُخرَج
V	$y + v_s + ta + f + v_1 + cc$ $+ v_2 + l$	**ya**tafa^{cc}al	$v_s \rightarrow u$	rare **yu**tafa^{cc}al	يُتَقَبَّل
VI	$y + v_s + ta + f + aa + {}^c$ $+ a + l$	**ya**tafaa^{c}al	$v_s \rightarrow u$	rare **yu**tafaa^{c}al	يُتَناوَل
VII	$y + v_s + nf + v_1 + {}^c +$ $v_2 + l$	yanfa^{c}il		none	
VIII	$y + v_s + ft + v_1 + {}^c +$ $v_2 + l$	**ya**fta^c**i**l	$v_s \rightarrow u$, $v_2 \rightarrow a$	**yu**fta^c**a**l	يُقتَرَح
IX	$y + v_s + f + {}^c + a + ll$			none	
X	$y + v_s + sta + f + {}^c +$ $v_2 + l$	**ya**staf^c**i**l	$v_s \rightarrow u$, $v_2 \rightarrow a$	**yu**staf^c**a**l	يُستَقبَل

Generalizations about the imperfect in the passive voice

v_1 is irrelevant.
v_s is always /**u**/.
v_2 is always /**a**/.
Rare passives for Forms V and VI.
No passives for Forms VII and IX because they are reflexive in meaning.

Active and passive forms of the imperfect tense

The following chart summarizes the imperfect active and passive.

Form	Active	Passive
I	يَفعَل	
	يَفعُل	يُفعَل
	يَفعِل	
II	يُفَعِّل	يُفَعَّل
III	يُفاعِل	يُفاعَل
IV	يُفعِل	يُفعَل
V	يَتَفَعَّل	rare يُتَفَعَّل
VI	يَتفاعَل	rare يُتَفاعَل
VII	يَنفَعِل	none
VIII	يَفتَعِل	يُفتَعَل
IX	يَفعَلّ	none
X	يَستَفعِل	يُستَفعَل

Exercise: inflecting the verb for the passive voice

Exercise 1

Change the following sentences from the active to the passive voice. Write the new sentences in the blank spaces below.

a) We heard a knock at the door.

سَمِعنا طَرقاً على الباب

---

b) The storm destroyed many houses and uprooted trees on the coast.

حَطَّمَت العاصِفةُ بيوتاً كثيرةً واِقتَلَعَت أشجاراً على الساحِلِ

____

c) The inspector checked the cargo on the ship before it was offloaded.

عايَنَ المُفَتِّشُ البضاعةَ على السفينة قبل تنزيلها

____

Workbook and Answers

Unit 4: the Arabic language writing system

Letter shapes and context

Unit 4: Answers to Exercise 1

Join the sets of letters to form words. Write the words in the space provided.

a) فَ + و + ا + ك + ه

فَواكه

b) كِ + ت + ا + بِ + ك

كِتابِك

c) رُ + ف + و + ف

رُفوف

d) يَ + ك + تُ + ب

يَكتُب

e) نُ + ق + و + د

نُقود

f) كِ + ت + ا + ب + ي

كِتابي

g) يَ + ن + ا + م

يَنام

h) ل + ي + ب + ي + ا

ليبيا

Unit 4: Answers to Exercise 2

Match each of the two groups of letters to one of the statements below. Draw a line under (a) or (b) to indicate your answer.

1 Letter(s) that cannot be joined by a following letter (i.e. the next letter to the left)

a) ا، د، ذ، ر، ز، و

b) ي

2 Letter(s) that cannot be in a word initial position

a) ا، د، ذ، ر، ز، و

b) ء

Unit 4: Answers to Exercise 3

Write examples of words with each of the following letters in the beginning, middle and end of the word. Write your words in the blank spaces in the table below.

Letter	*End of a word*	*Middle of a word*	*Beginning of a word*
ك ک	بَنك	رَكَدَ	كِتاب
	مَلِك	يكتُب	كَفّ
	فَكّ	كَلْب	كان
		تكوين	كيف
			كُرسي

ق قـ	فُندُق	رَقَدَ	قال
	فاروق	نُقود	قَمح
	فَريق	نَقَلَ	قول
ل لـ	بُرتُقال	تِلِفون	لا
	قال	كَلْب	لَيْمون
	مال	وَلَد	لن
	عمل	فَلافِل	
	فعل	كلمات	
		دولار	
م مـ	قَلَم	قَمَر	مَلِك
	يَنام	كَلِمَات	مَكتَب
	كَلام	لَيْمون	مَسْموع
			مَمْنوع
س سـ	مُدَرِّس	كُرسي	سامي
		فُستان	سَنة
			سيدات
			سادة
ش شـ	فِراش	الشاي	شاي
	قِرش	يمشي	شَمس
	دُهِشَ	مُشكِلة	شَبَكة
		الشهر	شخصيّة
		اكتشفنا	
ص صـ	خاص	بَصَل	صَباح
	نُصوص	قَصير	صُندوق
	فُصوص	مَصر	صاحِب

Hamza shapes and context

Unit 4: Answers to Exercise 4

Join the following letters to form words. Write the correct answer in the blank spaces below.

Read from right to left.

1 رِ + ئَ + ةٌ ri’atun

رِئَةٌ

2 ب + ي + ئِ + يٌّ bii’iyyun

بيئِيٌّ

3 ق + ا + رِ + ئ + و + ن qaari’uuna

قارِئون

4 بِ + ئ + س bi’sun

بِئس

5 رُ + ؤَ + س + ا + ء ru’asaa’un

رُؤَساء

6 رُ + ئِ + يَ ru’iya

رُئِيَ

7 رُ + ؤْ + ي + ةٌ ru’yatun

رُؤْيةٌ

8 رُ + ؤ + و + س ru’uusun

رُؤوس

9 لُ + ؤ + م   lu'mun

لُؤم

10 رَ + أَ + سَ   ra'asa

رَأَسَ

11 تَ + ق + رَ + ئ + ي + نَ   taqra'iina

تَقرَئينَ

12 تَ + ق + رَ + ؤ + و + نَ   taqra'uuna

تَقرَؤون

13 رَ + أ + يٌ   ra'yun

رَأيٌ

Hamza shape based on position in a word

Unit 4: Answers to Exercise 5

Below are examples of words that contain a hamza. Match each word to the corresponding statement describing the context of the hamza by rewriting the word in the space provided.

1 باءات	4 سوء	7 أسرة	10 مئة
2 لاءات	5 قَميء	8 سأل	11 شيء
3 شاء	6 درْء	9 قرأ	

a) on no seat and unjoined between two long vowels:

باءات، لاءات

b) on no seat and unjoined at the end of a word and preceded by a long vowel:

شاء، سوء، قَميء

c) on no seat and unjoined at the end of a word and preceded by a sukūn:

درْء

d) on the ا as seat at the beginning of a word:

أسرة

e) on the ا as seat in the middle of a word:

سأل

f) on the ا as seat at the end of a word:

قرأ

g) In the middle of a word:

مئة، با ءات، سأل، لاءات

Unit 4: Answers to Exercise 6

أ or ؤ or ئ? Which will be the seat of the hamza in the following contexts? To the right and to the left of the blank spaces below are vowels before or after the hamza. Fill in the blanks below with the correct hamza seat. The first answer is provided as an example.

Read from right to left	transcribed word
1 … + a +__________+ i + …	ri'atun
… + a + ئ + i + …	
2 … + i +__________+ i + …	bii'iyyun
… + i + ئ + i + …	
3 + u +__________+ i +	qaari'uuna
… + u + ئ + i + …	
4 … + ْ + __________ + i + …	bi'sun
… + ئ + ْ + i + …	
5 … + a + __________ + u + …	ru'asaa'un
… + a + ؤ + u + …	
6 … + i + __________ + u + …	ru'iya
… + i + ئ + u + …	
7 … i + ْ + __________ + u + …	ru'yatun
… i + ؤ + ْ + u + …	
8 + u + __________ + u +	ru'uusun
… + u + ؤ + u + …	

9 ... + ° + __________ + u + ... lu’mun

... + ؤ + ° + u + ...

10 ... + a + __________ + a + ... ra’asa

... + a + أ + a + ...

11 ... + i + __________ + a + ... taqra’iina

... + i + ئ + a + ...

12 ... + u + __________ + a + ... taqra’uuna

... + u + ؤ + a + ...

13 ... + ° + __________ + a + ... ra’yun

... + أ + ° + a + ...

Unit 5: Function of diacritics التشكيل وعلامات الإعراب

Diacritics as an integral part of a word

Unit 5: Answers to Exercise 1

What are the differences between the two words below?
The diacritics are different; there are three differences:

Meaning:

he studies/is studying	يَدْرُس	فتحة 1 سُكون 2 ضَمّة 3
he teaches/is teaching	يُدَرِّس	ضَمّة 1 فتحة 2 كسرة and شَدّة 3

Diacritics marking case of nouns علامات إعراب الأسماء

Unit 5: Answers to Exercise 2

In the blank spaces below, add the diacritic case marking for the first terms of the ’idafa phrase: شارع محمد. First, fill the blank spaces below with the ’idafa phrase شارع محمد so the second term in the ’idafa is the standalone proper noun محمد. Then add the diacritic case marking to the first term of the ’idafa phrase. As a reminder, please place the diacritic immediately before the possessives (i.e. the proper, standalone noun).

شارعُ محمد.	مَرفوع
شارعَ محمد.	مَنصوب
شارعِ محمد.	مَجرور

Unit 5: Answers to Exercise 3

In the blank spaces below, add the diacritic case marking for the first terms of the 'idafa phrase: شارع محمد. In this exercise, the second term in the 'idafa is a pronoun suffix ـه. So, first fill the blank spaces below with the 'idafa phrase شارعه. Then add the diacritic case marking to the first term of the 'idafa phrase. As a reminder, please place the diacritic immediately before the possessive (i.e. pronoun suffix).

شارعُه	مَرفوع
شارعَه	مَنصوب
شارعِه	مَجرور

Diacritics marking mood of verbs علامات إعراب الأفعال

Unit 5: Answers to Exercise 4

Add the mood marker of the imperfect verbs below. Reminder: please make sure the mood marker is in the appropriate location.

	المَجزوم	المنصوب	المرفوع
هو	لم يقمْ	لن يقومَ	يقومُ
أنا	لم أقلْ	لن أقولَ	أقولُ
أنتَ	لم تكتبْ	لن تكتبَ	تكتبُ
نحن	لم ندعوْ	لن ندعوَ	ندعوُ
هي	لم تتكلّمْ	لن تتكلّمَ	تتكلّمُ

Unit 5: Answers to Exercise 5

Study the following sentences. The underlined words are imperfect verbs in المرفوع mood. Add the mood marker for the underlined verbs. Reminder: please make sure the mood marker is in the appropriate locations.

A تحتاجُ تزيدُها

فإنَّ كُلَّ أُمَّةٍ تَحتاجُ إلى لُغَةٍ مُوَحَّدَةٍ

تَزيدُها تَجاوُباً وتَماسُكاً، فتكون مُوَحِّدة

Every nation needs a unified language (one language) that would make it more (mutually) responsive and more joined/connected/fused/fastened together, and thus be a unifying language.

B تختلفُ تختلفُ

تَختلفُ اختلافاً بَيِّنا

حتّى إنّها تَختلفُ بَعضَ الاختلافِ من حارةٍ إلى حارة

They differ considerably; they are even somewhat different from one alley to another.

Unit 5: Answers to Exercise 6

Study the following sentences. The underlined words are imperfect verbs in المنصوب mood. Add the mood marker for the underlined verbs. Reminder: please make sure the mood marker is in the appropriate location.

A تبسّطَ

من اللازِم أنْ تُبَسِّطَ لُغَتَك عندما تتكلّمُ مع الأطفال

You must simplify your language when speaking with the children.

B أغيّرَ

أحبّ أن أخرج معكم ولكنّي أريد أنْ أُغَيِّرَ ملابِسي أوّلاً

I would like to go out with you, but I would like to change my clothes first.

C تدخلَ

إذا تأخّرْتَ أكثر من خمس دقائق

فلا تستطيع أن تَدخلَ إلى الصف

If you are more than 5 minutes late, you will not be able to enter the class.

D تتحقّق

أتَمَنّى أنْ تَتَحَقّقَ كلُّ أحلامي

I hope (I wish) that all my dreams will come true.

E تستمعَ

أظُنُّ أنَّها لم تُريدْ أنْ تَستَمِعَ إلى رأيي في الموضوع

I think that she does not want to listen to my opinion on the subject.

Unit 5: Answers to Exercise 7

Study the following sentences. The underlined words are imperfect verbs in المَجزوم mood. Add the mood marker for the underlined verbs. Reminder: please make sure the mood marker is in the appropriate locations.

A يعرّبْ

لم يُعَرَّبْ تَدريسُ الطِّب في مُعظَم الجامعات العربية حتّى الآن

The teaching of medicine was not done in Arabic ("Arabized") in most Arab universities until now.

B تعتادْ

انتَ لا تُحبّ القهوة لأنّك لم تَعتادْ عليها

You do not like coffee because you are not used to it.

C يتغيّرْ

مَطَر مَطَر مَطَر! إذا لم يَتَغَيَّرْ الطقسُ قريباً

فلا أعرف ماذا سأفعل

Rain, rain, rain! If the weather does not change soon, I do not know what I will do.

D يحضرْ

أنا غاضِبةٌ مِنهُ لأنَّهُ لم يَحضُرْ لِزيارتي مُنذُ وقتٍ طويل

I am angry with him because he has not come to visit me in a long time.

E تريدْ

أظُنُّ أنّها لم تُريدْ أنْ تَستَمِعَ إلى رأيي في الموضوع

I think that she does not want to listen to my opinion on the subject.

Unit 6: Agreement تطابق

Unit 6: Answers to Exercise 1

Read the following passage carefully, then rewrite it in Arabic substituting محمّد for ياسمين. Rewrite the new passage in the blank spaces below. Make all the necessary changes to ensure agreement.

ياسمين تسكن في مدينة نيويورك، وهي طالبة تدرس الأدب الإنجليزي في جامعة نيويورك. والدها مصري، وهو يعمل في الأمم المتحدة، ووالدتها فلسطينية وهي سكرتيرة في نفس الجامعة. محمود وعادل وفاطمة أقارب ياسمين، وهم يسكنون في مدينة القاهرة.

محمّد يسكن في مدينة نيويورك، وهو طالب يدرس الأدب الإنجليزي في جامعة نيويورك. والده مصري، وهو يعمل في الأمم المتحدة، ووالدته فلسطينية وهي سكرتيرة في نفس الجامعة. محمود وعادل وفاطمة أقارب محمّد، وهم يسكنون في مدينة القاهرة

Unit 6: Answers to Exercise 2

Use the vocabulary in the glossary of adjectives below to fill in the blanks in the sentences. Make all the necessary changes to ensure agreement.

Glossary

كبير	big	واسع	wide, broad
مصريّ	Egyptian	جَديد	new

a) I am a new student أنا طالِبة ________

أنا طالِبة جديدة

b) New York is a big city نيويورك مدينة ________

نيويورك مدينة كبيرة

c) I live in a new house أسكن في بيت ________

أسكن في بيت جديد

d) My dad is Egyptian والدي ________

والدي مصريّ

e) This is a wide road هذا شارع ________

هذا شارع واسِع

Unit 7: Pronouns الضمائر

Possessive pronouns ضمائر المُلكيّة

Unit 7: Answers to Exercise 1

Fill in the blanks below with the Arabic noun and possessive pronoun suffixes that correspond to the underlined English words. The first answer is offered as an example.

Glossary

Word	meaning	Gender
كِتاب	a book	m.
بَيت	a house	m.
سَيّارة	a car	f.
شقّة	an apartment	f.

a) Whose book is this? This is his book

هذا ________

هذا كِتابه

b) Whose car is this? This is her car

هذه ________

هذه سَيّارتها

c) Whose house is this? This is my house

هذا ________

هذا بَيتى

d) Whose apartment is this? This is their (p., f.) apartment

هذه ________

هذه شقّتهُنّ

Object pronouns

Unit 7: Answers to Exercise 2

Fill in the blanks below with the Arabic words and object pronoun suffixes that correspond to the underlined English words.

Glossary

He loves	يُحِب	with	مع
We heard	سَمِعنا		

a) He loves the girl. — هو بيحب البنت

He loves her — هو ________

هو يُحِبها

b) We heard Samia — نحن سَمِعنا سامية

We heard her — نحن ________

نحن سَمِعناها

c) The girl is playing with her friend — البنت تلعب مع صديقتها

The girl is playing with her — البنت تلعب ________

البنت تلعب معها

d) The boy is playing with the neighbours — الوَلد يلعب مع الجران

The boy is playing with them — الوَلد يلعب ________

الوَلد يلعب معهُم

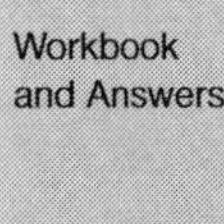

Free-standing pronouns الضمائر المُنفَصِلة

Unit 7: Answers to Exercise 3

Study the underlined subject pronouns in the statements. For each underlined subject pronoun, choose the correct person, gender, and number.

Person, gender, number	Statement
a) 2nd person masculine singular	هَل أنتَ جَوعان؟
b) 1st person singular	نَعَم، أنا جَوعان
c) 2nd person masculine plural	مِن أينَ أنتُم يا شَباب؟
d) 1st person plural	نَحنُ مِن مِصر
e) 2nd person feminine singular	هَل أنتِ مِصريّة يا عائشَة؟
f) 1st person singular	لا. أنا سودانِيّة
g) 3rd person feminine singular	مَن نادية؟ هِيَ خالَة عائشَة
h) 3rd person masculine singular	أينَ يَعمَل والِد مَها؟ هو يَعمَل في الأُمَم المُتَّحِدة
i) 3rd person feminine singular	أدرُس في جامِعة ميدلبِري، وهي جامِعة صَغيرة في وِلايَة فيرمونت
j) 3rd person feminine singular	أسكُن في مِنطقة المَزَّة، وهي مِنطقة قريبة مِن جامِعة

Free-standing and suffixed pronouns الضمائر المُنفَصِلة والمُتَّصِلة

Unit 7: Answers to Exercise 4

Fill in the blanks with the correct forms of the pronouns or noun and pronoun suffix combinations. The first answer is given as an example.

Glossary

صورة	picture	والدة	mother
سوريا	Syria		

a) Your (s., m.) picture is pretty — ________ جميلة

صورَتُك جميلة

b) My mother is Syrian — ________ سوريّة

والدتي سوريّة

c) I live in Beirut and it (s., f.) is a large city in the Middle East.

أسكن في مدينة بيروت و ______ مدينة كبيرة
في الشرق الأوسط

أسكن في مدينة بيروت و هي مدينة كبيرة
في الشرق الأوسط

d) Are you (s., f.) a translator? Yes, I specialize in Arabic.

هل ________ مترجمة؟
نعم. ______ متخصِّصة في العربيّة

هل أنتِ مترجمة؟
نعم. أنا متخصِّصة في العربيّة

Unit 7: Answers to Exercise 5

Change the statements below from the first person to the third person feminine. Make all other necessary changes. The first answer is provided as an example.

a) I am hungry (m.) — أنا جعان
She is hungry — هي جَوعانة

b) I am from Egypt — أنا مِن مِصر
She is from Egypt — ________

هي مِن مِصر

c) I am Dalia's aunt — أنا خالَة داليا
She is Dalia's aunt — ________

هِيَ خالَة داليا

d) I work at the United Nations — أنا أعْمَل في الأُمَم المُتَّحِدة
She works at the United Nations — ________

هِيَ تـعمَل في الأُمَم المُتَّحِدة

Unit 8: Demonstratives – أسماء الإشارة

Unit 8: Answers to Exercise 1

Fill in the blanks below with the appropriate pronoun and demonstrative. The first example is completed for reference.

Glossary

فنجان	tea cup (s., m.)	مُمَثِّل	actor (s., m.)
شَجَرة	tree (s., f.)		

a) This is a man. This is the man.

_____ رَجُل. _____ الرَجُل

هذا رَجُل. هذا هو الرَجُل

b) This is a tea cup. This is the tea cup.

_______ فنجان _______ الفنجان

هذا فنجان. هذا هو الفنجان.

c) This is a tree. This is the tree.

_______ شَجَرة _______ الشَجَرة

هذه شَجَرة. هذه هي الشَجَرة

d) These are actresses (dual). These are the actresses (dual).

_______ مُمَثلتان _______ المُمَثلتان

هاتان مُمَثلتان. هاتان هما المُمَثلتان

Unit 10: Noun type words: Syntactic function, case name, and case marking

Syntactic function

Unit 10: Answers to Exercise 1

Identify the syntactic function of the underlined words as subject of a verb (فاعِل), object of verb (مفعول به), object of preposition (اسم مجرور). For each underlined word, select the appropriate syntactic function from the three options provided.

A Mohamed travelled to Yemen in the winter of 2009.

سافر محمد إلى اليَمن في شتاء ٢٠٠٩

i) محمد

a) subject of a verb (فاعِل),

ii) اليَمن

c) object of a preposition (اسم مجرور)

iii) شتاء

c) object of a preposition (اسم مجرور)

B The wife listens to the radio while she has breakfast in the morning.

تستمع الزوجة إلى الإذاعة وهي تفطر في الصباح

i) الزوجة

a) subject of a verb (فاعِل),

ii) الإذاعة

c) object of a preposition (اسم مجرور)

iii) الصباح

c) object of a preposition (اسم مجرور)

C When I visit the family during the weekends, we eat dinner and watch TV together.

عندما أزور العائلة في نهاية الأسبوع نأكل العشاء ونُشاهد التلفزيون معا

i) العائلة

b) object of a verb (مفعول به)

ii) نهاية

c) object of a preposition (اسم مجرور)

iii) العشاء

b) object of a verb (مفعول به)

iv) التلفزيون

b) object of a verb (مفعول به)

D She saw the accident on TV then read an article about it.

شاهدَت الحادثة في التلفزيون ثُمّ قرأَت مقالة عنها.

i) الحادثة
   b) object of a verb (مفعول به)

ii) التلفزيون
   c) object of a preposition (اسم مجرور)

iii) مقالة
   b) object of a verb (مفعول به)

E The two friends met in the evening and had dinner, then went into the "Shuruuq" bookstore where Mustafa bought a magazine and Mahmoud bought a book.

تقابل الصديقان في المساء وأكلا العشاء وبعد ذلك دخلا مكتبة "الشروق" حيث اشترى مصطفى مجلة واشترى محمود كتابا.

i) الصديقان
   a) subject of a verb (فاعِل)

ii) المساء
   c) object of a preposition (اسم مجرور)

iii) العشاء
   b) object of a verb (مفعول به)

iv) مكتبة
   b) object of a verb (مفعول به)

v) مصطفى
   a) subject of a verb (فاعِل)

vi) مجلة
   b) object of a verb (مفعول به)

vii) محمود
   a) subject of a verb (فاعِل)

viii) كتابا
   b) object of a verb (مفعول به)

Unit 10: Answers to Exercise 2

Identify the case name of the underlined words as مرفوع (nominative), منصوب (accusative), or مجرور (genitive). For each underlined word, select the appropriate case name from the three options provided.

A Mohamed travelled to Yemen in the winter of 2009.

سافر محمد إلى اليَمن في شتاء ٢٠٠٩.

i) محمد
   a) مرفوع (nominative)

ii) اليَمن
   c) مجرور (genitive)

iii) شتاء
   c) مجرور (genitive)

B The wife listens to the radio while she has breakfast in the morning.

تستمع الزوجة إلى الإذاعة وهي تفطر في الصباح.

i) الزوجة
   a) مرفوع (nominative)

ii) الإذاعة
   c) مجرور (genitive)

iii) الصباح
   c) مجرور (genitive)

C When I visit the family during the weekends we eat dinner and watch TV together.

عندما أزور العائلة في نهاية الأسبوع نأكل العشاء ونُشاهد التلفزيون معا.

i) العائلة
   b) منصوب (accusative)

ii) نهاية
   c) مجرور (genitive)

iii) العشاء

b) منصوب (accusative)

iv) التلفزيون

b) منصوب (accusative)

D She saw the accident on TV then read an article about it.

شاهدَت الحادثة في التلفزيون ثُمّ قرأت مقالة عنها.

i) الحادثة

b) منصوب (accusative)

ii) التلفزيون

c) مجرور (genitive)

iii) مقالة

b) منصوب (accusative)

E The two friends met in the evening and had dinner, then went into the "Shuruuq" bookstore where Mustafa bought a magazine and Mahmoud bought a book.

تقابل الصديقان في المساء وأكلا العشاء وبعد ذلك دخلا مكتبة "الشرو" حيث اشترى مصطفى مجلة واشترى محمود كتابا.

i) الصديقان

a) مرفوع (nominative)

ii) المساء

c) مجرور (genitive)

iii) العشاء

b) منصوب (accusative)

iv) مكتبة

b) منصوب (accusative)

v) مصطفى

a) مرفوع (nominative)

vi) مجلة

b) منصوب (accusative)

vii) محمود

a) مرفوع (nominative)

viii) كتابا

b) منصوب (accusative)

Case marking

Unit 10: Answers to Exercise 3

Are case marks applied to any of the words or phrases below? Give the answer نعم (yes) or لا (no) in the blank spaces below.

	نعم	لا
a) singular, feminine noun	نعم	
b) singular, masculine noun	نعم	
c) dual, feminine noun	نعم	
d) sound, plural masculine	نعم	
e) verbal phrase		لا
f) nominal phrase		لا

Case marking by diacritics

Unit 10: Answers to Exercise 4

Study the sentence below. Add the appropriate case marker to the underlined words. If necessary, refer to sections on agreement, case marking, and syntactic functions of nouns and their case markers.

استجابت الحكومةُ الأمريكيةُ لدعوات الاتصال المباشر بسوريا وإيران، وقبلت، للمرةِ الأولى، الجلوسَ على طاولة واحدة مع مسئولين من البلدين في شهر مارس الماضي، وفي إطار مؤتمر بغداد الذي شارك فيه وفود أمريكية وعربية بهدف إيجاد حل لوقف دوامة العنف في العراق.

Unit 10: Answers to Exercise 5

Study the phrases below. Identify the syntactic function of the underlined words as subject of a verb (فاعِل), object of a verb (مفعول به), object of a preposition (مجرور اسم). For each underlined word, select the appropriate name of the case-marking diacritic (كسرة, فَتحة,ضَمّة).

a) ذهبت المهندسة للمرة الثانية
b) استجابت الحكومة لدعوات الاتصال
المباشر في ظل الضغوط
c) استجابت الحكومة الإطالية
d) قبلت (هى) الجلوس

For each of the four underlined words, fill in the blanks below with 1) the appropriate syntactic function and 2) the name of the case-marking diacritic. If necessary, refer to sections on case marking and syntactic functions of nouns and their case markers.

	Syntactic function	Case-marking diacritic
a) المرّة	إسم مجرور	كسرة
b) ظل	إسم مجرور	كسرة
c) الحكومة	فاعل	ضَمّة
d) الجلوس	مفعول به	فَتحة

Case marking by letters

Unit 10: Answers to Exercise 6

Rewrite the sentences below by transforming the underlined singular nouns into their dual form. Place the correct answer in the blank spaces below. Remember to make all necessary changes and add the letters marking the case of dual nouns.

a) وَجَدتُ عائلةً في هذه البناية

وَجَدتُ عائلتَيْنِ في هذه البناية

b) الكتابُ على الكرسي

الكتابانِ على الكرسي

c) الأستاذةُ في الكُلّيّة

الأستاذتانِ في الكُلّيّة

d) البنت كَسّـرة قَلَمٍ

البنت كَسّـرة قَلَمَيْنِ

e) كتبت الرسالة إلى الرجُلِ

كتبت الرسالة إلى الرَجُـلَـيْنِ

Unit 10: Answers to Exercise 7

Rewrite the sentences below by transforming the underlined singular nouns into their plural, masculine form. Place the correct answer in the blank spaces below. Remember to make all necessary changes and add the letters marking the case of plural nouns.

a) وَجَدتُ الرجلَ الطَـيِّـبَ في هذا الشارع

وَجَدتُ الرجالَ الطَـيِّـبيـنَ في هذه البناية

b) يصومُ المسلمُ شهرَ رمضان

يصومُ المسلمون شهرَ رمضان

c) المواطنُ معتادُ على دفع الضرائب

المواطنونَ معتادون على دفع الضرائبِ

Variations in case marking

Unit 10: Answers to Exercise 8

Study the eight sentences below. The underlined words are diptotes (ممنوع من الصرف). First add the appropriate case marker to the underlined words. Then write the case name for each of these eight words in the blank spaces below. The first answer is given as an example.

a) case name: منصوب

مع أنّي لا أكتُب رسائلَ عادةً، فإنّي أحياناً أكتُبُ إلى صديقة طفولتي.

b) case name: مرفوع

لماذا لا تُوجَدُ كَنائسُ كثيرةٌ في الأحياء الحديثة بالمُدُن الغربية؟

c) case name: منصوب

عملي يَضطَّرُني أن أُقيمَ في البحرين عدّةَ أسابيعَ من كلّ سنة.

d) case name: مجرور

مَرَرْتُ بِتَجارِبَ صَعبةٍ كثيرةٍ في حياتي جعلتني أكتَشِف نَفسي.

e) case name: منصوب

الناس الذين تعرّفتُ عليهم في العالم العربي كانوا لُطَفاءَ جِدّاً معي.

f) case name: منصوب

خَرَّجَت الجامعة الأمريكية في بيروت وُزَراءَ ورُؤَساءَ عرباً كثيرين.

g) case name: منصوب

عِندما زُرنا الشامَ رأَيْنا عِدَّةَ مَساجِدَ قَديمةً في منطقة ،،باب توما.

h) case name: منصوب

ناقَشَت المُتَحَدِّثَةُ باسم الحُكومة عِدّةَ مَشاريعَ جديدة تَنوي الحُكومةُ القيامَ بها.

An overview of case marking

Unit 10: Answers to Exercise 9

Complete the three tables below by making all necessary changes to the noun مُمَثِّلٌ (an actor).

A Fill in the blanks in this table with the noun in the singular. Please make all necessary changes to reflect all combinations of the following attributes: definite, indefinite, masculine, feminine, nominative case, accusative case, genitive case.

The singular (المُفرَد)				
Definite (مَعرِفَة)		*Indefinite* (نَكِرَة)		*Case*
Feminine (مُؤَنَّث)	*Masculine* (مُذَكَّر)	*Feminine* (مُؤَنَّث)	*Masculine* (مُذَكَّر)	
المُمَثِّلَةُ	المُمَثِّلُ	مُمَثِّلَةٌ	مُمَثِّلٌ	المرفوع
المُمَثِّلَةَ	المُمَثِّلَ	مُمَثِّلَةً	مُمَثِّلاً	المنصوب
المُمَثِّلَةِ	المُمَثِّلِ	مُمَثِّلَةٍ	مُمَثِّلٍ	المجرور

B Fill in the blanks in this table with the noun in the dual. Please make all necessary changes to reflect all combinations of the following attributes: definite, indefinite, masculine, feminine, nominative case, accusative case, genitive case.

The dual (المُثَنَّى)				
Definite (مَعرِفة)		*Indefinite* (نَكِرَة)		*Case*
Feminine (مُؤَنَّث)	*Masculine* (مُذَكَّر)	*Feminine* (مُؤَنَّث)	*Masculine* (مُذَكَّر)	
المُمَثِّلتانِ	المُمَثِّلانِ	مُمَثِّلتانِ	مُمَثِّلانِ	المرفوع
المُمَثِّلتَيْنِ	المُمَثِّلَيْنِ	مُمَثِّلتَيْنِ	مُمَثِّلَيْنِ	المنصوب
المُمَثِّلتَيْنِ	المُمَثِّلَيْنِ	مُمَثِّلتَيْنِ	مُمَثِّلَيْنِ	المجرور

C Fill in the blanks in this table with the noun in the plural. Please make all necessary changes to reflect all combinations of the following attributes: definite, indefinite, masculine, feminine, nominative case, accusative case, genitive case.

The plural (الجَمع)				
Definite (مَعرِفة)		*Indefinite* (نَكِرَة)		*Case*
Feminine (مُؤَنَّث)	*Masculine* (مُذَكَّر)	*Feminine* (مُؤَنَّث)	*Masculine* (مُذَكَّر)	
المُمَثِّلاتُ	المُمَثِّلونَ	مُمَثِّلاتٌ	مُمَثِّلونَ	المرفوع
المُمَثِّلاتِ	المُمَثِّلينَ	مُمَثِّلاتٍ	مُمَثِّلينَ	المنصوب
المُمَثِّلاتِ	المُمَثِّلينَ	مُمَثِّلاتٍ	مُمَثِّلينَ	المجرور

Unit 12: Noun types

The relative adjective النِّسبة

Unit 12: Answers to Exercise 1

Fill in the blanks with the appropriate relative adjectives. First, for each statement, identify the suitable word from the glossary below. Then make all the necessary changes to each selected word from the glossary to convert it to an adjective that agrees with the noun that it qualifies. That is, the relative adjective must agree with the noun that it qualifies in terms of number, gender, and definiteness.

Glossary

Saudi Arabia	السعودية	Egypt	مِصر
Italy	إيطاليا	Arab	عرب (s., m.)
Spain	إسبانيا	coffee	قهوة (s., f.)
France	فرنسا	bank	البنك (s., m.)
Turkey	تركيا	literature	الأَدَب (s., m.)

a) a <u>Saudi</u> man — رجل ______

رجل سعودي

b) the <u>Turkish</u> coffee (s., f.) — القهوة ______

القهوة التركية

c) the <u>Arab</u> bank (s., m.) — البنك ______

البنك العربيّ

d) <u>Italian</u> girl — بنت ______

بنت إطالية

e) The book, *Alf Leila Wa Leila*, is one of the great works in the history of <u>Arab</u> Literature (s., m.).

كتاب ‟ألف ليلة وليلة" من الأعمال العظيمة في تاريخ الأدب ______

كتاب ‟ألف ليلة وليلة" من الأعمال العظيمة في تاريخ الأدب العربيّ

f) I {study/am studying} <u>Spanish</u> literature (s., m.)

أدرُس الأَدَب ______

أدرُس الأَدَب الإِسبانيّ

g) She's an <u>Egyptian</u> from the city of Tanta

هي ______ من مدينة طنطا

هي مِصريّة من مدينة طنطا

h) the <u>Egyptian</u> student (s., m.) — الطالب ______

الطالب المصري

Gerunds المصدر

Unit 12: Answers to Exercise 2

Rewrite the following sentence by substituting the word مَشي (walking) with the prompts provided. Make all other necessary changes.

He likes walking because it strengthens the mind.

a) walking هو يحب المشي لِأنه يُقَوّى العَقل

b) reading هو يحب القِراءة لِأنها تُقَوّى العَقل

c) writing هو يحب الكِتابة لِأنها تُقَوّى العَقل

Unit 12: Answers to Exercise 3

Study the sentences below. Underline the مصدر in each sentence.

a) أكل الفطار مُفيد

b) الطفل لا يحب الاسْتِحمام

c) البنت تستمتع بقراءة الكتب

d) التاجر يُحِّب الإقامة في المدن الكبيرة

e) ازداد عددُ المُحجّبات في هذه المنطقة

f) الأُستاذ لا يحبُّ التَدريس في الصباح

g) عقيل كان يحب شُرب القهوة

h) الشُعور بالوحدة صعب على الجميع

i) داليا تُحِب السَّفَر

Unit 13: The "human" vs "non-human" classification of nouns

Gender and non-human nouns

Unit 13: Answers to Exercise 1

Fill in the blanks. Below is a glossary of terms for reference.

Glossary

سَيّارة	car	سريع	fast
إسعاف	ambulance		

1 The car (f.) is fast — السَيّارة سَريعة

2 It (the car, f.) is fast — هى سَريعة

3 The ambulance (m.) is fast — الإسعاف سريع

4 It (the ambulance, m.) is fast — هو سريع

Gender and human nouns

Unit 13: Answers to Exercise 2

Rewrite the following by turning the masculine human nouns into feminine. Please make all necessary changes to ensure agreement. Write the answers in the blank spaces below.

a) He is a professor — هو أُستاذ

She is a professor — هى أُستاذة

b) He is a student — هو طالب

She is a student — هى طالبة

c) He is American — هو أمريكي

She is American — هى أمريكية

Number in human and non-human nouns and their adjectives

Unit 13: Answers to Exercise 3

Fill in the blank spaces below with the appropriate adjective. Use the glossary below to identify the relevant adjective. Then make all the necessary adjustments to the number and gender of the adjective to ensure agreement with the noun.

Glossary

لُغات	languages (pl.)	جديد	new (s., m.)
أوروبيّ	European (s., m.)	أشياءَ	things
مُتَرجِمون	translators (pl., m.)	يابانـيّ	Japanese (s., m.)
عَرَب	Arab (pl.)	لُبنانيّ	Lebanese (s., m.)
موظّفات	employees (pl., f.)		

a) Italian, Spanish, and French are European languages.

الإيطالية والإسبانية والفرنسية لُغات أوروبيّة

b) Lebanese friends

أصحاب لُبنانيّون

c) Arab translators at the UN

مُتَرجِمون عَرَب في الأُمَم المُتَّحِدة

d) Miss Muna, Miss Wafa' and Mrs Mary are new employees.

الآنِسة مُنى والآنِسة وفاء والسيدة ماري موظّفات جديدات

e) Today, the history professor taught us new things about ancient Central Asian history.

اليومَ أستاذُ التاريخِ علَّمنا أشياءَ جديدةً
عن تاريخِ آسيا الوُسْطَى القديم.

f) Honda, Isuzu and Toyota are Japanese cars.

هوندا وإيسوزو وتويوتا سَيّارات يابانـيّـة

Unit 14: The human category nouns

Reference to singular masculine human nouns

Unit 14: Answers to Exercise 1

Study the sentences below and the pronouns and/or demonstratives in each sentence. Draw a line under each pronoun and/or demonstrative referencing a singular masculine human noun. In the blank spaces below, write the specific pronoun and/or demonstrative. Where, for example, the pronoun is affixed to part of another word, only write the independent pronoun. If there are no singular, masculine human nouns, write "none" in the blank spaces.

Glossary

pretty, scenic	جميلةُ المَناظِرِ	restless	كثيرُ الحركة
kind-hearted, generous	طَيّبة القلب	far-sighted	بعيدةُ النظر
in broad circulation	الواسعةِ الانتشار	cute/funny	خفيفةُ الدمِ
unpleasant	ثقيلُ الدّمِ	quick-witted	وسريعةُ البديهة
pale-faced or jaundiced	أصفَرُ الوَجه	tall	الطويلُ القامةِ
		handsome	الجميلُ الوجه
		silent, not wordy	قليلُ الكلام

a) هو

لا يستطيع أخي أن يجلس في مكان واحد مدة طويلة، فهو كثيرُ الحركة

b) None (no masculine human singular pronouns or demonstratives)

والدتي إنسانة بعيدةُ النظر تُفكّر دائماً في المُستقبل

c) None (no masculine human singular pronouns or demonstratives)

تعجبني شخصيتها لأنّها خفيفةُ الدمِ وسريعةُ البديهة

d) هذا

مَن هذا الشابّ الطويلُ القامةِ الجميلُ الوجه؟

e) هو هو

من الصعب أن يتعرّف عليهِ الناس لأنّه خجولٌ وقليلُ الكلام

f) None (no masculine human singular pronouns or demonstratives)

هذه منطقة جميلةُ المَناظِرِ ولذلك يَقصِدُها ناسٌ كثيرونَ كلّ عام

g) None (no masculine human singular pronouns or demonstratives)

جريدة الـ "واشنطون بوست" والـ "نيويورك تايمز" من الجرائد الواسعةِ الانتشار

h) None (no masculine human singular pronouns or demonstratives)

يبدو أنّك تعبان جداً وأصفَرُ الوَجه، هل أنتَ مَريض؟

i) None (no masculine human singular pronouns or demonstratives)

هي طَيّبة القلب، تحبّ كلّ الناس وتحاول أن تساعدهم

j) هو هو

هو شخص ثقيلُ الدّمِ،

لا أستطيع الجُلوس معهِ أكثر من دقيقتين

Reference to singular feminine human nouns

Unit 14: Answers to Exercise 2

Study the sentences below and the pronouns and/or demonstratives in each sentence. Draw a line under each pronoun and/or demonstrative referencing a singular feminine human noun. In the blank spaces below, write the specific pronoun and/or demonstrative. Where, for example, the pronoun is affixed to part of another word, only write the independent pronoun. If there are no singular, feminine human nouns, write "none" in the blank spaces.

Glossary

pretty, scenic	جميلةُ المَناظِرِ	restless	كثيرُ الحركة
kind-hearted, generous	طَيّبة القلب	far-sighted	بعيدةُ النظر
		cute/funny	خفيفةُ الدمِ
in broad circulation	الواسعةِ الانتشار	quick-witted	وسريعةُ البديهة
		tall	الطويلُ القامةِ
unpleasant	ثقيلُ الدّمِ	handsome	الجميلُ الوجه
pale-faced or jaundiced	أصفَرُ الوَجه	silent, not wordy	قليلُ الكلام

a) None (no feminine human singular pronouns or demonstratives)

لا يستطيع أخي أن يجلس في مكان واحد مدة طويلة،
فهو كثيرُ الحركة

b) None (no feminine human singular pronouns or demonstratives)

والدتي إنسانة بعيدةُ النظر تُفَكّر دائماً في المُستقبل

c) هي هي

تعجبني شخصيتها لأنّها خفيفةُ الدمِ وسريعةُ البديهة

d) None (no feminine human singular pronouns or demonstratives)

مَن هذا الشابّ الطويلُ القامةِ الجميلُ الوجه؟

e) None (no feminine human singular pronouns or demonstratives)

من الصعب أن يتعرّف عليه الناس لأنّه خجولٌ وقليلُ الكلام

f) هي هي

هذه منطقة جميلةُ المَناظِرِ ولذلك يَقصِدُها ناسٌ كثيرونَ كلّ عام

g) None (no feminine human singular pronouns or demonstratives)

جريدة الـ ''واشنطون بوست'' والـ ''نيويورك تايمز'' من الجرائد الواسعةِ الانتشار

h) None (no feminine human singular pronouns or demonstratives)

يبدو أنّك تعبان جداً وأصفرُ الوَجه، هل أنتَ مَريض؟

i) هي

هي طَيّبة القلب، تحبّ كلّ الناس وتحاول أن تساعدهم

j) None (no feminine human singular pronouns or demonstratives)

هو شخص ثقيلُ الدّمِ، لا أستطيع الجُلوس معه أكثر من دقيقتين

Summary: reference to singular human nouns

Unit 14: Answers to Exercise 3

Rewrite the sentences below and change pronouns and demonstratives that are singular masculine human to singular feminine human. Please make all necessary changes to ensure agreement. Write the answers in the blank spaces below.

a)

لا تستطيع أختي أن تجلس في مكان واحد مدة طويلة، فهي كثيرةُ الحركة

b)

مَن هذه الشابّة الطويلةُ القامةِ الجميلةُ الوجه؟

c)

من الصعب أن يتعرّف عليها الناس لأنّها خجولةٌ وقليلةُ الكلام

d)

هي شخصيّة ثقيلةُ الدّمِ، لا أستطيع الجُلوس معها أكثر من دقيقتين

Unit 14: Answers to Exercise 4

Rewrite the sentences below and change pronouns and demonstratives that are singular feminine human to singular masculine human. Please make all necessary changes to ensure agreement. Write the answers in the blank spaces below.

Glossary

area/place	منطقة (s., f.)	area/place	مكان (s., m.)

a)

تعجبني شخصيته لأنّه خفيفُ الدمِ وسريعُ البديهة

b)

هذا مكان جميلُ المَناظِرَ ولذلك يَقصِدُه ناسٌ كثيرونَ كلّ عام

c)

هو طَيّب القلب، يحبّ كلّ الناس ويحاول أن يساعدهم

Reference to masculine dual human nouns

Unit 14: Answers to Exercise 5

Study the sentences below and the pronouns and/or demonstratives in each sentence. Draw a line under each pronoun and/or demonstrative referencing a masculine dual human noun. In the blank spaces below, write the specific pronoun and/or demonstrative. If there are no references to masculine dual human nouns, write "none" in the blank spaces.

a) هذان هما

هذان هما المهندسان

b) هذان

هذان المهندسان أسسا شركة في العام الماضي

c) None

هاتان هما المُمَرضتان

d) None

هاتان المُمَرضتان أسستا عيادة مجانية في العام الماضي

Reference to feminine dual human nouns

Unit 14: Answers to Exercise 6

Study the sentences below and the pronouns and/or demonstratives in each sentence. Draw a line under each pronoun and/or demonstrative referencing a feminine dual human noun. In the blank spaces below, write the specific pronoun and/or demonstrative. If there are no references to feminine dual human nouns, write "none" in the blank spaces.

a) None

هذان هما المهندسان

b) None

هذان المهندسان أسسا شركة في العام الماضي

c) هاتان هما

هاتان هما المُمَرضتان

d) هاتان

هاتان المُمَرضتان أسستا عيادة مجانية في العام الماضي

Summary reference to dual human nouns

Unit 14: Answers to Exercise 7

Rewrite the sentences below and change the pronouns and demonstratives that are dual masculine human to dual feminine human. Please make all necessary changes to ensure agreement. Write the answers in the blank spaces below.

a) These are the (two m.) children

هذان هما الطفلان

These are the (two f.) children

هاتان هما الطفلتان

b) These (two m.) engineers founded a company last year

هذان المهندسان أسسا شركة في العام الماضي

These (two f.) engineers founded a company last year

هاتان المهندستان أسستا شركة في العام الماضي

Unit 14: Answer to Exercise 8

Rewrite the sentences below and change the pronouns and demonstratives that are dual feminine human to dual masculine human. Please make all necessary changes to ensure agreement. Write the answers in the blank spaces below.

a) These (two f.) nurses founded a free clinic last year

هاتان المُمَرضتان أسستا عيادة مجانية في العام الماضي

These (two m.) nurses founded a free clinic last year

هذان المُمَرضان أسسا عيادة مجانية في العام الماضي

b) These are nurses (d., f.)

هاتان هما مُمَرضتان

These are nurses (d., m.)

هذان هما مُمَرضان

Reference to masculine plural human nouns

Unit 14: Answers to Exercise 9

Study the sentences below and the pronouns and/or demonstratives in each sentence. Draw a line under each pronoun and/or demonstrative referencing a masculine plural human noun. In the blank spaces below, write the specific pronoun and/or demonstrative. If there are no references to masculine dual human nouns, write "none" in the blank spaces.

a) هؤلاء هم

هؤلاء هم العلماء

b) هؤلاء

هؤلاء علماء

c) None

هؤلاء هن المحترفات

d) هؤلاء هم

هؤلاء هم المحترفون

e) هؤلاء هم

هؤلاء هم التلاميذ

f) هؤلاء

هؤلاء تلاميذ (m.)

g) None

هؤلاء هن مُترجمات

h) None

هؤلاء المترجمات (f.)

Reference to feminine plural human nouns

Unit 14: Answers to Exercise 10

Study the sentences below and the pronouns and/or demonstratives in each sentence. Draw a line under each pronoun and/or demonstrative referencing a feminine plural human noun. In the blank spaces below, write the specific pronoun and/or demonstrative. If there are no references to feminine plural human nouns, write "none" in the blank spaces.

a) None

هؤلاء هم العلماء

b) None

هؤلاء علماء (m.)

c) هؤلاء هن

هؤلاء هن المحترفات

d) None

هؤلاء هم المحترفون

e) None

هؤلاء هم التلاميذ

f) None

هؤلاء تلاميذ (m.)

g) هؤلاء هن

هؤلاء هن مُترجمات

h) هؤلاء

هؤلاء المترجمات

Summary – reference to plural human nouns

Unit 14: Answers to Exercise 11

Rewrite the sentences below and change the pronouns and demonstratives that are plural feminine human to plural masculine human. Please make all necessary changes to ensure agreement. Write the answers in the blank spaces below.

a) These (pl. f.) are the skilled (individuals)

هؤلاء هن المحترفات

These (pl. m.) are the skilled (individuals)

هؤلاء هم المحترفون

b) These are translators (pl. f.)

هؤلاء هن مُترجمات

These are translators (pl. m.)

هؤلاء هم مُترجموت

Unit 15: The non-human category nouns

Singular masculine non-human nouns

Unit 15: Answers to Exercise 1

Fill in the blanks below with the appropriate noun and pronoun and/or demonstrative. The first example is completed for reference. For help, refer to the following glossary of objects found in a typical classroom:

Glossary

كُرسي	(s., m.) chair	كِتاب	(s., m.) book
باب	(s., m.) door	قَلَم	(s., m.) pen
شُبّاك	(s., m.) window		

a) What is this? ما هذا؟
This is a chair. هذا كرسي
This is the chair هذا هو الكُرسي

b) What is this? ما هذا؟
This is a door. هذا باب
This is the door. هذا هو الباب

c) What is this? ما هذا؟
This is a window. هذا شُبّاك
This is the window. هذا هو الشُبّاك

d) What is this? ما هذا؟
This is a book. هذا كِتاب
This is the book. هذا هو الكِتاب

e) What is this? ما هذا؟
This is a pen. هذا قَلَم
This is the pen. هذا هو القَلَم

Unit 15: Answers to Exercise 2

Fill in the blanks below with the appropriate noun and pronoun and/or demonstrative. The first example is completed for reference. For help, refer to the following glossary of objects found in a typical class room:

Glossary

طاوِلة	(s., f.) table	كَرّاسة	(s., f.) notebook

a) What is this? ما هذِهِ؟

This is a table. هذِهِ طاوِلة

This is the table. هذِهِ هي الطاوِلة

b) What is this? ما هذِهِ؟

This is a notebook. هذِهِ كَرّاسة

This is the notebook. هذِهِ هي الكَرّاسة

Dual, masculine non-human nouns

Unit 15: Answers to Exercise 3

Translate the English phrases below into Arabic with a noun and pronoun and/or demonstrative. Use a pronoun or demonstrative corresponding to non-human, dual masculine nouns. Refer to the glossary below for the noun and make the necessary changes to ensure agreement.

Glossary

كِتاب	book (s., m.)	كِتاب	book (s., m.)
باب	door (s., m.)	قَلَم	pen (s., m.)
شُبّاك	window (s., m.)		

i) These are two books

____

هذانِ كِتابانِ

ii) These are the two doors

____

هذان هم البابان

iii) These are the two windows

____

هذان هم الشباكان

iv) These two houses

____

هذان البيتان

____

v) These are the two pens

____

هذان هم القلمان

Dual, feminine non-human nouns

Unit 15: Answers to Exercise 4

Translate the English sentences below into Arabic with a noun and pronoun and/or demonstrative. Use a pronoun or demonstrative corresponding to non-human dual feminine nouns. Refer to the glossary below for the noun and make the necessary changes to ensure agreement.

Glossary

سيّارة	car (s., f.)	طاوِلة	table (s., f.)
شَجَرة	tree (s., f.)	شَقّة	apartment (s., f.)

i) These two cars

____

هاتان السَّرتان

ii) These are the two cars

____

هاتان هما السَّرتان

iii) These are the two trees

____

هاتان هم الشَجَرتان

iv) These two tables

____

هاتان الطاوِلتان

Reference to all non-human plural nouns

Unit 15: Answers to Exercise 5

Translate the English phrases below into Arabic with a noun and pronoun and/or demonstrative. Use a pronoun or demonstrative corresponding to non-human plural nouns. Refer to the glossary below for the noun and make the necessary changes to ensure agreement.

Glossary

كَرّاسة	notebook	شَقّة	apartment

i) These notebooks

____

هذه الكَرّاسات

ii) These apartments

____

هذه الشُقَق

iii) These are the apartments

____

هذه هي الشُقَق

iv) These are apartments

____

هذه شُقَق

Unit 16: Noun attributes: number, gender, case, definiteness

Decoding attributes of an unfamiliar noun

Unit 16: Answers to Exercise 1

Study the feminine, indefinite nouns below and determine whether they are singular or plural by underlining the correct choice.

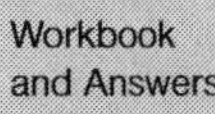

Noun	Answer choices
مُتَرجِمة	(plural feminine, indefinite) or (singular feminine, indefinite)
مهندسة	(plural feminine, indefinite) or (singular feminine, indefinite)
سَيِّدة	(plural feminine, indefinite) or (singular feminine, indefinite)
جامعة	(plural feminine, indefinite) or (singular feminine, indefinite)
مُتَرجِمات	(plural feminine, indefinite) or (singular feminine, indefinite)
مهندسات	(plural feminine, indefinite) or (singular feminine, indefinite)
سَيِّدات	(plural feminine, indefinite) or (singular feminine, indefinite)
جامعات	(plural feminine, indefinite) or (singular feminine, indefinite)

Singular الـمُفرَد

Unit 16: Answers to Exercise 2

Read the phrases below. Each one comprises a noun followed by an adjective. Draw a line under the adjectives in the singular form.

a) مُتَرجِمون يابانيّون

b) مُتَرجِمات يابانيّات

c) مُدُن يابانية

d) سيارات يابانية

e) لُغات أوروبيّة

f) مُتَرجِمون عَرَب

Dual المُثَنّى

Unit 16: Answers to Exercise 3

Change the following duals to their singular forms. Write the singular forms in the blank spaces below. For this exercise, diacritic case markings may be left out of the answers.

Dual	Singular
رَجُلانِ	رَجُل
رَجُلَيْنِ	رَجُل
مُمَثِّلَيْنِ	مُمَثِّل
كِتابانِ	كِتاب
اِبنَينِ	اِبن
مَكتَبَتَيْنِ	مَكتَبة
مَكتَبَتانِ	مَكتَبة
مُمَثِّلاتانِ	مُمَثِّلة
بِنتانِ	بِنت
اِمرأتَيْنِ	اِمرأة

Unit 16: Answers to Exercise 4

Fill in the blanks in the table below.

Dual مُثَنَّى		*Singular* مُفرد			
مَنصوب /مجرور	مرفوع	مَنصوب /مجرور	مرفوع		
عربيَّيْنِ	عربيّانِ	عربيّاً	عربيٌّ	Indefinite نكرة	Masculine مذكّر
العربيَّيْنِ	العربيّانِ	العربيَّ	العربيُّ	Definite معرفة	
عربيّتَيْنِ	عربيّتانِ	عربيّةً	عربيّةٌ	Indefinite نكرة	Feminine مؤنّث
العربيّتَيْنِ	العربيّتانِ	العربيّةَ	العربيّةُ	Definite معرفة	

Sound plurals جَمع السالم

Unit 16: Answers to Exercise 5

Change the following sound plurals to their singular forms. Place the singular forms in the blank spaces below.

Plural	Singular
a) مُمَثِّلات	مُمَثِّلة
b) طاوِلات	طاوِلة
c) مَكتَبات	مَكتَبة
d) مُمَثِّلين	مُمَثِّلً in المَنصوب case or مُمَثِّلٍ in المَجرور case
e) مُمَثِّلون	المرفوع مُمَثِّلٌ

Unit 16: Answers to Exercise 6

Once you have changed the sound plurals to their singular form, put them in four very simple sentences. Refer to the glossary below for help.

Glossary

a) مُمَثِّلات actresses (female actors)

b) طاوِلات tables

c) مَكتَبات bookstores/libraries

d) مُمَثِّلون actors (male actors)

Below are four blank spaces for four simple sentences.

a) هذه هي المُمَثِّلة

b) هذه هي الطاوِلة

c) هذه هي المَكتَبة

d) هذا هو المُمَثِّل

Definiteness

Unit 16: Answers to Exercise 7

The simple sentences below are written in English from least to most specific. Fill in the blank spaces below with the Arabic version of the simple sentences that are relatively more specific (i.e. that contains the definite version of the noun).

a) This is a Sudanese song — هذه غنوة سودانية

This is the Sudanese song — هذه الغنوة السودانية

b) This is an Egyptian song — هذه غنوة مصرية

This is the Egyptian song — هذه الغنوة المصرية

c) This is a Sudanese Muhammad — هذا محمد سوداني

This is the Sudanese Muhammad — هذا محمد السوداني

d) This is an Egyptian Muhammad — هذا محمد مصري

This is the Egyptian Muhammad — هذا محمد المصري

Summary of noun attributes

Unit 16: Answers to Exercise 8

Complete the table below by making all necessary changes to the singular form of the noun أمريكيٌّ (an American).

مفرد *(Singular)*		مجرور *(genitive)*	منصوب *(accusative)*	مرفوع *(nominative)*
نكرة (Indefinite)	(m.) مذكر	أمريكيٍّ	أمريكيّاً	أمريكيٌّ
	(f.) مؤنّث	أمريكيّةٍ	أمريكيّةً	أمريكيّةٌ
معرفة (Definite)	(m.) مذكر	الأمريكيِّ	الأمريكيَّ	الأمريكيُّ
	(f.) مؤنّث	الأمريكيّةِ	الأمريكيّةَ	الأمريكيّةُ

Unit 16: Answers to Exercise 9

Complete the table below by making all necessary changes to the dual form of the noun أمريكيٌّ (an American).

مُثَنّى (Dual)		مجرور (genitive)	منصوب (accusative)	مرفوع (nominative)
نكرة (Indefinite)	مذكر (m.)	أمريكيَّيْنِ	أمريكيَّيْنِ	أمريكيّانِ
	مؤنّث (f.)	أمريكيَّتَيْنِ	أمريكيَّتَيْنِ	أمريكيّتانِ
معرفة (Definite)	مذكر (m.)	الأمريكيَّيْنِ	الأمريكيَّيْنِ	الأمريكيّانِ
	مؤنّث (f.)	الأمريكيَّتَيْنِ	الأمريكيَّتَيْنِ	الأمريكيّتانِ

Unit 16: Answers to Exercise 10

Complete the table below by making all necessary changes to the plural form of the noun أمريكيٌّ (an American).

جَمع (Plural)		مجرور (genitive)	منصوب (accusative)	مرفوع (nominative)
نكرة	مذكر (m.)	أمريكيّينَ	أمريكيّينَ	أمريكيّونَ
(Indefinite)	مؤنّث (f.)	أمريكيّاتٍ	أمريكيّاتٍ	أمريكيّاتٌ
معرفة	مذكر (m.)	الأمريكيّينَ	الأمريكيّينَ	الأمريكيّونَ
(Definite)	مؤنّث (f.)	الأمريكيّاتِ	الأمريكيّاتِ	الأمريكيّاتُ

Unit 18: The sentence الجُملَة – the basics

Constituents of a basic sentence

Unit 18: Answers to Exercise 1

Name the constituents of a verbal clause (جُملة فِعليّة). Place the correct answer in the blank spaces.

a) ____ الفِعل ________________________________

b) ____ الفاعل ________________________________

Unit 18: Answers to Exercise 2

Name the constituents of a nominal clause (جُملة إسميّة).Place the correct answer in the blank spaces.

a) ____ الـمُبتَدأ ______________________________

b) ____ الـخَـبَر ______________________________

Subject of a verbal and a nominal sentence

Unit 18: Answers to Exercise 3

What is the sentence type of each of these sentences? Choose the correct answer.

أَلَّف مَحمودٌ رِوايةً — Mahmoud wrote a novel.

a) Verbal sentence

مؤَلِّف الرِواية محمود — The author of the novel is Mahmoud.

b) Nominal sentence

محمود مؤلِّف الرِواية — Mahmoud is the author of the novel.

b) Nominal sentence

لا! الرواية مؤلِّفها محمود — No! The novel's author is Mahmoud.

b) Nominal sentence

Unit 18: Answers to Exercise 4

Study the following sentence:

أنتَ تَكَلَّمتَ — You (2nd p. masc. sing.) spoke.

Rewrite the sentence above by replacing the subject with each of the following:

Subject

محمد

الرَجُلُ

ليلى

أنا

نحن

أنتُما

ليلى وسميرة

مُصطفى ومحمود وعائلاتُهم

a) محمد تَكَلَّمَ

b) الرَجُلُ تَكَلَّمَ

c) ليلى تَكَلَّمَت

d) أنا تَكَلَّمتُ

e) نَحنُ تَكَلَّمنا

f) أنتُم تَكَلَّمتُم

g) ليلى وسميرة تَكَلَّمَتا

h) مُصطفى ومحمود وعائلاتُهم تَكَلَّموا

Unit 18: Answers to Exercise 5

Study the following sentence:

أنتَ تَتَكَلَّمُ You (2nd p. masc. sing.) speak/are speaking.

Rewrite the sentence above by replacing the subject with each of the following:

Subject

a) الحَرامي

b) الشُرطِيّة

c) أنا

d) نحن

e) المُمَرِّضَتانِ

f) الطبيباتُ

g) الأَطِبّاءُ

a) الحَرامي يَتَكَلَّمُ
b) الشُرطِيّة تَتَكَلَّمُ
c) أنا أتَكَلَّمُ
d) نحنُ نَتَكَلَّمُ
e) الـمُمَرِّضَتانِ تَتَكَلّمانِ
f) الطبيباتُ يَتَكَلَّمْنَ
g) الأَطِبّاءُ يَتَكَلّمونَ

Basic verbal sentence

Unit 18: Answer to Exercise 6

Study the following sentence that starts with a perfect verb. What type of sentence is it? Choose the correct answer.

تَكَلَّمَت الـمَرأةُ The woman spoke

a) جُملة فِعليّة

Unit 18: Answer to Exercise 7

Copy the sentence above that starts with a perfect verb and identify the the subject (الفاعل) by drawing a line under the correct word. Write your answer in the blank space.

تَكَلَّمَت الـمَرأةُ The woman spoke
الـمَرأةُ

Unit 18: Answers to Exercise 8

Rewrite the sentence above which starts with a perfect verb by replacing the subject (الفاعل) with each of the common nouns below. Write the correct answers in the blank spaces.

Glossary

الرجُل	the man	الرِجالُ	the men
اَلرجُلانِ	the two men	النِساءُ	the women
الـمَرأتانِ	the two women		

a) تَكَلَّم الرَجُلُ

b) تَكَلَّمَ الرَجُلانِ

c) تَكَلَّمَت المَرأتانِ

d) تَكَلَّمَ الرِجالُ

e) تَكَلَّمَت النِساءُ

Unit 18: Answers to Exercise 9

Rewrite the sentences above and then identify the verb by drawing a line under the correct word. Write your answers in the blank spaces.

a) تَكَلَّم الرَجُلُ

b) تَكَلَّمَ الرَجُلانِ

c) تَكَلَّمَت المَرأتانِ

d) تَكَلَّمَ الرِجالُ

e) تَكَلَّمَت النِساءُ

Unit 18: Answer to Exercise 10

Study the following sentence that starts with an imperfect verb. What type of sentence is it? Choose the correct answer.

يُسافِرُ الرجُلُ The man travels/is travelling.

a) جُملة فِعليّة

Unit 18: Answer to Exercise 11

Copy the sentence above which starts with an imperfect verb and then identify the subject (الفاعل) by drawing a line under the correct word. Write your answer in the blank space.

يُسافِرُ الرجُلُ The man travels/is travelling.

الرجُلُ

Unit 18: Answers to Exercise 12

Study the following sentence.

يُسافِرُ الرجُلُ

Rewrite the sentence by replacing the subject (الفاعل) with each of the common nouns below. Place the correct answers in the blank spaces.

Glossary

محمد	Mohamed (singular m. proper noun)
ليلى	Laila (singular f. proper noun)
ليلى وسميرة	Laila and Samira (two singular f. proper nouns)
مُصطفى ومحمود وعائلاتُهم	Mostafa and Mahmood (two singular m. proper nouns) and their familiars

a) يُسافِرُ محمد

b) تُسافِرُ ليلى

c) تُسافِرُ ليلى وسميرة

d) يُسافِرُ مُصطفى ومحمود وعائلاتُهم

Unit 18: Answers to Exercise 13

Rewrite the sentences below and then identify the verb by drawing a line under the correct word. Write the verbs in the blank spaces.

a) يُسافِرُ محمد

b) تُسافِرُ ليلى

c) تُسافِرُ ليلى وسميرة

d) يُسافِرُ مُصطفى ومحمود وعائلاتُهم

a) يُسافِرُ

b) تُسافِرُ

c) تُسافِرُ

d) يُسافِرُ

Basic nominal sentence

Unit 18: Answers to Exercise 14

Write the sentences below in Arabic. Use the glossary if necessary. Remember to add the correct preposition based on the context and intended meaning.

Glossary

Hoda	هُدى
the car	السيارةِ
the file	الـملَفُّ
the secretary's desk	مَكتَبِ السكرتيرِ
Barbara	باربارة
Nashville	ناشڤيل
prize	جائزةُ
design	تصميم

a) Hoda is in the car

هُدى في السيّارةِ

b) The file is on the secretary's desk

الـملَفُّ على مَكتَبِ السكرتيرِ

c) Barbara is from Nashville

باربارة مِن ناشفيل

d) Magda is with Mounir

ماجدةُ مَعَ مُنير

e) The prize is for the best design

الجائزةُ لأحسن تصميم

Unit 18: Answers to Exercise 15

What type of sentence is each of the sentences below? Choose the correct answer.

a) هُدى في السيّارةِ

ii) جملة إسمية

b) الـمِلَفُّ على مَكتَبِ السكرتيرِ

ii) جملة إسمية

c) باربارة مِن ناشڤيل

ii) جملة إسمية

d) ماجدةُ مَعَ مـُنير

ii) جملة إسمية

e) الجائزةُ لأحسن تصميم

ii) جملة إسمية

Unit 18: Answers to Exercise 16

Copy the nominal sentences above and then identify the predicate (الخَبَر) by drawing a line under the word(s).

a) هُدى <u>في السيّارةِ</u>

b) الـمِلَفُّ <u>على مَكتَبِ السكرتيرِ</u>

c) باربارة <u>مِن ناشڤيل</u>

d) ماجدةُ <u>مَعَ مـُنير</u>

e) الجائزةُ <u>لأحسن تصميم</u>

Unit 18: Answers to Exercise 17

Fill in the blanks using the words provided on the left. Please make all necessary changes to ensure agreement.

a) الإيطالية والإسبانية والفرنسية لُغات أوروبيّة

b) مُحَمَّد وعَلي وسَعيد رِجال يَمَنيّون

c) هوندا وإيسوزو وتويوتا سيّارات يابانية

d) فيرمونت ونيوهامشير وكونيتيكت وِلايات أمريكية

e) منهاتن وبروكلين وبرونكس مَناطِق صغيرة في نيويورك

f) بيروت ودِمشق والقاهرة مُدُنْ عربية

Unit 18: Answers to Exercise 18

Study each of the sentences above that start with a noun. Determine what type of sentence each one is. Write the correct answer in the blank space.

جملة إسمية or جُملة فِعليّة

a) جملة إسمية ______________________

b) جملة إسمية ______________________

c) جملة إسمية ______________________

d) جملة إسمية ______________________

e) جملة إسمية ______________________

Unit 18: Answers to Exercise 19

Rewrite the sentences above and then identify the subject (الـمُبتَدأ) by drawing a line under the correct word. Write your correct answer in the blank space.

a) الإيطالية والإسبانية والفرنسية لُغات أوروبيّة

b) مُحَمَّد وعَلي وسَعيد رِجال يَمَنيّون

c) هوندا وإيسوزو وتويوتا سيّارات يابانية

d) فيرمونت ونيوهامشير وكونيتيكت وِلايات أمريكية

e) منهاتن وبروكلين وبرونكس مَناطِق صغيرة في نيويورك

f) بيروت ودِمشق والقاهرة مُدُنْ عربية

Unit 20: Adjectives: agreement with nouns

Adjectival agreement with nouns in the singular

Unit 20: Answers to Exercise 1

Fill in the blanks. Please make all necessary changes to ensure agreement. The first one is completed for reference.

Glossary

قَوِيّ الشَخصيّة	strong-willed (s., m.)
رَجُلٌ	a man
اِمرأةٌ	a woman

a) رَجُلٌ ______ الشَخصيّةِ — a strong-willed man

رَجُلٌ قَوِيُّ الشَخصيّةِ

b) الرَجُلُ القَوِيُّ الشَخصيّةِ — the strong-willed man

c) اِمرأةٌ قَوِيّةُ الشَخصيّةِ — a strong-willed woman

d) المَرأةُ القَوِيّةُ الشَخصيّةِ — the strong-willed woman

Unit 21: The ’idafa phrase الإضافة

Unit 21: Answers to Exercise 1

Turn each of the following English phrases into an Arabic إضافة phrase with a possessive pronoun suffix. Write the إضافة phrases in the blanks below. The first phrase is given for reference.

Glossary

بيت	house	خاتم	ring
قلم	pen	أرض	land
سيارة	car	أفكار	ideas
ساعة	watch	رأي	opinion

1 my house __________ __________

بيتي

2 your (m. s.) pen __________ __________

قلمَك

3 your (f. s.) car __________ __________

سيارتكِ

4 his watch __________ __________

ساعته

5 her ring __________ __________

خاتمها

6 our land __________ __________

أرضنا

7 their (m. pl.) opinion __________ __________

رأيهم

8 your (m. s.) ideas __________ __________

أفكارَك

Unit 21: Answers to Exercise 2

Turn each of the following English phrases into an Arabic إضافة phrase with a second term that is a noun, definite or indefinite. Write the إضافة phrases in the blanks below. The first example is answered for reference.

Glossary

حِذاء	shoe	بِداية	beginning
لاعِب	player	عام/سن	year
قميص	shirt	قطِ	cat
صفّارة	whistle	نـهاية	end
مُدرّب	trainer	يومِ	day
خطيبة	fiancée	صديق	friend
شارع	street	أخت	sister

1 Omar's shirt

__________ __________

قميص عمر

2 a player's shoe

__________ __________

حِذاء لاعِب

3 the trainer's whistle

__________ __________

صفّارة الـمُدرّب

4 the cat's meow

__________ __________

مواء القطِ

5 the day's end

__________ __________

نـهاية اليوم

6 my friend's (m.) sister

__________ __________

أخت صديقي

7 Salma's street

__________ __________

شارع سَلمى

8 Mahmoud's fiancée

__________ __________

خطيبة محمود

9 the beginning of the year ________ ________

بِداية العام/ بِداية السنة

Unit 21: Answers to Exercise 3

Turn each of the following English phrases into an Arabic إضافة phrase "x *of* y" to express ownership. Write the إضافة phrases in the blanks below. The first phrase is given for reference.

Glossary

قصر	palace	آلة	an instrument
أرستُقراطي	an aristocrat	مَلِك	king
موسيقار	a musician		

1 a palace of an aristocrat ________ ________

قصر أرستُقراطي

2 an instrument of a musician ________ ________

آلة موسيقار

3 the palace of the king ________ ________

قصر المَلِك

Unit 21: Answers to Exercise 4

Turn each of the following English phrases into an Arabic إضافة phrase "x *of* y" that does not express ownership. Write the إضافة phrases in the blanks below. The first phrase is given for reference.

Glossary

زجاجة	bottle	فنجان	(coffee) cup
إستقلال	independence	قهوة	coffee
مياه	water	طَعم	taste
صُندوق	a case	الحِساب	reckoning (the day of, religious)
بيرةٍ	beer	عَسَل	honey
عام	year		

1 a case of beer

صُندوق بيرةٍ

2 the bottle of water

زجاجة المياهِ

3 the year of independence

عام الاستقلال

4 a cup of coffee

فنجان قهوة

5 the taste of honey

طَعم العَسَل

Unit 21: Answers to Exercise 5

Turn each of the following English phrases into an Arabic إضافة phrase with a second noun offering amplification or specification to the first noun, with no overt expression of ownership. Write the إضافة phrases in the blanks below. The first phrase is given for reference.

Glossary

مطار	Cairo	مقهى	Café
القاهرة	Airport	البرامجِ	Software
ستاربَكس	Starbucks	تصميم	Design

1 Cairo Airport

مطار القاهرةِ

2 Starbucks café

مقهى ستاربَكس

3 software design

تصميم البرامجِ

4 gas station

محطة بنزين

5 the history department

قسم التاريخِ

6 the ticket office

مكتب التذاكرِ

7 football shoes

حذاء كرةِ القدمِ

Unit 21: Answers to Exercise 6

Turn each of the following into an Arabic إضافة phrase. Write the the answers in the blank spaces below. The first phrase is given for reference.

Glossary

جهاز	Machine/unit	زيت	oil
فاكس	Fax	خـزّان	tank
تـكييف	air conditioning	بنزين/وقود	gas
تـكييف	building	طبيب	physician
مدخل	entrance	جامعة	university
عمارة/مَبنى	building	غـُرفة	room
فِلتَر/مُرَشِّح	filter	اِجتماع	meeting

1 a fax machine

جهاز فاكس

2 the air conditioning unit

جهاز التـكييف

3 the building entrance

مدخل المَبنى

4 oil filter

مـُرَشّح زيت

5 the gas tank ________ ________

خـزّان البنزين

6 the university physician ________ ________

طبيب الجامعة

7 a meeting room ________ ________

غرفة اِجتماع

Unit 21: Answers to Exercise 7

Answer the questions below with a second noun that adds a measure of specificity to the first noun. Place the correct responses in the blank spaces below. The first question is answered for reference.

Glossary

عائلة	family
شيكاغو	Chicago
فرجينيا	Virginia
الشرق الأوسط	the Middle East region
عمّ	uncle (father's brother)
بِنت	girl/daughter
خالة	aunt (mother's sister)
مَكتَب القُبول	the office of admissions
داليا	Dalia

1) What picture? أيّ صورة؟

The family picture صورة ______

صورة العائلة

2) What city? أيّ مَدينة

The city of Chicago مدينة ______

مدينة شيكاغو

3) What state? أيّ وِلاية؟
The state of Virginia ولاية ______
ولاية فرجينيا

4) What region? أيّ منطقة؟
The Middle East region منطقة ________
منطقة الشرق الأوسط

5) Whose son? اِبن مَن؟
My cousin (my uncle's son) اِبن ______
اِبن عمّي

6) Whose address? عُنوان مَن؟
The girl's address عنوان ______
عنوان البِنت

7) Whose husband? زَوج مَن؟
My aunt's husband زوج ______
زوج خالتي

8) Which office? أيّ مَكتَب؟
The office of admissions مَكتَب ______
مَكتَب القُبول

9) Whose room? غرفة مَن؟
Dalia's room غُرفة______
غُرفة داليا

Unit 22: The 'idafa-adjective phrase

Unit 22: Answers to Exercise 1

Express the following in Arabic using an 'idafa-adjective phrase:

Hameeda, her hearing is weak حَميدةُ سَمَعُها ضَعيفٌ

Glossary

her hearing سَمَعها
weak ضَعيف

Reading old books قِراءةُ كُتُبٍ قَديمةٍ

Glossary

reading	قِراءة
books	كُتُب
old	قديم (m.) قديمة (f.)

Reading the books is boring قِراءةُ الكُتُبِ مُمِلَّةٌ

Glossary

reading	قِراءة
books	كُتُب
boring	مُمِلّة

Unit 26: To have عِندَ، لِ، مَع، في

Unit 26: Answers to Exercise 1

Study the phrases below, all of which convey the following meanings: "to hold in the hand" or "in control", "to own", to "possess" (e.g. "to have wealth"). Fill in the blank spaces below with the appropriate preposition and pronoun suffix. Refer to the list of pronoun suffixes below for assistance. The first answer is given as an example.

Pronoun suffixes attached to prepositions:

ـي، ـكَ، ـكِ، ـهُ، ـها، ـكُما، ـهُما، ـنا، ـكُم، ـكُنَّ، ـهُم، ـهُنَّ

A He has half the land.

____ نصف الأرض

لَ + هو (he) = لَه

لَه نصف الأرض

B She only has her house.

ليس ______ إلا بيتها

ليس لَها إلا بيتها

C If you have to sell land, you (2nd p. s. m.) have your father's land.

إذا كان لازم تبيع أرض ____ أرض أبوك

إذا كان لازم تبيع أرض، عِندَكَ أرض أبوك

D He has tons of money. (Note: قارون is a historic figure who was exceptionally wealthy).

____ مال قارون

عِندَهُ مال قارون

E In the countryside, people used to give the merchant some of their produce if they wanted to buy something and did not have money.

في الريف كان الناسُ يُعطون التاجر شيئاً مِن إنتاجهم

الزراعي إذا أرادوا شراء شيءٍ ولم يكُن ______ مال

في الريف كان الناسُ يُعطون التاجر شيئاً مِن إنتاجهم

الزراعي إذا أرادوا شراء شيءٍ ولم يكُن عِنْدَهُم مال

Unit 26: Answers to Exercise 2

Study the phrases below, all of which convey the following meanings: "to possess or contain as a part, a characteristic or attribute" (e.g. "she has blue eyes"). Fill in each blank space with the appropriate or preposition and noun and pronoun suffix. Refer to the list of pronoun suffixes below for assistance. The first answer is given as an example.

Pronoun suffixes attached to prepositions:

ـي، ـكَ، ـكِ، ـهُ، ـها، ـكُما، ـهُما، ـنا، ـكُم، ـكُنَّ، ـهُم، ـهُنَّ

A She has a beautiful smile.

______ ابتسامة جَميلة

لَ + هي (she) = لَها

لَها ابتسامة جَميلة

B Rooms that have high windows.

غُرَف —— شبابيك عالية

غُرَف لَها شبابيك عالية

C It (non-human) has no effect on him.

لا أثرَ —— عليه

لا أثرَ لَها عليه

D He said that his country has youth who are very understanding.

Glossary

بلاد country

قال إنّ —— شبابًا يتحلّون بتفهّم واسع

قال إنّ لِبلاده شبابًا يتحلّون بتفهّم واسع

Unit 26: Answers to Exercise 3

Fill in the blanks below with the appropriate 1) prepositions that convey the meaning "to possess by way of experience", "experience", "undergo" (e.g. "have a good time") and 2) pronoun suffixes attached to these prepositions. The first answer is given as an example.

a) God has his own plans for mankind.

لله في خلقه شؤون

b) I have an idea.

—— فكرة.

عِندي فكرة.

c) She has aspirations.

—— طموحات.

لَها طموحات.

d) He has a view.

—— رؤية.

لَه رؤية.

Unit 26: Answers to Exercise 4

Fill in the blank space below with the appropriate 1) preposition that conveys the meaning “to perform”, “carry on”, “engage in something” (e.g. “to *have* an argument”) and 2) pronoun suffixes attached to these prepositions.

She had a meeting.

كان ــــ اجتماع.

كان عِندَها اجتماع.

Unit 26: Answers to Exercise 5

Fill in the blanks below with the appropriate 1) prepositions that convey the meaning to have a certain relation with someone (e.g. “to have brothers and sisters”) and 2) noun or pronoun suffixes attached to these prepositions. The first answer is given as an example.

a) Baher bek only had one son. (باهر)

ولم يكن ــــ بك غير ابن واحد.

ولم يكن لِباهر بك غير ابن واحد.

b) We have no enemies.

ليس ــــ أعداء

ليس لَنا أعداء

c) He has three daughters.

__________ ثلاث بنات

عنده ثلاث بنات.

d) She has a pretty daughter.

__________ بنت حلوة

عندها بنت حلوة.

e) Denmark has a soldier in the peace-keeping forces. (دنمارك)

__________ جندي ضمن قوات حفظ السلام

للدنمارك جندي ضمن قوات حفظ السلام.

Unit 27: Questions

Interrogative participles

Unit 27: Answers to Exercise 1

Fill in the blank with the correct prepositions and interrogative participles.

1 With whom do you (m.) live? ______ تَسكُن؟

With whom do you (m.) live? مَع مَن تَسكُن؟

2 In which university? ______ جامعة؟

In which university? في أي جامعة؟

3 Where are you (f.) from? ______ اَنتِ؟

Where are you (f.) from? مِن أينَ اَنتِ؟

4 How much is this dress? ______هذا الفُستان؟

How much is this dress? بِكَم هذا الفُستان؟

5 How much is a kilo of potatoes? ______كيلو البطاطس؟

How much is a Kilo of potatoes? بِكَم كيلو البطاطس؟

Unit 27: Answers to Exercise 2

Translate the following from English to Arabic. Use the vocabulary in the glossary below to identify the appropriate interrogative articles and nouns. Write the answers in the blank spaces below. The first answer is given as an example.

Glossary

how many?	كَم؟	American (m.)	أمريكيّ
time	مَرّة	American (f.)?	أمريكيّة
day (m. s.)	يَوم	idea? (f.)	فِكرَة
Week (m. s.)	أُسبوع		

1 How many times? ______

كَم مَرّةً؟

(Note: the تنوين فَتح diacritic case marking is added to the end of the noun مَرّة)

2 How many days? ________________

How many days? كَم يَوماً؟

3 How many weeks? ________________

How many weeks? كَم أُسبوعاً؟

4 How many Americans (m.)? ________________

How many Americans (m.)? كَم أمريكيّاً؟

5 How many Americans (f.)? ________________

How many Americans (f.)? كَم أمريكيّةً؟

6 How many ideas? ________________

How many ideas? كَم فِكرَةً؟

Unit 27: Answers to Exercise 3

The following seven items each represent a question followed by an answer. Write the appropriate question item in the blank.

1 Where are you from, Magda? I am from Lebanon.

______ أنتِ يا ماجدة؟

مِن أينَ أنتِ يا ماجدة؟

أنا مِن لُبنان

2 Are you (f.) Syrian? No. I am Lebanese.

______ انتِ سوريّة؟

هَل انتِ سوريّة؟

لا أنا لُبنانيّة

3 Where is the University of Michigan? In the city of Ann Arbor.

______ جامعة ميشيجان؟

أينَ جامعة ميشيجان؟

في مدينة آن آربور

4 Who is she? The new professor.

__________ هي؟

مَن هي؟

الأستاذة الجديدة

5 What do you study at university? Spanish literature.

__________ تَدرُس في الجامعة؟

ماذا تَدرُس في الجامعة؟

الأدب الأسباني

6 What is this? Coffee.

______ هذِهِ؟

ما هذِهِ؟

قهوة

7 How do we say "bathroom" in Arabic? حَمّام

______ نَقول "bathroom" بالعربية؟

كَيفَ نَقول "bathroom" بالعربية؟

حَمّام

Unit 30: Conjugating the perfect verb

Unit 30: Answers to Exercise 1

Conjugate the following verb stems by suffixing all possible subject markers to them:

	Stem	*Meaning*
ذَهَب	dhahab	past of: to go
ذَهَبْتُ	I went	1st person singular
ذَهَبْتَ	you went	2nd person masculine singular
ذَهَبْتِ	you went	2nd person feminine singular
ذَهَبَ	he went	3rd person masculine singular
ذَهَبَت	she went	3rd person feminine singular
ذَهَبْتُما	you went	2nd person dual

	Stem	*Meaning*
ذَهَبَا	they went	3rd person masculine dual
ذَهَبَتَا	they went	3rd person feminine dual
ذَهَبنا	we went	1st person plural
ذَهَبتُم	you went	2nd person masculine plural
ذَهَبتُنَّ	you went	2nd person feminine plural
ذَهَبوا	they went	3rd person masculine plural
ذَهَبنَ	they went	3rd person feminine plural
تَكَلَّم	takallam	past of: to speak
تَكَلَّمتُ	I spoke	1st person singular
تَكَلَّمتَ	you spoke	2nd person masculine singular
تَكَلَّمتِ	you spoke	2nd person feminine singular
تَكَلَّمَ	he spoke	3rd person masculine singular
تَكَلَّمَت	she spoke	3rd person feminine singular
تَكَلَّمتُما	you spoke	2nd person dual
تَكَلَّما	they spoke	3rd person masculine dual
تَكَلَّمَتا	they spoke	3rd person feminine dual
تَكَلَّمنا	we spoke	1st person plural
تَكَلَّمتُم	you spoke	2nd person masculine plural
تَكَلَّمتُنَّ	you spoke	2nd person feminine plural
تَكَلَّموا	they spoke	3rd person masculine plural
تَكَلَّمنَ	they spoke	3rd person feminine plural

Unit 31: Conjugating the imperfect

Subject markers of the imperfect verb in the singular

Unit 31: Answers to Exercise 1

How many distinct forms of the singular subject marker exist for an imperfect verb? Choose the correct answer:

b) 4

Subject markers of the imperfect verb in the dual

Unit 31: Answer to Exercise 2

How many distinct forms of the dual subject marker exist for an imperfect verb? Choose the correct answer:

a) 2

Subject markers of the imperfect verb in the plural

Unit 31: Answer to Exercise 3

How many distinct forms of the plural subject marker exist for an imperfect verb? Choose the correct answer:

c) 5

Conjugating the imperfect verb

Unit 31: Answers to Exercise 4

Conjugate the following verb stem by suffixing all possible subject markers:

stem	v	*meaning*
ـقابِـل qaabil	/u/	present of: to meet

أُقابِـلُ	I meet	1st person singular
تُـقابِـلُ	you meet	2nd person masculine singular
تُـقابِـلِينَ	you meet	2nd person feminine singular
يُـقابِـلُ	he meets	3rd person masculine singular
تُـقابِـلُ	she meets	3rd person feminine singular
تُـقابِـلانِ	you meet	2nd person dual
يُـقابِـلانِ	they meet	3rd person masculine dual
تُـقابِـلانِ	they meet	3rd person feminine dual
نُـقابِـلُ	we meet	1st person plural
تُـقابِـلُونَ	you meet	2nd person masculine plural
تُـقابِـلْنَ	you meet	2nd person feminine plural
يُـقابِـلُونَ	they meet	3rd person masculine plural
يُـقابِـلْنَ	they meet	3rd person feminine plural

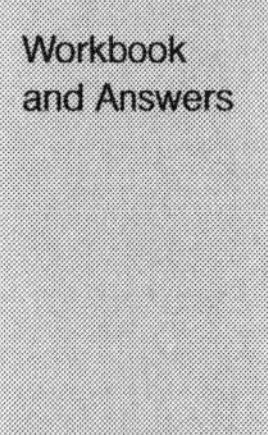

Unit 31: Answers to Exercise 5

Conjugate the following verb stem by suffixing all possible subject markers.

stem	v	*meaning*
سمـع sma^{c}	/a/	present of: to hear

أسمَعُ	I hear	1st person singular
تَسمَعُ	you hear	2nd person masculine singular
تَسمَعين	you hear	2nd person feminine singular
يَسمَعُ	he hears	3rd person masculine singular
تَسمَعُ	she hears	3rd person feminine singular
تَسمَعانِ	you hear	2nd person dual
يَسمَعانِ	they hear	3rd person masculine dual
تَسمَعانِ	they hear	3rd person feminine dual
نَسمَعُ	we hear	1st person plural
تَسمَعونَ	you hear	2nd person masculine plural
تَسمَعنَ	you hear	2nd person feminine plural
يَسمَعونَ	they hear	3rd person masculine plural
يَسمَعنَ	they hear	3rd person feminine plural

Unit 31: Answers to Exercise 6

Fill in the blanks by conjugating the two verbs for the second person singular masculine and the second person singular feminine.

	أدرُس	أسكُن	أنا
يَعمَل	يَدرُس	يَسكُن	هُوَ
تَعمَل	تَدرُس	تَسكُن	هِيَ

Unit 33: Verb patterns أوزان الفعل

Unit 33: Answers to Exercise 1

Use the chart below to help you replace ف ع ل with the root, ق ب ل (from right to left)[1]:

	الماضِي	المُضارع
I		
II	قَبَّلَ	يُقَبِّل
III	قابَلَ	يُقابِل
IV	أَقبَلَ	يُقبِل
V	تَقَبَّلَ	يَتَقَبَّل
VI	تَقابَلَ	يَتَقابَل
VII		
VIII		
IX		
X	اِستَقبَلَ	يَستَقبِل

Verb patterns, الماضي*, Forms I–X*

Unit 33: Answers to Exercise 2

Write the perfect form stems I–X in Arabic, replacing the consonants "f" with "ف", "c" with "ع", and "l" with "ل"; and the vowels /a/ with a فتحة, /u/ with a ضمة, and /i/ with a كسرة. For example, Form VII would be written like this: اِنفَعَلَ.

[1] The search and replace function of a word processor is a fast way of replacing ف ع ل with actual roots.

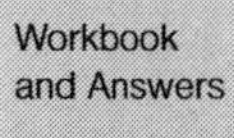

When done, you should have the 10 forms – without the subject marker – written in Arabic.

	Perfect (الماضي)	Arabic
Form I stem:	fa^{c}vl	
	{fa^{c}al}	فَعَل
	{fa^{c}ul}	فَعُل
	{fa^{c}il}	فَعِل
Form II stem:	fa^{cc}al	فَعَّل
Form III stem:	faa^{c}al	فاعَل
Form IV stem:	'af^{c}al	أفعَل
Form V stem:	tafa^{cc}al	تَفَعَّل
Form VI stem:	tafa^{ac}al	تَفاعَل
Form VII stem:	infa^{c}al	اِنفَعَل
Form VIII stem:	ifta^{c}al	اِفتَعَل
Form IX stem:	if^{c}all	اِفعَلّ
Form X stem:	istaf^{c}al	إستَفعَل

Unit 33: Answers to Exercise 3

Conjugate the perfect Form II by adding the appropriate subject markers. Use the following root radicals to conjugate Form II in the perfect:

ف for the first radical,

ك for the second, and

ر for the third.

فَكَّرتُ	I thought	1st person singular
فَكَّرتَ	you thought	2nd person masculine singular
فَكَّرتِ	you thought	2nd person feminine singular
فَكَّرَ	he thought	3rd person masculine singular
فَكَّرَت	she thought	3rd person feminine singular
فَكَّرتما	you thought	2nd person dual

فَكَّرا	they thought	3rd person masculine dual
فَكَّرَتا	they thought	3rd person feminine dual
فَكَّرنا	we thought	1st person plural
فَكَّرتُم	you thought	2nd person masculine plural
فَكَّرتُنَّ	you thought	2nd person feminine plural
فَكَّروا	they thought	3rd person masculine plural
فَكَّرنَ	they thought	3rd person feminine plural

Verb patterns, المُضارِع, Forms I–X

Unit 33: Answers to Exercise 4

Write the imperfect form stems I–X replacing the consonants "f" with "ف", "c" with "ع", and "l" with "ل"; and the vowels /a/ with a فتحة, /u/ with a ضمة, and /i/ with a كسرة. For example, Form VII would be written like this, نفَعِل, without the subject marker. When done, you should have the 10 forms, without the subject marker, written in Arabic.

	Imperfect (المُضارِع)	Arabic
Form I stem:	f^{c}vl	
	{f^{c}al}	فْعَل
	{f^{c}ul}	فْعُل
	{f^{c}il}	فْعِل
Form II stem:	fa^{cc}il	فَعِّل
Form III stem:	faa^{c}il	فاعِل
Form IV stem:	f^{c}il	فعِل
Form V stem:	tafa^{cc}al	تَفَعَّل
Form VI stem:	tafaa^{c}al	تَفاعَل
Form VII stem:	nfa^{c}il	نفَعِل
Form VIII stem:	fta^{c}il	فتَعِل
Form IX stem:	f^{c}all	فعَلّ
Form X stem:	staf^{c}il	ستَفعِل

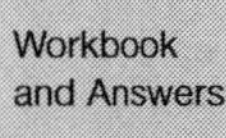

Unit 34: The perfect, Form I فعَل

Unit 34: Answers to Exercise 1

Conjugate the perfect Form I verb فتَح for all possible 13 subjects. See Conjugating the perfect if necessary.

فتَحتُ	1st person singular
فتَحتَ	2nd person masculine singular
فتَحتِ	2nd person feminine singular
فتَحَ	3rd person masculine singular
فتَحَت	3rd person feminine singular
فتَحتُما	2nd person dual
فتَحا	3rd person masculine dual
فتَحتا	3rd person feminine dual
فتَحنا	1st person plural
فتَحتُم	2nd person masculine plural
فتَحتُنَّ	2nd person feminine plural
فتَحوا	3rd person masculine plural
فتَحنَ	3rd person feminine plural

Unit 34: Answers to Exercise 2

Conjugate the perfect Form I verb كبُر for all possible 13 subjects. See Conjugating the perfect if necessary.

كبُرتُ	1st person singular
كبُرتَ	2nd person masculine singular
كبُرتِ	2nd person feminine singular
كبُرَ	3rd person masculine singular
كبُرَت	3rd person feminine singular
كبُرتُما	2nd person dual
كبُرا	3rd person masculine dual

كَبُرَتا	3rd person feminine dual
كَبُرنا	1st person plural
كَبُرتُم	2nd person masculine plural
كَبُرتُنَّ	2nd person feminine plural
كَبُروا	3rd person masculine plural
كَبُرنَ	3rd person feminine plural

Unit 34: Answers to Exercise 3

Conjugate the perfect Form I verb سَمِع for all possible 13 subjects. See Conjugating the perfect if necessary.

سَمِعتُ	1st person singular
سَمِعتَ	2nd person masculine singular
سَمِعتِ	2nd person feminine singular
سَمِعَ	3rd person masculine singular
سَمِعَت	3rd person feminine singular
سَمِعتُما	2nd person dual
سَمِعا	3rd person masculine dual
سَمِعَتا	3rd person feminine dual
سَمِعنا	1st person plural
سَمِعتُم	2nd person masculine plural
سَمِعتُنَّ	2nd person feminine plural
سَمِعوا	3rd person masculine plural
سَمِعنا	3rd person feminine plural

Unit 35: The perfect, Form II (فَعّل)

Unit 35: Answers to Exercise 1

Conjugate the perfect Form II verb نَوَّرَ for all possible 13 subjects. See Conjugating the perfect if necessary.

Form II	Perfect (الماضي)	Meaning
fa^{cc}al	نَوَّر	to turn (lights) on
	نَوَّرتُ	1st person singular
	نَوَّرتَ	2nd person masculine singular
	نَوَّرتِ	2nd person feminine singular
	نَوَّرَ	3rd person masculine singular
	نَوَّرَت	3rd person feminine singular
	نَوَّرتُما	2nd person dual
	نَوَّرا	3rd person masculine dual
	نَوَّرَتا	3rd person feminine dual
	نَوَّرنا	1st person plural
	نَوَّرتُم	2nd person masculine plural
	نَوَّرتُنَّ	2nd person feminine plural
	نَوَّروا	3rd person masculine plural
	نَوَّرنَ	3rd person feminine plural

Unit 35: Answers to Exercise 2

Conjugate the perfect Form II verb وَلَّع for all possible 13 subjects. See Conjugating the perfect if necessary.

Form II	Perfect (الماضي)	Meaning
fa^{cc}al	وَلَّع	to set fire to
	وَلَّعتُ	1st person singular
	وَلَّعتَ	2nd person masculine singular
	وَلَّعتِ	2nd person feminine singular
	وَلَّعَ	3rd person masculine singular
	وَلَّعَت	3rd person feminine singular
	وَلَّعتُما	2nd person dual
	وَلَّعا	3rd person masculine dual
	وَلَّعَتا	3rd person feminine dual
	وَلَّعنا	1st person plural

	وَلَّعتُم	2nd person masculine plural
	وَلَّعتُنَّ	2nd person feminine plural
	وَلَّعوا	3rd person masculine plural
	وَلَّعنَ	3rd person feminine plural

Unit 35: Answers to Exercise 3

Conjugate the perfect Form II verb كَسَّر for all possible 13 subjects. See Conjugating the perfect if necessary.

Form II	Perfect (الماضي)	Meaning
fa^{cc}al	كَسَّر	to smash
	كَسَّرتُ	1st person singular
	كَسَّرتَ	2nd person masculine singular
	كَسَّرتِ	2nd person feminine singular
	كَسَّرَ	3rd person masculine singular
	كَسَّرَت	3rd person feminine singular
	كَسَّرتُما	2nd person dual
	كَسَّرا	3rd person masculine dual
	كَسَّرَتا	3rd person feminine dual
	كَسَّرنا	1st person plural
	كَسَّرتُم	2nd person masculine plural
	كَسَّرتُنَّ	2nd person feminine plural
	كَسَّروا	3rd person masculine plural
	كَسَّرنا	3rd person feminine plural

Unit 36: The perfect, Form III فاعَل

Unit 36: Answers to Exercise 1

Conjugate the perfect Form III verb ناوَل for all possible 13 subjects. See Conjugating the perfect if necessary.

Form III	Perfect (الماضي)	Meaning
faacc al	ناوَل	to hand (something to someone)
	ناوَلتُ	1st person singular
	ناوَلتَ	2nd person masculine singular
	ناوَلتِ	2nd person feminine singular
	نَاوَلَ	3rd person masculine singular
	ناوَلَت	3rd person feminine singular
	ناوَلتُما	2nd person dual
	ناوَلا	3rd person masculine dual
	ناوَلَتا	3rd person feminine dual
	ناوَلنا	1st person plural
	ناوَلتُم	2nd person masculine plural
	ناوَلتُنَّ	2nd person feminine plural
	ناوَلوا	3rd person masculine plural
	ناوَلنَ	3rd person feminine plural

Unit 36: Answers to Exercise 2

Conjugate the perfect Form III verb حاوَل (in حاوَل أنْ) for all possible 13 subjects. See Conjugating the perfect if necessary.

Form III	Perfect (الماضي)	Meaning
faac al	حاوَل أنْ	to try to (do something)
	حاوَلتُ أنْ	1st person singular
	حاوَلتَ أنْ	2nd person masculine singular
	حاوَلتِ أنْ	2nd person feminine singular
	حاوَلَ أنْ	3rd person masculine singular
	حاوَلَت أنْ	3rd person feminine singular
	حاوَلتُما أنْ	2nd person dual
	حاوَلا أنْ	3rd person masculine dual
	حاوَلَتا أنْ	3rd person feminine dual
	حاوَلنا أنْ	1st person plural

	حاوَلتُم أنْ	2nd person masculine plural
	حاوَلتُنَّ أنْ	2nd person feminine plural
	حاوَلوا أنْ	3rd person masculine plural
	حاوَلنَ أنْ	3rd person feminine plural

Unit 36: Answers to Exercise 3

Conjugate the perfect Form III verb قاوَم for all possible 13 subjects. See Conjugating the perfect if necessary.

Form III	Perfect (الماضي)	Meaning
faa^cal	قاوَم	to resist (someone or something)
	قاوَمتُ	1st person singular
	قاوَمتَ	2nd person masculine singular
	قاوَمتِ	2nd person feminine singular
	قاوَمَ	3rd person masculine singular
	قاوَمت	3rd person feminine singular
	قاوَمتُما	2nd person dual
	قاوَما	3rd person masculine dual
	قاوَمَتا	3rd person feminine dual
	قاوَمنا	1st person plural
	قاوَمتُم	2nd person masculine plural
	قاوَمتُنَّ	2nd person feminine plural
	قاوَموا	3rd person masculine plural
	قاوَمنا	3rd person feminine plural

Unit 37: The perfect, Form IV أَفعَل

Unit 37: Answers to Exercise 1

Conjugate the perfect Form IV verb أحضَر for all possible 13 subjects. Write down all 13 possibilities in the blank spaces below. See Conjugating the perfect if necessary.

Form III	Perfect (الماضي)	Meaning
afᶜal	أحضَر	to bring (someone or something)
	أحضَرتُ	1st person singular
	أحضَرتَ	2nd person masculine singular
	أحضَرتِ	2nd person feminine singular
	أحضَرَ	3rd person masculine singular
	أحضَرَت	3rd person feminine singular
	أحضَرتُما	2nd person dual
	أحضَرا	3rd person masculine dual
	أحضَرَتا	3rd person feminine dual
	أحضَرنا	1st person plural
	أحضَرتُم	2nd person masculine plural
	أحضَرتُنَّ	2nd person feminine plural
	أحضَروا	3rd person masculine plural
	أحضَرنَ	3rd person feminine plural

Unit 37: Answers to Exercise 2

Conjugate the perfect Form IV verb أخبَر for all possible 13 subjects. Write down all 13 possibilities in the blank spaces below. See Conjugating the perfect if necessary.

Form III	Perfect (الماضي)	Meaning
afᶜal	أخبَر	to inform (someone about (عن) something)
	أخبَرتُ	1st person singular
	أخبَرتَ	2nd person masculine singular
	أخبَرتِ	2nd person feminine singular
	أخبَرَ	3rd person masculine singular
	أخبَرَت	3rd person feminine singular
	أخبَرتُما	2nd person dual

أخبَرَا	3rd person masculine dual
أخبَرَتا	3rd person feminine dual
أخبَرنا	1st person plural
أخبَرتُم	2nd person masculine plural
أخبَرتُنَّ	2nd person feminine plural
أخبَروا	3rd person masculine plural
أخبَرنَ	3rd person feminine plural

Unit 37: Answers to Exercise 3

Conjugate the perfect Form IV verb أجبَر for all possible 13 subjects. Write down all 13 possibilities in the blank spaces below. See Conjugating the perfect if necessary.

Form III Perfect (الماضي)		Meaning
afʿal	أجبَر	to force (someone into (على) doing something)
	أجبَرتُ	1st person singular
	أجبَرتَ	2nd person masculine singular
	أجبَرتِ	2nd person feminine singular
	أجبَرَ	3rd person masculine singular
	أجبَرَت	3rd person feminine singular
	أجبَرتُما	2nd person dual
	أجبَرا	3rd person masculine dual
	أجبَرَتا	3rd person feminine dual
	أجبَرنا	1st person plural
	أجبَرتُم	2nd person masculine plural
	أجبَرتُنَّ	2nd person feminine plural
	أجبَروا	3rd person masculine plural
	أجبَرنَ	3rd person feminine plural

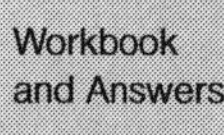

Unit 38: The perfect, Form V تَفَعَّلَ

Unit 38: Answers to Exercise 1

Conjugate the perfect Form V by adding the appropriate subject markers. Use the following root radicals to conjugate Form V in the perfect for all 13 possibilities. Write the answers in the blank spaces below.

ج for the first radical,
م for the second, and
ع for the third.

تَجَمَّعتُ	1st person singular
تَجَمَّعتَ	2nd person masculine singular
تَجَمَّعتِ	2nd person feminine singular
تَجَمَّعَ	3rd person masculine singular
تَجَمَّعَت	3rd person feminine singular
تَجَمَّعتُما	2nd person dual
تَجَمَّعا	3rd person masculine dual
تَجَمَّعتا	3rd person feminine dual
تَجَمَّعنا	1st person plural
تَجَمَّعتُم	2nd person masculine plural
تَجَمَّعتُنَّ	2nd person feminine plural
تَجَمَّعوا	3rd person masculine plural
تَجَمَّعنا	3rd person feminine plural

Unit 39: The perfect, Form VI تَفاعَلَ

Unit 39: Answers to Exercise 1

Conjugate the perfect Form VI by adding the appropriate subject markers. Write the answers in the blank spaces below. Use the following root radicals to conjugate Form VI in the perfect for all 13 possibilities:

س for the first radical,
ل for the second, and
م for the third.

تَسالَمتُ	1st person singular
تَسالَمتَ	2nd person masculine singular
تَسالَمتِ	2nd person feminine singular
تَسالَمَ	3rd person masculine singular
تَسالَمَت	3rd person feminine singular
تَسالَمْتُما	2nd person dual
تَسالَمَا	3rd person masculine dual
تَسالَمَتا	3rd person feminine dual
تَسالَمْنا	1st person plural
تَسالَمتُم	2nd person masculine plural
تَسالَمتُنَّ	2nd person feminine plural
تَسالَموا	3rd person masculine plural
تَسالَمنا	3rd person feminine plural

Unit 40: The perfect, Form VII إنفَعَلَ

Unit 40: Answers to Exercise 1

Conjugate the perfect Form VII by adding the appropriate subject markers. Use the following root radicals to conjugate Form VII in the perfect for all 13 possibilities. Write the answers in the blank spaces below.

ح for the first radical,
ر for the second, and
ف for the third.

إنحَرَفتُ	1st person singular
إنحَرَفتَ	2nd person masculine singular
إنحَرَفتِ	2nd person feminine singular
إنحَرَفَ	3rd person masculine singular
إنحَرَفَت	3rd person feminine singular
إنحَرَفتُما	2nd person dual

إنحَرَفا	3rd person masculine dual
إنحَرَفَتا	3rd person feminine dual
إنحَرَفنا	1st person plural
إنحَرَفتُم	2nd person masculine plural
إنحَرَفتُنَّ	2nd person feminine plural
إنحَرَفوا	3rd person masculine plural
إنحَرَفنَ	3rd person feminine plural

Unit 40: Answers to Exercise 2

Conjugate the perfect Form VII by adding the appropriate subject markers. Write the answers in the blank spaces below. Use the following root radicals to conjugate Form VII in the perfect for all 13 possibilities:

ع for the first radical,
ك for the second, and
س for the third.

إنعَكَستُ	1st person singular
إنعَكَستَ	2nd person masculine singular
إنعَكَستِ	2nd person feminine singular
إنعَكَسَ	3rd person masculine singular
إنعَكَسَت	3rd person feminine singular
إنعَكَستُما	2nd person dual
إنعَكَسا	3rd person masculine dual
إنعَكَسَتا	3rd person feminine dual
إنعَكَسنا	1st person plural
إنعَكَستُم	2nd person masculine plural
إنعَكَستُنَّ	2nd person feminine plural
إنعَكَسوا	3rd person masculine plural
إنعَكَسنَ	3rd person feminine plural

Unit 41: The perfect, Form VIII اِفتَعَل

Unit 41: Answers to Exercise 1

Conjugate the perfect Form VIII by adding the appropriate subject markers. Write the answers in the blank spaces below. Use the following root radicals to conjugate Form VIII in the perfect for all 13 possibilities:

ق for the first radical,
ن for the second, and
ع for the third.

اِقتَنَعتُ	1st person singular
اِقتَنَعتَ	2nd person masculine singular
اِقتَنَعتِ	2nd person feminine singular
اِقتَنَعَ	3rd person masculine singular
اِقتَنَعَت	3rd person feminine singular
اِقتَنَعتُما	2nd person dual
اِقتَنَعا	3rd person masculine dual
اِقتَنَعَتا	3rd person feminine dual
اِقتَنَعنا	1st person plural
اِقتَنَعتُم	2nd person masculine plural
اِقتَنَعتُنَّ	2nd person feminine plural
اِقتَنَعوا	3rd person masculine plural
اِقتَنَعنَ	3rd person feminine plural

Unit 41: Answers to Exercise 2

Conjugate the perfect Form VIII by adding the appropriate subject markers. Write the answers in the blank spaces below. Use the following root radicals to conjugate Form VIII in the perfect for all 13 possibilities:

ز for the first radical,
ح for the second, and
م for the third.

ازدَحَمتُ	1st person singular
اِزدَحَمتَ	2nd person masculine singular
ازدَحَمتِ	2nd person feminine singular
ازدَحَمَ	3rd person masculine singular
ازدَحَمَت	3rd person feminine singular
ازدَحَمتُما	2nd person dual
ازدَحَمَا	3rd person masculine dual
ازدَحَمَتا	3rd person feminine dual
ازدَحَمنا	1st person plural
ازدَحَمتُم	2nd person masculine plural
ازدَحَمتُنَّ	2nd person feminine plural
ازدَحَموا	3rd person masculine plural
ازدَحَمنَ	3rd person feminine plural

Unit 41: Answers to Exercise 3

Conjugate the perfect Form VIII by adding the appropriate subject markers. Write the answers in the blank spaces below. Use the following root radicals to conjugate Form VIII in the perfect for all 13 possibilities:

ص for the first radical,
د for the second, and
م for the third.

اِصطَدَمتُ	1st person singular
اِصطَدَمتَ	2nd person masculine singular
اِصطَدَمتِ	2nd person feminine singular
اِصطَدَمَ	3rd person masculine singular
اِصطَدَمَت	3rd person feminine singular
اِصطَدَمتُما	2nd person dual
اِصطَدَمَا	3rd person masculine dual
اِصطَدَمَتا	3rd person feminine dual
اِاصطَدَمنا	1st person plural

اِصطَدَمـتـُم	2nd person masculine plural
اِصطَدَمـتـُنَّ	2nd person feminine plural
اِصـطَـدَمـوا	3rd person masculine plural
اِصطَدَمـنَ	3rd person feminine plural

Unit 42: The perfect, Form IX اِفعَلَّ

Unit 42: Answers to Exercise 1

Find the perfect Form IX verb for the following three roots. Write down the verbs in the blanks spaces below.

The root الأصل	The perfect الماضي
a) خ ض ر	اِخضَرَّ
b) ز ر ق	اِزرَقَّ
c) ص ف ر	اِصفَرَّ

Unit 43: The perfect, Form X اِستَفعَلَ

Unit 43: Answers to Exercise 1

Conjugate the perfect Form X by adding the appropriate subject markers. Use the following root radicals to conjugate Form X in the perfect:

خ for the first radical,
د for the second, and
م for the third.

اِستَخدَمتُ	1st person singular
اِستَخدَمتَ	2nd person masculine singular
اِستَخدَمتِ	2nd person feminine singular
اِستَخدَمَ	3rd person masculine singular
اِستَخدَمَت	3rd person feminine singular
اِستَخدَمتُما	2nd person dual
اِستَخدَما	3rd person masculine dual
اِستَخدَمَتا	3rd person feminine dual

اِستَخدَمنا	1st person plural
اِستَخدَمتُم	2nd person masculine plural
اِستَخدَمتُنَّ	2nd person feminine plural
اِستَخدَموا	3rd person masculine plural
اِستَخدَمنَ	3rd person feminine plural

Unit 43: Answers to Exercise 2

Conjugate the perfect Form X by adding the appropriate subject markers. Use the following root radicals to conjugate Form X in the perfect. Write down all 13 possibilities in the blank spaces below.

ث for the first radical,
م for the second, and
ر for the third.

اِستَثمَرتُ	1st person singular
اِستَثمَرتَ	2nd person masculine singular
اِستَثمَرتِ	2nd person feminine singular
اِستَثمَرَ	3rd person masculine singular
اِستَثمَرَت	3rd person feminine singular
اِستَثمَرتُما	2nd person dual
اِستَثمَرا	3rd person masculine dual
اِستَثمَرتا	3rd person feminine dual
اِستَثمَرنا	1st person plural
اِستَثمَرتُم	2nd person masculine plural
اِستَثمَرتُنَّ	2nd person feminine plural
اِستَثمَروا	3rd person masculine plural
اِستَثمَرنَ	3rd person feminine plural

Unit 44: Noun–verb paradigm chart

Unit 44: Answers to Exercise 1

For Form I, find the perfect – الـماضي – and imperfect – الـمُضارع – of the following six roots.

ف ت ح	ف ر ح
ن ص ر	ض ر ب
ح س ن	ح س ب

Root	Perfect	Imperfect
ن ص ر	نَصَر	يَنْصُرب
ض ر ب	ضَرَب	يَضرِب
ف ت ح	فَتَح	يَفتَح
ف ر ح	فَرِح	يَفرَح
ح س ن	حَسُن	يَحسُن
ح س ب	حَسِب	يَحسِب

Unit 44: Answers to Exercise 2

For Form I, find the gerund – المصدر – of the following 12 roots.

Root	Form I	Gerund
خ ط ر	فَعَل	خَطَر
د ر س	فَعْل	دَرس
ل غ ز	فُعْل	لُغز
ش ع ر	فِعْل	شِعر
خ ر ب	فَعال	خَراب
ن د م	فَعالَة	نَدامة
ك ت ب	فِعالَة	كِتابة
ط ل ع	فُعول	طُلوع
ب ط ل	فُعولة	بُطولة

ل ق م	فُعلة	لُقمة
خ د م	فِعلة	خِدمة
غ س ل	فَعلة	غَسلة

Unit 44: Answers to Exercise 3

Fill in the blanks.

Gerund المصدر	*Imperfect* المُضارِع	*Perfect* الماضي	*Form* الوزن
الاشتِهار بِـ	يَشتَهِرُ بِـ	اِشتَهَر بِـ	Form VIII اِفتَعَل
الاهتِمام بِـ	يَهتَمُّ بِـ	اِهتَمَّ بِـ	Form VIII اِفتَعَل

Unit 44: Answers to Exercise 4

For Form IX, find the perfect and imperfect verbs, the gerund, and the active participle of the following seven roots. As mentioned above, these roots correspond to colours ألوان.

خ ض ر	ز ر ق	ص ف ر
ح م ر	س م ر	
ب ي ض	س و د	

The root الأصل	*The perfect* الماضي	*The imperfect* المُضارِع	*The gerund* المصدر	*The active participle* اسم الفاعِل
ح م ر	اِحمَرَّ	يَحمَرُّ	اِحمِرار	مُحمَرٌّ
خ ض ر	اِخضَرَّ	يَخضَرُّ	اِخضِرار	مُخضَرٌّ
ز ر ق	اِزرَقَّ	يَزرَقُّ	زُرقَة	مُزرَقٌّ
ص ف ر	اِصفَرَّ	يَصفَرُّ	صُفرة/اِصفِرار	مُصفَرٌّ
س و د	اِسوَدَّ	يَسوَدُّ	سَواد	مُسوَدٌّ
ب ي ض	اِبيَضَّ	يَبيَضُّ	بَياض	مُبيَضٌّ
س م ر	اِسمَرَّ	يَسمَرُّ	سُمرة	مُسمَرٌّ

Unit 48: Verb types (sound, hamzated, doubled, weak radicalled)

Unit 48: Answers to Exercise 1

The following verb, أَحَبَّ, is doubled (مضعّف). Conjugate the perfect and imperfect Form IV verb أَحَبَّ for the subjects identified in the table below. The first answer is filled out as an example.

الضمير	الماضي	المُضارع		
		المرفوع	المنصوب	المجزوم
هو	أَحَبَّ	يُحِبُّ	لن يُحِبَّ	لم يُحِبَّ
هُم	أَحَبّوا	يُحِبّونَ	لن يُحِبّوا	لم يُحِبّوا
هي	أَحَبَّتْ	تُحِبُّ	لن تُحِبَّ	لم تُحِبَّ
أنتَ	أَحبَبْتَ	تُحِبُّ	لن تُحِبَّ	لم تُحِبَّ
أنتُم	أَحبَبْتُم	تُحِبّونَ	لن تُحِبّوا	لم تُحِبّوا
أنتِ	أَحبَبْتِ	تُحبّينَ	لن تُحِبّي	لم تُحِبّي
أنا	أَحبَبْتُ	أُحِبُّ	لن أُحِبَّ	لم أُحِبَّ

Unit 48: Answers to Exercise 2

The following verb, أعطى, is final weak radicalled (ناقص). Conjugate the perfect and imperfect Form IV verb أعطى for all possible 13 subjects.

الضمير	الماضي	المُضارع
	أفعَل	يُفعِل
أنا	أعطَيْتُ	أُعطي
أنتَ	أعطَيْتَ	تُعطي
أنتِ	أعطَيْتِ	تُعطينَ
هو	أعطَى	يُعطي
هي	أعطَت	تُعطي
أنتُما	أعطَيْتُما	تُعطيانِ

يُعطِيانِ	أعطَيا	هُما
تُعطيانِ	أعطَتا	هُما
نُعطي	أعطَيْنا	نحن
تُعطونَ	أعطَيْتُم	أنتُم
تُعطينَ	أعطَيتُنَّ	أنتُنَّ
يُعطونَ	أعطَوْا	هُم
يُعطينَ	أعطَيْنَ	هُنَّ

Unit 50: The passive voice

Unit 50: Answers to Exercise 1

Change the following from the active to the passive voice. Write the new sentences in the blank spaces below.

Reminder: when doing passive transformations remember the following:

- the subject of the original sentence is deleted
- the direct object becomes the new subject
- the verb in the passive agrees with the new subject

The following are the passives of the three verbs: سُجِّل ،كُتِب ،تُرِك.

1 The father left the keys in the room on the table.

تَرَكَ الأبُ المفاتيح في الغُرفةِ على الطاولة

تُرِكَت المفاتيحُ في الغُرفةِ على الطاولة

2 I wrote the report yesterday.

كَتَبْتُ التقريرَ أمس

كُتِبَ التقريرُ أمس

3 The team scored a goal in the fifth minute of the match/game.

سجَّلَ الفريق هدفاً في الدقيقة الخامسة مِن المُباراة

سُجِّلَ هدفٌ في الدقيقة الخامسة مِن المُباراة

Unit 51: Inflecting the verb for the passive voice

Unit 51: Answers to Exercise 1

Change the following sentences from the active to the passive voice. Write the new sentences in the blank spaces below.

a) We heard a knock at the door.

سَمِعنا طَرقاً على الباب

سُمِعَ طَرقٌ على الباب

b) The storm destroyed many houses and uprooted trees on the coast.

حَطَّمَت العاصِفةُ بيوتاً كثيرةً واِقتَلَعَت أشجاراً على الساحِل

حُطِّمَت بيوتٌ كثيرةً واقتَلَعَت أشجاراً على الساحِل

c) The inpector checked the cargo on the ship before it was unloaded.

عايَنَ المُفَتِّشُ البضاعةَ على السفينة قبل تنزيلها

عويِنَة البضاعةُ على السفينة قبل تنزيلها

INDEX

'idafa phrases
  and adjectives, see 'idafa-adjective phrases
  in comparison to English, 145–149
  meanings generated from, 143–144
  morphology of, 141–142
  rules of, 142
  syntax of, 141, 144–145
  types of, 141
  word order in, see 'idafa phrases, syntax of
'idafa-adjective phrases
  agreement in, 159
  definite article in, 159
  word order in, 159

adjectival noun, 62
adverbials
  and case, 171
  as first term of an 'idafa, 172–180
  and subordinating conjunctions, 171, 173
  عِنْدَ, 167–169
  بَعْدَ, 169–171
  قَبْلَ, 171–173
  أمامَ, 173–174
  وَراءَ, 174–180
  فَوقَ, 175
  تَحتَ, 176
  قُربَ, 176
  جانِبَ, 176
  وَقتَ, 177
  ساعةَ, 177
adverbs, marked by accusative case, 250

agreement
  of adjectives with dual nouns, 127–132
  of adjectives with human vs nonhuman nouns, 121, 136–140
  of adjectives with nouns, 120–140
  of adjectives with plural nouns, 132–136
  of adjectives with singular nouns, 122–127
  and case, 120–121
  and gender, 134–140
  grammatical categories contributing to, 27
  verb-subject, 245
    gender, 245
    number, 245
    word order, 245
  see also noun-adjective phrases

case marking, 39, 48–60
  by diacritics, 50–51
  by letters
    accusative case, 52
    genitive case, 52
    nominative case, 51
  overview, 57–58
case names
  accusative, 44
  genitive, 44
  nominative, 44
charts, noun-verb paradigm, 240–242
colours, 209
computational linguistics, 3
copula, absence of, 3
counting, see numbers and counting

definite articles
  and the 'idafa, 161
  and the 'idafa-adjective phrase, 159

effect on word count, 3
with nouns and adjectives, 161
definiteness, 103–105
rule of, 104
see also indefiniteness
demonstratives, 37, 74–88
with dual human nouns, 75–76
with dual non-human nouns, 85–87
with plural human nouns, 77–78, 77–81, 78–81
with plural non-human, 87–88
with singular human nouns, 74
with singular non-human, 82–85
diacritics
definition, 8
first term of an 'idafa, 22–23
marking case, 21–22, 48–51
definiteness/indefiniteness, 22
marking mood, 23–24
dictionaries, Arabic, 241

Form I, 214
Form II, 218
Form III, 220
Form IV, 223
Form V, 227
Form VI, 229
Form VII, 231
Form VIII, 233
Form IX, 237
Form X, 238

gender
human nouns, 68–89
non-human nouns, 68
and nouns
feminine dual, 99–101
feminine plural, 100–101
feminine singular, 98–101
masculine dual, 75–76
masculine plural, 78–79
masculine singular, 98
genitive case, 44
second term in an 'idafa is in the, 143
gerund, 65–66
grammatical categories, 4–5

hamza, as character in the alphabet, 7
have, to, 178–184
عِندَ, 179–181
لِ, 181
مَع, 181
في, 181

indefiniteness
rules of, 104
see also definiteness
inter-digitization, see plurals, broken, 93

letters, 8–11
shape of, 10–11

mood, 203–205
mood markers
imperfect verbs, 203–206
see also diacritics, marking mood
mood markings, see diacritics, marking mood
mood names, imperfect verbs, 205
morphology, 6

negation
nominal sentences, 190
past tense sentences, 190
present tense sentences, 190
noun types, 283–304
noun-adjective phrases, 120–121
agreement, 120–121, 122–140
word order, 120
nouns
dual human, 75–78
human vs non-human, 89–106
agreement of adjectives with, 121, 136–140
demonstratives, 37, 81, 82–88
plural human, 78–81
singular human, 71–75
number
human nouns, 69–70
non-human nouns, 69–70
numbers and counting, 107–108

passive vocalization
imperfect tense, 256–257
perfect tense, 254–255
passive voice, 251–253
steps in transformation of, 252–253
phonology, 8
plurals
broken, 93, 98, 101
sound, 96–97, 102–103, 133, 136, 138–139
prepositions, 158–166
pronominal suffixation, 29, 158
and verbs, 158
في, 158–160
على, 160–161

مِن, 161–162
إلى, 162–163
بِـ, 163–164
لِ, 165
مَع, 165–166
pronominal suffixation, 2, 29–32, 34–35, 158
pronouns, 29–33
freestanding, 32–35
suffixed, see pronominal suffixation
pronouns, effect on word count, 3
possessive
pronouns, 30
pronouns suffix, 34–35
see the 'idafa phrase, 143

questions
how many, 191
what, 185
where, 186
who, 186
yes-no, 185
هَل, 185
ما, 185
ماذا, 185
كيف, 185
أي, 186
مَن, 186
أينَ, 186
بِكَم, 186
كَم, 187

relative adjectives, 62–63

sentence, 109–119
constituents of, 109
nominal, 115–119
verbal, 109–115
sound, 93, 101
stem, 204
subject markers, 2
effect on word count, 3
imperfect verbs, 199
dual, 200
plural, 201–202
singular, 199–200
perfect verbs, 195
dual, 196
plural, 196–197
singular, 199
substantive nouns, 63–64
syntactic functions, 3
case markings, 6, 23, 57–58, 60, 101–103
case names, 60
object of a verb, 40
object of preposition, 40
subject of verb, 40

tashkeel, see diacritics
tense
and time, 243
types of, 192
time
and participles, 243
and tense, 243

verb forms, 208
triliteral, 193–194
verb patterns
quadriliteral root, 193
triliteral root, 193
verbs
'Hamzated,' 247
imperfect tense
and future time, 243
and present time, 243
imperfect verb
mood, 203–26
plural, 199
singular, 199–202
subject markers
dual, 200
and mood, 194
neutral "it," 193
object suffix, 246
perfect tense
and future time, 243
and past time, 243
perfect verb
subject markers
gender, 196–197
plural, 196–197
singular, 195
and syllabic structure rules, 247
with two objects, 246
voice: active and passive, 193
weak radicalled, 247, 248
voice: active and passive, 193

white space in written language, 1, 3, 8, 10
word boundaries, 1–3
word count, 3
writing system, 7